THE CATERPILLAR WAY

LESSONS IN LEADERSHIP, GROWTH, AND SHAREHOLDER VALUE

CRAIG T. BOUCHARD
AND JAMES V. KOCH

New York Chicago San Francisco Athens London Madrid Mexico City
Milan New Delhi Singapore Sydney Toronto

1 2 3 4 5 6 7 8 9 0   DOC/DOC   1 8 7 6 5 4 3

ISBN   978-0-07-182124-7
MHID   0-07-182124-4

e-ISBN   978-0-07-182125-3
e-MHID   0-07-182125-2

Library of Congress Cataloging-in-Publication Data

Bouchard, Craig T.
 The Caterpillar way : lessons in leadership, growth, and shareholder value / by Craig Bouchard and James Koch.
     pages cm
  ISBN 978-0-07-182124-7 — ISBN 0-07-182124-4 1. Caterpillar Tractor Company.
 2. Tractor industry—United States   Management. I. Title.
   HD9710.4.U64C324 2014
   338.7'62'92250973—dc23
                                                                    2013025617

McGraw-Hill books are available at special quantity discounts to use as premiums and sales promotions, or for use in corporate training programs. To contact a representative, please visit the Contact Us page at www.mhprofessional.com.

Dedications

Craig T. Bouchard

Thank you to my fiercely loyal best friend and wife, Melissa.

Kai, Justin, Patrick, Shale, Cambelle, and Braidy, beautiful and wondrous kids all.

Raj Maheshwari at Charlestown Capital, my brilliant wing man in the business wars.

John Weber, one of the truly great analysts on Wall Street, whose help on our model was invaluable.

My career-long friend and mentor, the incredible James V. Koch.

James V. Koch

To Donna, Elizabeth, Marcus, Oliver, Felix, Mark, Tera and Calvin Augustus.

To my colleagues and friends at Old Dominion University— too many to mention, but three in particular are critical to my productivity—Vinod Agarwal, Vicky Curtis and Ayush Toolsidass.

To Craig T. Bouchard—from whom I have learned more than I ever taught him.

Contents

CHAPTER 1

THE QUEST FOR THE HOLY GRAIL

This book is about greatness and specifically about Caterpillar Inc., a superb example of a once struggling company made great by a deliberate sequence of astute management decisions. Caterpillar today is the world's leading manufacturer of construction and mining equipment, diesel and natural gas engines, industrial gas turbines, and diesel-electric locomotives. Financial analysts say that its global market share is increasing and that it is churning out profits.

But things weren't always this way. In 1984, Caterpillar lost $1.17 million every day as it suffered through its third down year in a row. There were whispers that bankruptcy could be somewhere down the street if CAT (this is how most people close to the company affectionately refer to it) could not turn things around.

However, turn things around is precisely what Caterpillar did even as many similarly situated firms fell into the ditch. In 2012, Caterpillar was ranked number 46 on the Fortune 500 list of the largest American corporations, up from number 58 the previous year. Its composite revenues and sales were $65.88 billion in 2012, a tenfold increase since 1984. In November 2012, Caterpillar's annual sales were 1.9 times as large as those of its nearest

American competitor, Deere, and 2.7 times the size of those of its largest international competitor, Komatsu.

Between January 2, 2001, and January 2, 2013, CAT's stock price rose an amazing 443 percent while the S&P 500 increased only 12.3 percent. Further, the company's dividend per share increased 269 percent between 2001 and 2012 and now has increased 20 years in a row.

By any standard, these achievements represent conspicuous success and help define what it means to be great. Nevertheless, the topic of good versus great is once again in vogue because on closer inspection, so few things seem genuinely great. Not in the United States, not in Europe, and not in the BRICs (Brazil, Russia, India, and China) either. Consider the implications of this assessment. It's increasingly difficult to find the qualities usually associated with greatness either in countries or in companies. The BRICs, for example, used to be synonymous with dynamic economic growth, but now that their growth has decelerated, they appear more vulnerable, and it is possible that they may lead the world into recession. It seems apparent that the global economic environment has changed, perhaps not forever but certainly for the foreseeable future.

As authors and as businessmen, we have glimpsed greatness a few times during our careers. Truth be told, getting a small whiff of it in our prior experience building Esmark, Inc., and Shale-Inland (both billion-dollar steel-related enterprises) made us eager to explain why some organizations are able to scale to higher levels of productivity and performance while others flame out and fall short. We sense that we're not the only ones who want to know why. This is a topic of great interest not only to directors, CEOs, and managers of companies but also to investors large and small.

Unfortunately, never in our lifetimes have so many managers and investors been so confused and uncertain about what constitutes the path to great business performance.

In today's equity and bond markets, this insecurity translates into massive doubts about how and where one should invest. It is not a mystery why this is so. Unmistakable uncertainties exist with respect to Europe's ability to work through its financial crises, the Middle East is a tinderbox, the Chinese economy has slowed, and Japan appears to be in the middle of yet another lost decade.

In the United States, no one really knows how the new health-care legislation will work or what it will cost. Nor do we know what our tax rates will be next year, much less five years from today. How will we pay for anticipated spending on entitlements? Our burgeoning national debt waits to be paid by future generations. The list of uncertainties is long.

Hanging like a cloud above all our heads is the reality that 14.3 percent of Americans were unemployed or underemployed in June 2013. Regrettably, this means that many millions of individuals are being forced to start over in their careers, sometimes at a terrifyingly late stage of their lives.

Some have responded bravely to these circumstances by taking the plunge and starting a new company. Not only do these entrepreneurs need to make the right choice with respect to what kind of business they should start, but also they need an understanding of what generates organizational greatness so that they can rely on these principles from the very start. In light of the fact that only 8 percent of new businesses reach 29 employees within 10 years, individuals investing their precious cash reserves want to know how new firms can grow to become great firms as well as how to plan for the troughs in economic activity that inevitably will occur.

Even the more fortunate among us face uncertainties because the world is in constant flux. Who is willing to stake his or her 401(k) balance on what the relationship between Israel and Iran will be five years from now? Who is capable of telling us what the capital gains tax rate will be five years from today or whether the promising "reshoring" of manufacturing into the United States will continue? Hence, even those who are invested intelligently today could experience unanticipated financial distress tomorrow. We all have a need to know how to identify management excellence within firms so that we can utilize that knowledge in the stock market.

Thinking About Today's Investment Environment

James Tobin and Harry Markowitz are academic titans. Each won a Nobel Prize in economics for advancing our knowledge of the best ways to invest funds and develop optimal financial portfolios. However, in the decades since Tobin and Markowitz won their Nobel Prizes, investing has become more complicated, ways to invest have grown appreciably since the 1980s, and these new opportunities usually are more complex. Consider financial derivatives. Although some kinds of derivatives have been around since the 1700s, until recent decades, they were not much more than a gleam in a financial innovator's eye. Today, a bewildering variety of derivatives exists, the most simple of which are forwards, futures, and options. Less than 1 percent of investors in the stock market ever dabble in derivatives because it is too difficult for most of them to estimate and price the risks involved.

Structured investments such as those containing subprime mortgages did not exist when Tobin and Markowitz were doing their pioneering work. Investment opportunities in commodities and real estate certainly did exist, but the alternatives were plain vanilla compared with the intricate opportunities that exist today. Exchange-traded mutual funds had yet to appear on the scene. Thus, the number of available investment opportunities has multiplied in number and increased in complexity, and this has made investing more complicated.

James Tobin *(1918–2002) won the Nobel Prize in 1981. He is notable not only for his work in portfolio theory but also for developing the Tobin regression specification for censored dependent variables and his proposal for a financial transactions tax (the Tobin tax).* **Harry Markowitz** *(1927–) won the Nobel Prize in 1990 primarily for his groundbreaking work in identifying efficient investment portfolios. He was involved in starting one of the very first hedge funds and in that context developed computerized trading algorithms to optimize that hedge fund's decisions.*

One of the biggest changes in the habits of investors is that many now choose to index their investments to reflect the entire stock market. Sometimes they don't know they are doing this because their pension fund invests their contributions and they don't pay much attention. In other cases, they personally choose to invest in indexed mutual funds sold by firms such as Fidelity and Vanguard, funds that attempt to imitate the entire stock market. For most investors, indexing turns out to be the optimal strategy. After all, accumulated evidence suggests that the typical individual investor or hedge fund that targets individual stocks does not do as well as the market overall and frequently does worse.

This means that many individual retail investors no longer spend much time consciously evaluating the characteristics of specific firms. Most investors have given up investing in people; that is, they no longer take into account the values and behavior of those who lead companies. We believe this is a mistake. *We believe it makes a huge difference not only what one invests in but also who leads the companies in which one invests.* "Who is going to lead the parade?" remains a salient investment question because leadership makes a significant difference in company performance.

Who is leading the firm? What are their values? How do they go about conducting their business? Private equity funds continually ask these questions, though their collective performance suggests that they often don't end up with the right answers. Institutional money managers ask the same questions. Alas, most retail investors don't know how to ask these questions or discover the answers.

In an odd way, the investment models of Tobin and Markowitz are responsible for the modern de-emphasis on the human component when one invests in stocks. Their classic models focused on two critical variables: the mean return one could earn on an asset and the standard deviation of that return. The duo didn't worry about the identity or values of the leaders of the companies whose financial assets they were analyzing. Tobin and Markowitz passed over any complications in this regard by making the usual ceteris paribus assumption that underpins so much of economic theory. That is, they held constant quite a few variables, such as managerial abilities and values, and implicitly assumed that those factors were not crucial considerations.

The work of Markowitz and Tobin was pathbreaking and deserving of a Nobel Prize because their theory underpins modern portfolio analysis and the well-known capital asset pricing model. Wall Street fell in love with their formulations and adopted their way of looking at things. Of course, it is essential to know which firms have generated the highest average returns in the past and how variable those returns have been. But portfolio analysis is not helpful in figuring out when a star performer on the New York Stock Exchange (NYSE) or Nasdaq will hit the wall and bog down with management issues associated with fast growth and scale.

We've cited Caterpillar's magnificent performance and could assemble a portfolio of firms to invest in by relying on similar track records of growth and stock appreciation. However, as television ads constantly warn us, past performance is no guarantee of future returns. Next year will bring different circumstances. What will the firm's managers do when faced with adversity? How will they react when, like Caterpillar, they are faced with strong new international competition and their exports are burdened by a strong U.S. dollar? What path will they choose when, like Caterpillar, they face a well-funded entrenched labor union, such as the United Auto Workers, that is insistent on imposing an industry pattern bargain solution on their firm that they believe is not in the best interest of the shareholders? What course of action will they take when, like Caterpillar, they conclude that their current organizational structure is obsolete and ought to be changed?

Great firms have managers who answer these questions as well as the questions we do not yet know. This underlines a basic reality: if you are not going to index your investments, you must pay attention to the quality of managers, the nature of the managerial processes they follow, and the way they arrive at decisions.

The Changing Investment Environment

Take a peek at your 401(k) or pension account. How has it been doing? The answer for many people is a bit embarrassing: their account balances are smaller today than they were 10 years ago. This should come as no surprise. As already noted, between January 2, 2001, and January 2, 2013, the S&P 500 stock index actually rose only 12.3 percent. During that period, the consumer price index (CPI) rose 30.0 percent. In real terms, the S&P 500 index declined by about 18 percent. No wonder many investors feel they have been bashed by the market.

> **Bad Management Makes a Difference:** *The Montana Power Company's very name suggests that it was a company involved in generating electric power. It was highly regarded in the 1990s, and its annual sales exceeded $1 billion. However, late in the 1990s, advised by Goldman Sachs, the company's management decided to get out of the power generating business and instead go into telecommunications. It sold its power plants for more than $3 billion and restructured itself into Touch America Holdings, which constructed a 21,000-mile fiber optic network. Alas, this turned out to be disastrous, and by 2003 Touch America had filed for Chapter 11 bankruptcy. Bad management choices = bad results.*

These computations don't include dividends paid by S&P 500 firms, but if we generously approximate those dividends at 1.5 percent per year, the total value of an investment that imitated the S&P 500 rose by about 30 percent, or about 2.5 percent per year. However, if we once again deflate this gain by the CPI, the real value of an investment that imitated the S&P 500 over this period virtually stood still. Buying and holding the S&P 500 was a disappointing proposition in the period 2000–2012.

The moral of the story? Today it is folly for most investors to assume or expect high rates of return on equity or debt portfolios. After all, in early July 2013, a one-year U.S. government note yielded only 0.124 percent and a 30-year U.S. government bond yielded only 3.683 percent. Federal Reserve Chairman Ben Bernanke informed all who cared to listen that these rates could persist for some time into the future. If he's right, rates of return earned on bonds are likely to be minimal. If he's wrong and interest rates rise, the prices of bonds will decline substantially. This rise in rates will hurt bondholders because lower bond prices will puncture what easily could be interpreted as a bond price bubble encouraged by Federal Reserve policies.

There have been changes in the nature of the risks attached to investments as well. In the past, individual investors could reasonably assume that their investments in the stocks of large banks and public utilities and the money they put into corporate bonds were safe, secure, and substantially immune to bankruptcies or default. This view of the world, however, was badly damaged by the 2008 demise of Washington Mutual ($307 billion in assets), the meltdown of the Fortune 500 public utility Montana Power, the sudden disappearance of Wall Street's Lehman Brothers, and the bursting of the real estate price bubble. Investors now realize that the size and fame of a firm provide no guarantee of intelligent management of that firm. Lehman Brothers, for example, had accumulated assets of approximately $600 billion and enjoyed a sterling reputation. But it became overleveraged during the 2008 financial crisis and had to declare bankruptcy—still the largest one in history.

Meanwhile, investments in residential real estate turned out to be notoriously bad between 2008 and 2011. The average equity that homeowners held in their houses fell from almost 60 percent of market value in 2000 to only 43.1 percent in the second quarter of 2012. Our homes may be our castles, but they haven't been wonderful investments. Declining real estate values are an important reason the Pew Foundation reported in August 2012 that median household net worth had fallen from $152,950 in 2008 to only $93,150 in 2010.

Contrast these dismal results with the performance of Caterpillar. As already noted, between January 2, 2001, and January 2, 2013, the price of CAT stock rose 443 percent. Add to this a dividend payment that averaged about 2.3 percent annually. Such dividend payments are likely to continue; the company's public commitment is that it will pay dividends that will rank CAT in the top 25 percent of all S&P 500 dividend payers.

This leads us to the central question: How can we identify the qualities and characteristics of firms that become better as they grow larger and reach higher levels of scale? As we will discuss later in the book, it's not a foregone conclusion that bigger is better when it comes to return on shareholder equity. One need look no further than the performance of famous brands such as Microsoft, Walmart, Bank of America, and General Electric (GE) to illustrate this point. A shareholder buying and holding these stocks for the last decade did not do well.

There are many reasons why these large firms did not excel, but the simplest one—diseconomies of scale—is probably the best one. At some point these firms became so large and complex that their managers and directors lost their grasp of their basic business drivers. It doesn't take lots of analysis to reach this conclusion; just read the newspapers. JPMorgan lost $8 billion in 2012 because a small, decentralized trading group incurred losses in European sovereign risk markets. JPMorgan's CEO, Jamie Dimon, acknowledged that he was taken by surprise, a rare circumstance for a CEO labeled "the best banker in the world."

The Mexican management team of Walmart embarrassed its CEO and the Walmart board during 2012 by earning front-page headlines in the *New York Times* for what the *Times* described as rampant violations of the Foreign Corrupt Services Act. These alleged violations involved Walmart personnel bribing local Mexican officials to grant permits for new stores. Walmart's grief was the product of two corporate deficiencies: the absence of a strong corporate ethical tradition that would have discouraged or eliminated such behavior and the difficulty Walmart's central managers had in managing and monitoring a huge, decentralized company with a large global reach.

GE Capital and Bank of America expanded into the home mortgage business, and both found reason to regret it during the Great Recession of 2008–2009. Both companies lost billions of dollars despite their large scale and seeming competence. Bank of America's acquisition of Countrywide later was mocked by the *Wall Street Journal* as possibly "the worst deal in history."

Microsoft enjoyed a near monopoly position in the computer desktop software industry with its Windows products. The global market for its software grew by leaps and bounds, and the company accumulated large cash balances. Nevertheless, the price of its stock began to languish when it became clear that the company had become a follower rather than a leader in reacting to developments such as the Internet, could not fully exploit search engine technology, was unable to capitalize on social media, was slow to find ways to harness cloud computing, and was a laggard in producing actual machines rather than software.

Why Focus on Caterpillar?

Caterpillar has taught itself how to scale to higher and higher levels of performance even as its bitter rivals Komatsu and Deere give it their best shots but nevertheless fall back. The story of how Caterpillar did this was told to us by the very people who made it happen as well as by their competitors. These conversations and our own observations provide an instructive journey through the corporate decision-making process.

But why focus on Caterpillar rather than on other successful firms? Because our research led us to the conclusion that CAT has been an exemplar in dealing with change, confronting challenges, and positioning itself for the future. It has been flexible and intelligent in its decision making. Plainly expressed, Caterpillar has met the market test better than has any other large industrial firm in the United States. Its ability to scale its size and performance upward is a remarkable story, as is its ability to cope with economic recession.

However, before we tell you the Caterpillar story, it will be helpful if you know a bit more about us. This will help you evaluate what we have to say.

The authors of this book, Craig Bouchard and Jim Koch, have run large businesses and have a firsthand sense of the kinds of choices, often unexpected, that confront leaders. Craig Bouchard has been a manufacturing company CEO, president, board member, or board chairman for two decades and in the 1990s ran a global derivatives trading room that spanned four continents. Jim Koch is a highly regarded economist and was a university president for 15 years. Jim was named one of the 100 most effective college presidents in the United States. When we assumed our various leadership positions, we inherited institutions that either appeared to be drifting or were wracked by problems. We turned them around. Craig masterminded what is still the only successful "hostile reverse tender merger" in Wall Street history when Esmark, the firm he founded, took over the Wheeling-Pittsburgh Steel Corporation in 2007. (Craig, however, wasn't finished. In June 2013 he won another hostile proxy battle, this time taking the reins of Signature Financial Holdings.)

We described these exciting times in our 2009 book *America for Sale: How the Foreign Pack Circled and Devoured Esmark*. Here's a nutshell description of what happened. In the friendliest way possible, we asked Wheeling-Pitt's 2,000-plus shareholders (including a score of large institutional share owners such as Tontine Associates, Fidelity, Wellington, and Mellon) to vote out 9 of the company's 11 directors at its annual shareholders' meeting. To the surprise of virtually everyone, we convinced the investors of the superiority of our plan for Wheeling-Pitt's future and won the proxy battle. We (Jim was a member of the Esmark board) subsequently dispatched the nine directors, the CEO, and many of the senior managers. Hostile moves of this nature had been tried by Carl Icahn and others. None had ever been successful on the scale we accomplished.

In August 2008, we sold Esmark to AO Severstal, the Russian steelmaker, for nearly $1.3 billion, with the founding investors receiving 20 to 40 times their investment. However, this wasn't easily accomplished either. We first had to defeat the attempt of the United Steel Workers (USW) to force us to sell at a price less than what the market commanded. We won that battle with the USW in a binding arbitration before the National Labor Relations Board in Washington, D.C. The $1.3 billion closing on the Severstal deal occurred less than a month before the most devastating crash on Wall Street since the Great Depression. Esmark became the highest-appreciating stock on the Nasdaq for the full year 2008.

Great timing? To be sure. We confess that we did not anticipate the intensity of the Great Recession, though we did predict that the U.S. steel industry was in for extended hard times and did see a credit crunch building up like Hurricane Sandy. *Forbes* magazine covered the story nicely in its January year-in-review edition, branding Craig and his brother Jim Bouchard as the American "Men of Steel."

We're a nonpartisan team politically. We'd best be described as middle-of-the-roaders, politically speaking. We don't have any political axes to grind and often cross party lines in our voting.

So now you know something about us. However, the key to understanding us is that we are investors who don't like to lose money. Who does? As managers, we don't like to make strategic mistakes that cost us money and will devastate our employees and stockholders. As a result, we've spent many hours and days together talking about investment fundamentals, arguing about how efficient equity markets really are, speculating about the impact high-speed trading is having on markets, and attempting to zero in on how one can identify great investments. For us, this means identifying companies with management teams and processes that will fare well into the next generation.

Although we recognize that no one can perfectly predict the future, our discussions increasingly led us to two critical factors: markets and management. Our focus on markets meant that we would concentrate our attention on firms that serve dynamic markets that almost surely will grow in the future. We don't deny that one can make money investing in declining markets and selling short, but this is a very tough game to play, carries with it substantial risk, and often comes back to haunt those who participate.

Caterpillar immediately appealed to us on the markets score because its prosperity is predicated on population and economic growth in Asia, Africa, and Latin America. As the populations in those regions grow and urbanize, infrastructure must be built to support that growth. Roads, schools, water and sanitation supplies, public and private buildings, the extraction of natural resources—all will be required in copious amounts.

No one is better situated than Caterpillar to supply those needs. When Caterpillar almost casually notes that nearly 70 percent of its sales and revenues already are made outside the United States, it is a signal that it is well positioned in countries such as Brazil, China, India, and Russia and that it intends to be the market leader in satisfying their burgeoning infrastructure needs.

With respect to our management focus, we sorted through large batches of companies that are well known, are diversified across geographic boundaries, and historically have offered consistent above-average returns. We then looked to see if they had strong management teams, were organized in a way that empowered their management teams, had developed a deep and highly qualified bench behind the CEO, had a history of managing through up *and* down business cycles, and had successfully confronted major bumps in the road. In so doing, we found ourselves in a process of developing criteria that we could use to sort winners from losers.

We spent quite a bit of time analyzing other large global companies, including Apple, Boeing, Coca-Cola, Exxon, General Electric, IBM, McDonald's, Microsoft, and Walmart. Each of these firms has a well-established reputation and has developed a brand ranked among the 100 most valuable in the world. In the not too distant past, each collected blue-ribbon awards for the quality of its management. All but Apple are counted among the 30 firms that inhabit the Dow Jones Industrial Average.

Taken as a group, these firms have been good investment vehicles. If one had invested $1,000 in each of these nine companies plus Caterpillar on January 3, 2000, by October 15, 2012, that $10,000 would have grown to $43,013 (see Table 1.1).

As one can see in Table 1.1, however, large size and a famous brand do not always augur immediate success. In the case of two of the firms—General Electric and Microsoft—the price of their shares, adjusted for stock splits, declined over the 12-year period. This underlines once again that success in the marketplace is never guaranteed, not even for Microsoft, which the U.S. Department of Justice accused of exercising monopoly power in the 1990s. Apparently, Microsoft's monopoly power was not enough to guarantee it success in a rapidly changing marketplace. General Electric's case is different. Under Jeffrey Immelt's leadership, GE deliberately has been restructuring and repositioning itself for future growth even while it has been generating significant amounts of cash. In our opinion, a decade from now, Immelt may well be acknowledged as the greatest strategist in GE's distinguished historical lineup of CEOs.

Table 1.1 also discloses that Walmart, the largest mass retailer in the world, barely eked out an increase in the value of its shares over the 12-year period. Despite the fact that it sold $418.9 billion

Table 1.1 *The Big 10: Comparing Caterpillar's Performance to that of Other Prominent Companies**

Name	Stock Symbol	Oct. 30, 2012 Market Cap ($ billions)	Share Price Jan. 1, 2000	Share Price Oct. 30, 2012	Percent Change in Share Price	Oct. 30, 2012 Share Price Beta	Revenue Growth Percent 2000–TTM Oct. 2012	Oct. 2012 Brand Value ($ billions)
Caterpillar	CAT	55.07	17.67	84.25	376.8	1.79	232.3	7.00
Apple	AAPL	567.28	27.87	604.00	2067.2	0.86	1861.2	87.10
Boeing	BA	53.62	31.15	71.11	128.3	1.10	153.3	5.70
Coca-Cola	KO	166.16	20.78	37.04	78.2	0.41	132.6	50.20
Exxon	XOM	418.30	29.40	90.62	208.2	0.83	0.8	18.32
General Electric	GE	222.14	34.25	21.11	**-38.4**	1.43	13.1	33.70
IBM	IBM	218.40	99.44	193.27	94.4	0.61	18.4	48.50
McDonald's	MCD	87.44	29.93	86.71	189.7	0.31	92.7	37.40
Microsoft	MSFT	237.43	44.57	28.21	**-36.7**	1.12	215.2	54.70
Walmart	WMT	252.48	55.52	75.11	38.3	0.42	179.2	20.30

*All brand values taken from "Apple Tops List of the World's Most Powerful Brands," *Forbes* (October 22, 2012), www.forbes.com/sites/kurtbadenhausen/2012
/10/02/apple-tops-list-of-the-worlds-most-powerful-brands, except Exxon, which comes from the Brand Directory, http://brandirectory.com/profile
/exxonmobil.
Stock prices are adjusted for stock splits.
All price and market capitalization data taken from www.yahoofinance.com.
Revenue growth in 2012 is for the trailing 12 months (TTM).

of goods and services in 2011, Walmart did not succeed in winning the favor of investors.

Thus our first-order analysis eliminated General Electric, Microsoft, and Walmart from our potential list of truly great firms that have managed to scale themselves over time. One can easily argue that each member of this well-known trio continues to exhibit many of the characteristics of great firms and that in at least one case (General Electric) it is restructuring itself for the future. Nevertheless, they all currently fall a bit short of Caterpillar.

As this book progresses, we will explain why the remaining six firms on the list also do not quite measure up to Caterpillar. This will give us an opportunity to explain our model for evaluating managerial effectiveness and how it measures financial and stock market effectiveness as well.

> **Even Apple**, *whose share price has catapulted upward, has run into rough times as it has encountered difficulties attempting to scale its operations even larger. The* New York Times *publicly questioned its ability to continue its profitable run and speculated that its stock was "headed straight for the discount rack."*

Could we have chosen a different list of firms to demonstrate our points? Of course. This particular list, however, contains companies that are familiar to nearly everyone; therefore, the comparisons we draw will be more easily understood.

The reader already knows how this story ends. We identify Caterpillar as our paragon not only because of its sterling performance but also because it has achieved that performance when confronted with significant challenges and unexpected adverse developments. What has differentiated Caterpillar from other firms?

There was only one way to find out. We had to get inside the company. To confirm or refute our basic hypotheses with respect to Caterpillar, we needed to learn more about the company and gain greater access to it than any outsiders had ever had before.

This meant we needed abundant access to Caterpillar executives, employees, and data. Never bashful, we asked Caterpillar for exactly those things. We asked the company to give us unfettered access to its executive managers (current and retired), board members, and dealers. It was generous in doing so. We also needed to talk with some of the company's customers, workers, retirees, unions, and Wall Street analysts; Caterpillar did not discourage us from doing so.

We weren't confident Caterpillar would agree, and initially the company did not. No doubt the corporation had other fish to fry and perhaps wondered if we could be trusted. Subsequently, however, Doug Oberhelman, CAT's energetic and visionary chairman/CEO, decided to grant our request. We don't know the thinking that led to his decision. However, outsiders have suggested to us that Caterpillar may have assessed us as experienced authors with the ability to examine the company's performance objectively, and we may have been seen as individuals who understood the company's distinctive history. As a young sprout, Jim Koch delivered the *Peoria Journal-Star* to Caterpillar employees, and a grown-up Craig Bouchard has dealt with many Caterpillar suppliers and customers.

Whatever Caterpillar's rationale was, once the company signaled its approval, it opened its gates and granted us access to its employees at all levels. We were honored by this access, because very few other corporate titans have ever done this unless the end product was to be a rigidly controlled version of events.

Our Criteria

We began our investigative process by spending generous amounts of time with Chairman of the Board and Chief Executive Officer Doug Oberhelman, followed by Caterpillar's group presidents and senior executives in areas such as operations, labor, international activities, and finance. We interviewed on the record legendary former CEOs such as Donald Fites, Glen Barton, and Jim Owens. We talked with independent Caterpillar directors such as Eugene Fife (Caterpillar's former presiding director and the former chairman of Goldman Sachs International), David Goode (the former CEO of Norfolk Southern Railroad), and Ed Rust (the CEO of State Farm Insurance Company and now the presiding director). We toured facilities and supplemented those conversations with numerous meetings with Caterpillar dealers and employees. We met with labor union leaders, financial analysts, and community leaders and had open and candid conversations. We are happy to report that most of those individuals were refreshingly frank. Political correctness is not a mandatory characteristic in Peoria, Illinois. We took good notes and, like Yogi Berra, found that "you can observe a lot just by watching."

The Bouchard-Koch Scale Efficiency Model

Having completed our behind the curtains inspection of Caterpillar's management process, we found the company in compliance with the 25 criteria we use to qualify scale efficiency:

1. Manufacture products in growing markets close to the customers.

2. Globalize but become a "local" in foreign countries.

3. Create a process/bible to negotiate labor contracts.

4. Own the process of continuously retooling and reducing costs.

5. Understand commodity, interest rate, and foreign exchange risk and take prudent actions to hedge positions and locate assets.

6. Nourish a global network of motivated dealers and distributors.

7. Use branding as a weapon.

8. Foster a culture of just-in-time delivery and service quality.

9. Excel in supply chain management and inventory control.

10. Disperse production to reduce costs and hedge supply disruptions.

11. Focus intensely on positive net working capital.

12. Maximize free unlevered cash flow.

13. Maintain research and development (through the business cycle).

14. Finance the customers (through the credit cycle).

15. Expand through the core and avoid small or noncore acquisitions.

16. Promote managers willing to take (career) risks.

17. Annually budget a growth scenario as well as a trough scenario.

18. Create a culture that generates esprit de corps.

19. Measure and reward employees on the basis of accurate profit and return on investment (ROI) metrics.

20. Influence government decisions.

21. Respond quickly and transparently to unexpected challenges.

22. Sustain the environment.

23. Allocate capital throughout the firm to its highest and best use.

24. Develop a deep managerial bench.

25. Maintain the CEO as the chairman of the board. This runs against the grain of fiduciary trends but has formed a critically important component of the CAT fabric.

This is a long list. The reader's first impression may be that it is too long. It's not. Managers and investors would like a simple answer or formula that would lead to the Holy Grail of investing, but life is more complicated. We cannot offer the equivalent of a new drug that will cure cancer or a cost-effective substitute for fossil fuels. The true Holy Grail of business is nothing like that. We believe the Grail is the rare combination of great leadership combined with these 25 business practices firing on all cylinders over an extended period. It is this rare mixture that propels a corporation to become better and better as it scales itself and becomes bigger.

Interestingly, all reasonably successful large companies do most of these 25 things well. If they did not, they wouldn't have become large and successful. But very few do all of them well.

We ask you to visualize the 25 factors as links in a lengthy chain. All the links eventually must be able to stand up to the myriad stresses of competition. Large companies are susceptible to the breakdown of weak links in their chains. Often, their very large size prevents them from anticipating or fixing those weak links. Unfortunately, if one link breaks, the entire chain will falter or fail.

Over the last 20 years, as Caterpillar has scaled upward, it has simultaneously become better; in fact, it has become the global leader in its product category. Figure 1.1 shows that Caterpillar's worldwide market share in construction and mining equipment is substantially larger than that of the number two firm (Komatsu). Further, CAT has been number one worldwide for some time; it is hardly an arriviste.

Caterpillar's shareholders have realized the economic benefits. Other firms grew to be as large or larger during this period yet stagnated in value creation. It is not sufficient to be big like JPMorgan, Microsoft, or Walmart. Further, it isn't enough to have a dominant market position like General Motors or Kodak. Even companies that have owned iconic names such as Montgomery Ward and Pan American Airways have found that this is not enough to cut the mustard if other links in the corporate chain malfunction.

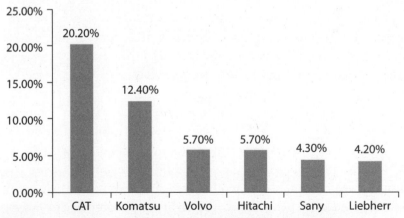

Figure 1.1 Bloomberg's estimate of worldwide market shares in the sales of construction and mining equipment, Caterpillar and its major competitors, 2011.

The reality is that the larger (and more successful) a company becomes, the more difficult that company becomes to manage. At some point, without the difficult-to-nurture management process and culture we write about in this book, many large firms gradually become less and less manageable. This is why large market shares dissipate, unexpected losses come seemingly from nowhere, and these firms are unable to scale successfully.

Caterpillar has not been immune to the challenges that accompany rapid growth, large size, and global reach. What is distinctive about Caterpillar, however, is the manner in which it has dealt with those challenges. This is what makes the Caterpillar story so interesting.

The very length of our list tells us why there are few truly great global companies. It's hard to do all these things well. In our view, this is also the reason it's so difficult to pick a winning stock. The average retail investor has insufficient access to the information necessary to evaluate a typical company's operations and management processes. The stock market battlefield is littered with the carcasses of companies that were great when they were small. Achieving scale requires vaulting over a much higher bar.

In the remainder of this book, we describe what we learned in our exhaustive investigation and interview process. Caterpillar satisfies each of our criteria (some much more clearly than others). It has figured out how to structure itself to enable it to achieve scale in size without forfeiting performance. This is among the reasons we expect Caterpillar to continue to excel in the future. Managers and investors who understand the principles that have propelled Caterpillar stand to benefit enormously.

Are there other great companies? Absolutely. Can a company be considered great even if it doesn't obviously fulfill all the criteria? Probably, because complex matters seldom are completely black and white. Exceptional performance in one area may compensate for less impressive performance in another area. However, in our view, the ultimate measure of success is the ability of a company to deliver exceptional returns for stockholders even while it treats other stakeholders—such as its employees and its community—equitably and prepares for the future.

Our analysis strongly suggests that the very best companies seldom if ever fall completely off the table with respect to any of our criteria. For example, great companies don't destroy the environment and don't take reckless risks even if it later turns out that the risks paid off. They do obey environmental laws and do assume carefully calculated risks. Some, like Caterpillar, do these things better than others, and ultimately this is what separates the merely good from the great.

In the following chapters, when we identify a factor that differentiates Caterpillar from many other companies, we will highlight it for readers by labeling it an "Insider's Edge." By no means do we mean that Caterpillar is the only company that possesses such an edge. Ultimately, however, it is the accumulation of these edges that has made CAT the great company it is today.

CHAPTER 2

CHANGE OR DIE: CATERPILLAR RETOOLS AND RESTRUCTURES

"Nothing concentrates one's mind like a date with the hangman's noose," English author Samuel Johnson (1719–1784) pungently observed. A succession of Caterpillar CEOs and board members might well have seen such a metaphoric corporate noose looming in the distance in the 1980s and 1990s. That was a period when CAT's leadership incrementally came to believe that the corporation might be at serious risk if it could not change from a centrally controlled cost center culture to a global collection of profit centers with powerful general managers at the helm of every important business.

Even so, the consensus that Caterpillar had to change or die did not appear as a revelation springing from a blinding flash of light. This was not Saul being converted on the road to Damascus, and by no means did all key leaders on the Caterpillar team come to the "we must change" conclusion at the same time. Instead, their epiphanies were the gradually emerging product of a diverse set of influences, events, and people.

Following Samuel Johnson, the attention of Caterpillar executives and board members was concentrated by the series of financial losses that the corporation sustained early in the 1980s. In short, the company hemorrhaged net working capital and cash. In 1982, it lost $180 million. Matters deteriorated in 1983, when the company lost $345 million, and topped out with a $428 million loss in 1984. CAT was losing more than $1.17 million per day in 1984, and that could not continue. The deficits constituted a cold shower for the company, its employees, the United Auto Workers, and the communities in which Caterpillar was situated. To make matters worse, CAT's confident rival, the Japanese competitor Komatsu, was winning customers on a global basis.

To CAT executives, a once unthinkable thought had crept into play. CAT might just lose the war. Komatsu brandished slogans such as, "Squash the Caterpillar," and, "Surround Caterpillar." The Japanese company had newer manufacturing facilities, had become a first mover on a process that would later be labeled lean manufacturing, offered a well-designed alternative to CAT's best products, and rode the wave of Japan's weak currency, the yen, to conquer territory quickly. Musashi's *Book of Five Rings*, written in 1645, became a must-read for key executives at CAT. Executives on both sides of the Pacific followed the rules of engagement advised in the classic text.

Would (could) Caterpillar change? CAT executives could have been forgiven if they harbored some doubts. They could easily observe that the post–World War II U.S. business landscape was littered with manufacturing firms that failed to continuously improve and consequently fell into bankruptcy. What Joseph Schumpeter had picturesquely labeled perennial waves of "creative destruction" a half century earlier became reality in the final two decades of the twentieth century. During this period, firms such as Allis-Chalmers, Harnischfeger, and International Harvester, struggling with issues similar to those facing Caterpillar, bit the dust. Further, well-known industrial titans such as Texaco, Bethlehem Steel, LTV, Colt, Kaiser Aluminum, Polaroid, Owens Corning, Lionel, Delphi, Braniff, the Milwaukee Road, and Wheeling Pittsburgh would fall along the wayside via bankruptcies or forced restructurings.

This rearrangement of economic furniture has not stopped since the challenging days of the 1980s and 1990s. Witness the near-death experience of General Motors and the 2012 demise of Kodak, which once occupied a dominant, seemingly unassailable position in the area of cameras and film. Creative destruction continues today, and firms that are unable to adjust to rapidly changing circumstances or technology simply fail in our instantly adapting markets.

Under these circumstances, it could not have been much of a surprise when in the late 1980s a Harvard University Business School case examined Caterpillar and came close to predicting Caterpillar's marginalization or eventual demise. CAT, according to the study, had a sense of "arrogance" and seemingly was not prepared for the demanding new world that confronted it.

The early 1980s financial losses underlined the idea that Caterpillar was a company stuck in the mud. Put another way, CAT gradually evolved into a larger and larger company that was built on a foundation of a high cost structure even as daily management decisions were based on financial data that were not always useful. In short, CAT had become increasingly harder to manage as a global enterprise. While the company tottered along a path that eventually could have led to bankruptcy, the mere possibility of bankruptcy being whispered sotto voce in financial circles represented a sea change in CAT's situation.

Yet Caterpillar sailed through those turbulent waters and emerged as an exemplar for manufacturing firms everywhere. How did it succeed where so many others failed? The answer is not mysterious, but it is complex. This chapter lays out the critical path implemented by a sequence of the company's CEOs to stabilize the business model, stem the losses, reinvent the physical facilities, reorganize from the ground up, motivate its employees to work as a global team, localize the empowerment of its business units, and redefine the relationship with its powerful labor union. In other words, the company changed nearly everything it did. Its executives made deliberate, well-informed, and sometimes risky choices to move it from uncertain financial conditions into the realm of acknowledged industrial leaders. The magnitude of this change and the duration and eventual success of this process may be unprecedented in corporate history. The CAT management teams worked feverishly for 30 years to make it happen.

Caterpillar has made decisions that have differentiated it from most U.S. manufacturing firms. Like Robert Frost's traveler, who prophetically came to a fork in a "yellow wood," Caterpillar on several occasions confronted a series of difficult, almost existential choices. Frost's traveler made a choice of path and said that "I took the one less traveled by, and that has made all the difference." Analogously, Caterpillar frequently chose the less traveled path in areas ranging from its decentralized management approach to its labor relations.

The truth is that firms seldom attain greatness by doggedly imitating their competitors or parroting their approaches. Instead, great firms carve their own paths by the nature of the choices they make and their willingness to swim against the tide. Sometimes their choices have appeared to be improbable or even unwise (witness Steve Jobs deciding to attempt to rescue Apple from near bankruptcy). Regardless, the great firms of our era frequently have listened to their own drummers and in the process have cultivated their own distinctive cultures.

So it has been with Caterpillar. It was CAT's choices in the 1980s and 1990s, especially with reference to the company's organization and manufacturing processes, that paved the way for it to go forth and double in size and then return to generating large amounts of cash as a result of enjoying market premium gross profit margins.

Turning the Aircraft Carrier

Sometimes it's better to be lucky than good. Coming off a miserable performance in 1984, Caterpillar caught a break, though one partially of its own making. When the final story is told of the Caterpillar turnaround and ascendancy, one of the sparks that turned into a flame was a political agreement that become known as the Plaza Accord. This was an agreement among the governments of the United States, Japan, France, West Germany, and the United Kingdom to depreciate the U.S. dollar in relation to the Japanese yen and the German deutsche mark by actively intervening in currency markets. The five governments signed the accord on September 22, 1985, at the Plaza Hotel in New York City. Between 1980 and 1985, as Caterpillar slid into an uncompetitive position against its toughest competitor, Komatsu, the dollar appreciated by about 50 percent against the Japanese yen, the deutsche mark, and the British pound (the currencies of the next three biggest economies at that time). That appreciation inflicted great pain on American exporters and created considerable difficulties for American industry, and those exporters responded by lobbying the U.S. government for relief. However, their lobbying fell on deaf ears. One reason was that the U.S. financial sector was profiting considerably from the rising dollar, and its lobbying counterbalanced that of the exporters. Also, a depreciation of the dollar would have run counter to the Reagan administration's plans for bringing down inflation.

Major players interested in reducing the value of the U.S. dollar relative to major currencies included (in addition to Caterpillar) grain exporters, automobile producers, and high-tech giants such as IBM and Motorola. By 1985, their campaign had begun to bear fruit, and Congress moved closer to mandating intervention in international markets to overcome the effect of the strong U.S. dollar. This "voice of the people" spurred the White House to begin the negotiations that led to the Plaza Accord. This situation was not unlike the current state of affairs in which the United States and Western Europe hope to persuade China to increase the value of the yuan.

The goals for the 1985 depreciation of the dollar were twofold: (1) reduce the U.S. current account deficit, which had reached 3.5 percent of gross domestic product, and (2) help the U.S. economy escape from a deep recession that began in the early 1980s and was injuring firms such as Caterpillar. Paul Volcker and the Federal Reserve had brought an end to the double-digit inflation rates of the 1970s by pushing up interest rates, but that had throttled economic activity and pushed the United States further into recession. The high interest rates (30-year U.S. government bond yields rose above 15 percent in 1982) were a magnet for capital worldwide, and the resulting flows into the United States pushed up the value of the dollar.

What happened next can only be described as remarkable. Within a year of the Plaza Accord, the yen/dollar exchange rate plummeted by 40 percent. Between 1985 and 2001, the yen appreciated almost 50 percent, from 238 to 128 yen per dollar. Meanwhile, Japan's monetary reserves increased by a factor of 8—a 13 percent compound annual rate of increase—although this did not occur at a constant rate. In the 1990s, Japanese monetary reserves once again doubled and then redoubled. During that time, the yen/dollar exchange rate fluctuated over a wide range, approximately 20 percent on both sides of 115 yen per dollar.

The Plaza Accord heralded a long-term strengthening of the yen relative to the dollar. The 1985 yen/dollar rate was 240. By Election Day 2012, the rate had fallen to 80. This constituted a long-term turning of the tables that decimated the ability of Japan to export its manufactured goods. This forced Komatsu and most other globalized Japanese manufacturers to move manufacturing plants to the countries where they wanted to sell product. At the same time, it gave CAT a pause that enabled it to reinvent itself.

The positive impact of the depreciation of the U.S. dollar on Caterpillar was vital to the company. Figure 2.1 reports the stock price of Caterpillar and the yen/dollar exchange rate beginning when the Plaza Accord was signed in 1985 and follows those two variables through April 2013. The weaker dollar and strengthened yen between 1987 and 2011 caused Caterpillar to prosper, and investors took note. In early 2013, however, the Japanese reversed field and began a deliberate campaign to weaken the yen. It remains to be seen what the effects of this will be.

The Plant with a Future (PWAF)

In 1986, on the heels of the Plaza Accord, George Schaefer announced a $1.8 billion plant modernization plan that he labeled the "Plant with a Future" (PWAF). His vision was to build Caterpillar plants that would be so modern and efficient that CAT would beat Komatsu at its own game. In 1990 alone, Caterpillar spent $358 million on PWAF plant modernization efforts, and it was to continue such investments even in years in which it recorded financial losses.

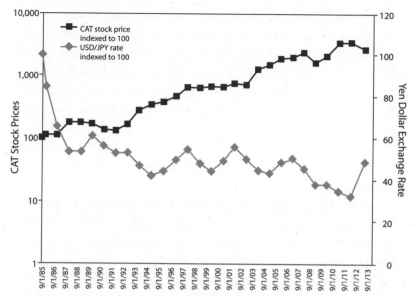

Figure 2.1   *Dollar decline/yen appreciation has helped Caterpillar.*

Sources: www.yahoofinance.com for Caterpillar's stock prices; St. Louis Federal Reserve Bank, www.research.stlouisfed.org/fred2.

Already in 1992, Caterpillar's annual report boasted of a 20 percent rate of return on capital invested in the PWAF. Stripped to its bare essentials, PWAF contained four identifiable initiatives:

1. Just-in-time inventory control systems

2. Automation of Caterpillar factories

3. Computerization and networking of machine tools on assembly lines

4. Flexible manufacturing systems

George Schaefer drew up the plan and sold it internally. Donald Fites, who assumed the helm at Caterpillar in 1990, drove it home. They each understood that the company's manufacturing facilities had become dated, high-cost, and inflexible. CAT needed to leapfrog Komatsu and its other competitors by becoming the low-cost, lean, premium brand in its industry.

The PWAF initiative does not receive the credit it deserves as a vital link in the chain of management decisions that together saved the company. The leaders of the reorganization recognized that in the world of manufacturing, it's very difficult to scale up to higher levels of output and performance if you are not a flexible, low-cost provider. Schaefer knew this and orchestrated what turned out to be an industrial experiment of a size never before seen in his industry. It involved a complete makeover of the entire company manufacturing platform and multi-billion-dollar investments in plant and equipment.

Rather than simply installing new production technology, CAT resolved to reconfigure the length and breadth of its production processes, beginning with research and development and extending to reshaping the floors of its manufacturing plants as it moved away from batch production methods. The movement away from batch production methods is instructive and did not occur immediately. The essence of batch production at Caterpillar was a final factory assembly point where the finished version of a product such as a tractor or wheel loader was assembled, with components such as engines, transmissions, and fuel tanks supplied in small lots by other production lines. To operate this model, large inventories of the individual components were required and the tasks of workers were highly specialized and repetitive. One worker might be tasked with a very narrow assignment, such as inserting and tightening several bolts, which he or she would do repetitively throughout his or her shift.

An obvious problem associated with the batch approach was that it was boring and workers' concentration tended to flag when they had to perform the same monotonous task hundreds of times each day. This boredom led to mistakes that tended to be time-consuming and expensive to correct. Hence, what Caterpillar wanted to do was not only provide workers with the latest tools and technology to do their jobs but also configure the production process so that each worker was cross-trained and could contribute in a variety of ways and have a greater personal investment in the volume and quality of production. The company's "soft" goal was audacious at the time: give every worker the feeling that his or her individual contribution to production was critically important to product quality and company profitability. Workers now were problem solvers, not simply repetitive assemblers, a role most came to relish. CAT was very pleased because this approach to production reduced downtime and slashed costs.

Caterpillar's Structural Challenges

Donald Fites, Caterpillar's chairman/CEO between 1990 and 1999, is regarded by many close to CAT as the most important and influential executive in the company's history. This is high praise in view of the star performers (including current chairman/CEO Doug Oberhelman) who have led the company since World War II. Fites modernized Caterpillar's organizational structure and operations.

In the 1980s Caterpillar was organized on a hierarchical, functional basis: there were divisions within the company for manufacturing, engineering, pricing, human resources, marketing, and so on. In our interview with Fites he described them as "silos." Those silos frustrated Fites and lots of other energetic and ambitious managers. To get anything accomplished, they had to plod through a hierarchy in which it might be necessary for a lower-level manager in the field to obtain approvals from as many as a half dozen upper-level managers, including someone at the GO. ("General Office," or GO, was the term used to describe the headquarters in Peoria.)

The general officers who oversaw the functional divisions had become especially powerful individuals. As one observer put it, "Everything revolved around them, and they rarely communicated with each other."

Our interview with A. J. Rassi and Gerry Flaherty in the Rassi living room in Peoria in November 2012 revealed the culture that existed before Caterpillar reorganized in 1990. Rassi was the plant manager of Caterpillar's large Aurora facility, and Flaherty was his predecessor until he was elevated to head the company's human resources efforts. They described a company that had become bureaucratic and slow to respond. CAT had become so hierarchical that it emitted whiffs of the heavy-handed and ill-fated economic planning mechanisms that characterized Central and Eastern European economies. Incentives to innovate were largely absent, and there was no internal transfer pricing mechanism that encouraged Caterpillar's managers to use the company's limited resources wisely.

In Caterpillar in the 1980s, corporate overhead, commodities, accounting services, and components of selling, general, and administrative expenses (SG&A) were allocated to divisions, sometimes with little regard for market competitive prices. Managers had to acquire needed inputs from inside Caterpillar even though there were better priced alternatives in outside markets. There wasn't a job description of "general manager" inside Caterpillar in 1989.

Though Rassi was a plant manager, there wasn't a job description for this position inside Caterpillar in 1989, and he did not receive a profit and loss statement for his plant. Rassi had responsibility for human resources, engineering, product design, and accounting but not for areas such as customer sales and marketing. Managers such as Rassi and Flaherty devised a capital plan each year to submit to the company's centralized General Office; however, because no charge was assessed for the use of capital by units within the company, it was difficult for Flaherty and Rassi, or anyone else, to understand if capital was being allocated wisely. Hence, most Caterpillar managers were making decisions on the basis of partial information.

The Japanese proverb "The nail that sticks out gets hammered down" applied to "nearly everything and everybody at Caterpillar," remembers another former Caterpillar administrator. (Many CAT executives have a tendency to use Japanese aphorisms and metaphors to make their points.) "There were lots of rules, formal and informal, and it quickly became clear that if you wanted to get along, you had to go along." Hence, if you wanted to manage outside the box, you had to be sure you were going to be successful, because otherwise you might ruin your career. As one might suspect, in such a culture managers willing to take career risks were hard to find.

One former Caterpillar manager remembers the criticism he received when he went to work attired in what he thought was a very nice sport coat. He soon learned that this was not the Caterpillar way; the approved attire was a suit and tie and perhaps even a hat in the 1970s. How things have changed. Caterpillar Chairman/CEO Doug Oberhelman often shows up for work today at the company headquarters in Peoria in an open-necked shirt.

Caterpillar in the 1970s and 1980s became a culture where it was difficult to assign responsibility. Layers of administrative approval were often required, and independent initiative was stifled. Failure or success frequently could be judged only at the corporate level. It was a struggle to determine if a specific Caterpillar product such as a D7 tractor was profitable because of the company's penchant for supplying inputs without accurate transfer pricing inside the company.

Suppose a manager discovered that an outside supplier could give his unit a better price on the steel he needed to make his product. Perhaps the outsider could provide higher quality and reliability or deliver needed items more promptly. Alas, CAT managers found that they often could not take advantage of such opportunities. This discouraged cost-effective behavior and exasperated ambitious, productive managers.

Don Fites commented, "I lived under this regime for many years, and it was frustrating." Managers couldn't manage efficiently. Further, one division or manager might not be on the same page as another, and it was an almost impossible job to persuade everyone to cooperate and coordinate. "People had different drivers of their perceived success" (Fites), and what individual managers or general office executives wanted was not always in the best overall interests of Caterpillar, much less the most efficient or cost-minimizing solution.

INSIDER'S EDGE *The foundation for successful profit center management is the transfer pricing of direct and indirect charges. Transfer prices must be calculated to reflect the real "market ask." This requires a culture in which managers negotiate transfer prices with one another without making it personal. If manager A quotes a price that is too high, manager B can buy it somewhere else. This includes home office overhead charges of all types. It is equally*

*important to avoid all forms of double counting. The general
managers must have accurate daily profit and loss calculations
with detail at the EBITDA level or they will make poor business
decisions.*

Finding a Better Way

Several Caterpillar CEOs, especially George Schaefer and Donald
Fites, arrived at the conclusion that the company's organizational
structure was flawed and had to change. CAT had become excessively bureaucratic and slow to make decisions at nearly every level.
Further, it was difficult for the company to determine whether particular business lines within the corporation or even specific products were profitable.

Schaefer, who led Caterpillar between 1985 and 1990, created
the company's first corporate-wide strategy team in 1988 after holding a series of meetings with company personnel. The team con-
sisted of a small group of very bright, mostly young managers drawn
from throughout the company. If one did not know them personally, they might have seemed to be young Turks. However, they were
thoroughly loyal Caterpillar managers who "bled yellow" (one of the
greatest compliments that can be paid to a CAT employee). Schaefer
wanted the group to do nothing less than outline Caterpillar's future
and in particular to answer a fundamental question: Was there a better way for Caterpillar to organize itself? Should the company junk
its General Office–driven silos for a profit-center model? Schaefer
had strong ideas in this area but wanted to hear it from line managers before recruiting support from his executive managers.

Schaefer had a good sense of the political minefield he would
encounter in trying to make major changes in the company's
entrenched culture. Future chairman/CEO Glen Barton remembers that about six months before Schaefer succeeded Lee Morgan
as chairman, Schaefer was assigned a project by Morgan to look at
Caterpillar's organization to see if modifications were needed. Schaefer
subsequently recommended several changes, but they were rejected.
Barton believes this experience drove Schaefer to pursue the Corporate
Strategy Group approach as a means to stimulate change.

The young members of the Corporate Strategy Group (CSG) followed Schaefer's direction and began to lean toward making major changes in the General Office functional model. To build support for their position, they embarked on a series of visits to other large corporations to learn about best practices. The CSG interviewed the CEOs and executive managers of iconic firms such as Kodak, Hewlett-Packard, and Ford. (Each later was to have its own organizational nightmares. None proved adept at scaling to better performance with larger global operations.)

Glen Barton, who became Caterpillar's CEO in 2004, was a member of the CSG. He told us, "We visited Kodak. We sat there for a day, and we concluded that they were similar to us. You could almost substitute CAT for Eastman Kodak in many ways." Kodak was in the process of reorganizing as well but was moving very slowly. Kodak's approach was entirely too leisurely in the view of board member Lou Gerstner (then the CEO of RJR Nabisco and later to gain fame as the CEO of IBM), and he likened it to the "Chinese water torture method."

Glen Barton told us that Gerstner was adamant that Caterpillar should move quickly and decisively. Gerstner wanted to let the gavel fall, reorganize thoroughly and promptly, and in the process force people to begin to work differently. Barton remembers this as a tipping point.

Retrospectively, it is telling that the group (and the board members) visited Kodak. We now know that that prestigious corporation would gradually forfeit its dominant market position and eventually declare bankruptcy in 2012. In our discussion, Barton mused about what a different road Caterpillar traveled in the subsequent two decades even though at the time Caterpillar personnel thought Kodak and CAT faced similar problems and challenges. This was an accurate assessment, but the two companies reacted to their similar problems and challenges very differently.

When the Corporate Strategy Group was formed, few in the corporation were aware of its existence. Six months later, George Schaefer clued in his senior management on the consensus taking hold in the strategic planning group. He then cleverly invited select senior managers (CEO-to-be Donald Fites and vice chairman-to-be

James Wogsland) into the group. Fites and Wogsland initially were taken aback by the revolutionary nature of the ideas and solutions being bandied about, and they told Schaefer that the changes to the Caterpillar model being discussed couldn't be accomplished.

Schaefer won them over. It helped that Fites had become personally frustrated with the General Office silos and was worried about the future of the company. The managers we spoke with who had participated in the Corporate Strategy Group say that Schaefer originated the concepts but Fites became the primary driver of the massive organizational change. He had already taken the reins of the reorganization when he was promoted to become Schaefer's successor as chairman/CEO in June 1990. Fites oversaw the new organizational wave, which would destroy the general offices and put in their place semiautonomous business units run by real general managers and staked his own career and future on making it work.

D-Day: Friday, January 26, 1990

On Friday, January 26, 1990, a structural reorganization was announced that would cause seismic changes in the ways Caterpillar employees would do their business. On Monday, January 29, every CAT employee who came to work not only was a part of a different administrative structure but also was operating under profoundly different rules of the road. The general offices had vanished, and in their place were 17 business units. Each would now have its own profit and loss statement along with dramatically increased freedom to determine its own fate. The business units represented both specific product lines and several geographic areas.

Each business unit manager was commanded to run a profitable business. Bottom line profitability, return on assets (ROA), and numerous measures of quality would be used to assess performance and compensate the managers. Further, each business unit would have to pay a transfer price for any inputs it acquired from another business unit (including corporate overhead expense such as human resources, legal, and marketing). Caterpillar would price inputs at market prices. Each business unit now had a general manager (GM) who owned the customer and his or her production process. A GM now would be measured by his or her profit and loss statement and compensated accordingly. Some of the operations managers who were given these GM jobs were able to adapt to the broader responsibilities, and some were not.

If there were entrepreneurial spirits being repressed at Caterpillar before the reorganization, the new structure would provide them with generous opportunities to flourish (or fail). Still, it was one thing to say that each business unit would be run as a semiautonomous business and quite another to conclude that Caterpillar's new general managers knew how to manage a business. CAT managers were told that their business units now faced the market and that they had the freedom to operate as they saw best. Not surprisingly, many of them didn't know how to act. Most of the company's managers had never had such flexibility, and as a CAT vice president at the time observed to us, "There weren't a whole lot of guidebooks."

> In 2013, the Caterpillar analogue to ROA (return on assets) is OPACC (operating profit after capital charge). CAT deducts from each business unit's profits a charge for the company capital that that unit uses. In addition, it assigns shadow prices to all other internal inputs the business units consume to reflect their costs.

Each business unit now had its own profit and loss statement, and several managers were astonished by what they found when they were handed the financial results for their units. Some learned that their operations were losing money, and others found that they were churning out profits.

As time passed, managers were progressively able to identify actual costs and isolate the profitability of individual plants, products, and processes. Nonetheless, there were many hiccups. Some managers could not adjust and moved on to other pursuits or retired. However, most managers flourished under the new arrangements because the new structure allowed them to behave efficiently. Caterpillar's world became very much like the world of big-time football coaches: be good or be gone. Or as CAT executives are apt to put it, "Everyone owned their own numbers."

Several decades later, the same rules and logic still apply at Caterpillar. Frank Crespo, CAT's vice president for global purchasing, leaves no doubt: "I tell my teams that I don't measure performance on intent or effort but instead on results. Being busy is not a measure of results."

But nothing was quite that certain in 1991. A. J. Rassi, who was managing the company's Aurora plant at the time, explained to us, "Executive management wasn't certain that plant managers actually could do everything that was required in this new world. When they saw that I could do it, I was promoted to vice president." Perhaps the 102 percent ROA that Rassi generated in the Aurora plant at that time had something to do with this.

Donald Fites became Caterpillar's chairman/CEO only five months after the new structure was announced. Clearly, it was up to him how quickly the plan would be implemented. He left no doubt that it would occur rapidly. Fites remarked, "I sat down with our accountants. I told them that each business unit was going to have its own profit and loss statement, balance sheet, and financial statements. I asked, 'How long will this take?' The response I received was, 'Three years.' No, I told them, it will happen at the end of this year because we are going to budget on this basis. Six months later, we had it done."

> **Caterpillar's** business unit approach was in evidence in October 2012 when it announced several cutbacks in production and employment. But those changes would depend on the product and the location. The company's statement at the time noted that "each business unit manages its operations. These actions vary by business unit and even from factory to factory within a business unit."

INSIDER'S EDGE Rapid change may not suit organizations that do not face emergencies, but it was precisely what Caterpillar needed to avoid drifting into bankruptcy. Rapid change can happen only if the most senior managers are committed to it at nearly any cost.

The Advent of Transfer Prices

The establishment of transfer pricing turned out to be one of the two most important behavioral aspects of the structural reorganization. From that point on, if a business unit wanted inputs from other units within Caterpillar, it had to buy those inputs rather than get them for nothing. Transfer prices would be set by external markets. If a muffler cost $300 externally, it would cost $300 inside Caterpillar. Everyone and everything had to be market competitive.

Further, a business unit head could purchase needed inputs and supplies from the open market rather than internally if that made sense. For example, a business unit could buy legal services from the outside. Managers could test the marketplace to see what prices and sales arrangements were available. Donald Fites said, "This made us more competitive. We found that we were doing some things quite well and very competitively, but other things needed improvement because outsiders were doing them better and less expensively."

Of course, one of the inputs that every business unit needed was capital. No longer would capital and financing be free inside the company. Business units would pay for the capital they used, and the price of that capital would approximate the cost of procuring external capital. Thus, each business unit had to decide if it wanted to proceed with modernization and expansion projects.

As time passed, Caterpillar established a hurdle rate of return for projects. If a project could not promise at least a 17 percent pretax return on investment, it probably was not a good use of the corporation's capital and would not be pursued.

Changes in Compensation and Incentives

Another important behavioral innovation connected to the reorganization involved a change in the company's compensation plan. Before the establishment of business units, a manager's bonus had depended primarily on the overall performance of the company. Now, however, managerial performance could be tracked more specifically. As a consequence, managers now could receive bonuses ranging from 7 to 45 percent if their business units met or exceeded their performance targets, which typically were tied directly or indirectly to the return on assets of individual units, their profitability, and several quality metrics. Senior executives' bonuses were tied to overall corporate ROA, profitability, and quality metrics.

Donald Fites was straightforward in his assessment of Caterpillar at the time: "The great motivator was survival—survival of the company, your personal survival as an important player, survival of this product that you love and that you designed, the survival of your plant." It was a culture change of the first magnitude.

> **INSIDER'S EDGE** *Incentives count. Allocate capital correctly— pay for profitable performance and customer satisfaction. This sounds simple but is rarely done properly as companies achieve larger scale.*

Some people and facilities survived; some did not. Caterpillar went on to close five American manufacturing plants. One of the largest, the company's York, Pennsylvania, plant, was closed in 1992 at a cost of more than $250 million. Multiple other operations were consolidated in single locations, and a variety of products were abandoned because, purely and simply, they were not profitable.

Glen Barton, the company's chairman/CEO between 1999 and 2004, told us that these were "draconian decisions" because of their impact on Caterpillar. Clearly, it was a painful time that is not remembered fondly by CAT personnel and even less fondly by the communities that saw their Caterpillar plants shrink or close. The company's employee base fell from 86,350 in 1980 to 53,770 in 1987 and 52,339 in 1992. Even so, these tough downsizing, cost-cutting, and company-focusing decisions laid the groundwork for the company's dramatic expansion and recovery of profitability.

The United Auto Workers (UAW), which still represents most of the company's line workers in the Upper Midwest, criticized Caterpillar's cost-cutting moves as hurting worker morale. The UAW was especially disparaging of CAT's outsourcing of input purchases to vendors in countries outside the United States. Nevertheless, that move made sound financial sense in the 1980s because the U.S. dollar was quite strong relative to most foreign currencies. This meant that CAT often could buy inputs less expensively outside the country than it could inside.

The Critical Role of Caterpillar's Dealers

Prepared simultaneously with the reorganization that shook the very foundations of the company, Caterpillar's 1990 annual report sent a message to the customer: Our "worldwide dealer organization is the best in the business and one of the primary sources of Caterpillar's competitive advantage." Partly as a result of work done by the Corporate Strategy Group, CAT had decided to place increased emphasis on its highly proficient, long-standing dealer network and therefore rely on its dealers to make nearly all sales to customers. This would prove to be an important factor differentiating the company from its competitors and also would smooth the way for CAT to scale itself to much larger sizes.

Caterpillar rarely has sold products directly to end users. Instead, it is the dealers who, working in concert with CAT, make the sales and subsequently service those products and sell parts to CAT customers. Hence, the dealers are the company's frontline troops in the competitive battle for market penetration. Because the dealers are not in competition with the company (i.e., they are not competing for sales), they become strategic and tactical partners. Their success with customers would be CAT's success.

Except in rare instances, CAT's 190 dealerships never have been owned by the company and to this day often are led by highly proficient third- and fourth-generation owners who are devoted to the company. The dealers were and are intertwined with Caterpillar's customer base and sell, rent, and service machines, engines, and parts to customers. Typically, they are well capitalized, and this is one of the reasons the network constitutes a major barrier to the entry of competitors into Caterpillar's markets.

During times of economic recession, the rental, service, and parts activities of Caterpillar dealers sustain them and the company even when they are not selling many machines. A succession of Caterpillar CEOs strategically concluded that the dealer network provided the corporation with a very difficult to replicate comparative advantage, but they needed to find additional ways to exploit that advantage.

> **INSIDER'S EDGE**   *It is the human being wearing your logo and sitting in the customer's office who cements customer loyalty. Unless you're an Internet-dominated firm, your sales force and the way it is organized, controlled, and motivated are the lifeline to your survival.*

Six Sigma Standards

A prominent feature of the reorganization as it matured was its emphasis on improving quality. "Our products have to be good because we typically charge more for them than our competitors," a current Caterpillar dealer told us. A firm can pursue such a strategy, however, only if its products actually are good and if it also promises highly competitive life-cycle ownership and operation costs.

Beginning in 2001, Caterpillar plunged into the world of Six Sigma quality standards to enhance its products and improve its market position. An immediate goal was to reduce overall costs about 10 percent while it was dramatically reducing errors and defects, improving product quality, and driving increased profits.

> **Six Sigma** *is a business management strategy originally developed by Motorola in 1986. The practice attained fame when Jack Welch made it a central focus of his business strategy at General Electric in 1995, and GE under Jeffrey Immelt has accentuated that emphasis as it has restructured. Today, Six Sigma is widely used in many sectors of industry. Six Sigma is used to improve the quality of process outputs by identifying and removing the causes of defects (errors) and minimizing variability in manufacturing and business processes. Each Six Sigma project carried out in an organization follows a defined sequence of steps and has quantified financial targets (cost reduction and/or profit increase). A Six Sigma process is one in which 99.99966 percent of the products manufactured are expected to be free of defects (3.4 defects per million).*

Six Sigma methods enabled CAT, already regarded as a high-quality producer, to put additional distance between itself and its competitors, at least for several years. Today, almost one-third of Caterpillar's employees are directly involved in Six Sigma implementation. Although the company is not eager to disclose its production costs to competitors, there have been conspicuous successes. The Caterpillar plant in Sanford, North Carolina, was able to increase its production by 26 percent even as it lowered assembly costs per unit by 25 percent in 2003.

The perception—and the reality—that its products exude quality and are the best in the market is critical to the company's prosperity. One cannot charge premium prices for products (which CAT tends to do) unless the products are superior both immediately when they are deployed in the field and over the years in terms of reduced life-cycle operational costs. CAT is zealous in testing and comparing its products with those of its competitors so that it can demonstrate to prospective customers the attractiveness of its value proposition.

Caterpillar would not be the largest firm in its industry if it had not generally been successful in creating and supporting its quality-driven value proposition. Even so, the value struggle is continuous. Competition is not static, and Caterpillar's competitors—particularly Cummins, Deere, and Komatsu—have fully implemented Six Sigma cultures. At the same time, low-price competitors such as China's Sany have appeared and established themselves in North America. Thus, CAT faces challengers with many different value propositions and has very little competitively that it can take for granted.

The 2004–2005 Structural Adjustments

In 2004, under Owens's leadership, Caterpillar instructed its strategic planning committee to create Vision 2020, a set of specific goals for improvements in products, operations, and growth that would guide the company between 2004 and 2020. From this examination came a fresh look at manufacturing. One of the group's conclusions was that it took too long for new CAT products to move from the development phase to production and final sales. Inventory problems persisted, and there was not enough communication among key individuals involved with production.

When the reorganization was announced in 1990, Glen Barton says most of the business units were eager to assume responsibility for their own purchasing. However, it soon became apparent that this was not optimal because it resulted in the company developing different purchasing processes that often perplexed suppliers. It also made it more difficult for the company to control costs. Barton remembers that the purchasing of tires provided a good example. Caterpillar could reduce costs and diminish supplier confusion if it purchased tires centrally.

This recognition led to the establishment of a global purchasing group inside the human resources (HR) department. Although the move to centralized purchasing proved to be wise, the administrative location for purchasing was not. Subsequently, Jim Owens recognized this and made the supply chain function a corporate office with the authority and power to cut costs.

Owens's assessment was that the business unit approach adopted in 1990 enabled each business unit to optimize its own situation, but this did not necessarily optimize Caterpillar's overall situation. Once again, he was interested in knowing how other companies dealt with similar challenges. CAT's leaders benchmarked a wide variety of companies ranging from Boeing to Sara Lee.

Owens observed that Caterpillar now had 15 or 20 different processes for sourcing inputs, taking orders, assembling products, distributing those products, and invoicing customers. As in the case of purchasing, he believed that it was possible to save time and money by standardizing such processes across the company and to do so without losing the entrepreneurial thrust and increased productivity that the business units had generated. Hence, the company moved in the direction of developing common processes in areas where that made sense, but it did not abandon the entrepreneurial "you own your own numbers" approach that had made the business units so successful.

Owens also concluded that there should be stronger emphasis on business units taking responsibility for specific products or product lines throughout the entire life cycle of development, production, and sale. For example, there would now be increased "back and forth" between those involved in research and development, those involved in production, and those in the field, including customers. Thus, whether the products in question were D11 tractors or 24M motor graders, increased attention would be paid to coordinating and integrating all the activities that related to those products. Caterpillar made significant changes in the way it trained and utilized its workers. It began to cross-train workers on production and assembly lines so that they would have multiple skills and the ability to do a variety of jobs. The aim, says Chuck Laurenti, now CAT's director of order delivery processes, was to empower workers so that they could quickly identify problems, fix them, and thus avoid costly disruptions. Laurenti estimates that the number of job descriptions in a typical CAT plant was reduced by 90 percent. This provided the company with more flexibility, reduced costs, and increased output.

INSIDER'S EDGE   *To achieve scale, great companies need highly talented employees; the more who are cross-trained, the better. Managers evolve from this pool of talent. Internal talent development provides flexibility and helps the Six Sigma culture take hold.*

Six Sigma and this burst of strategic planning also placed additional emphasis on lean manufacturing techniques and made possible just-in-time delivery to the customer. The company's goal was to reduce greatly the amount of inventory it held on premises, and in this it succeeded. Ultimately, Caterpillar was able to reduce its production costs by more than 10 percent. Glen Barton unambiguously declared this initiative a success when he said, "We lowered our costs significantly" by adopting disciplined, coordinated Six Sigma production processes and inventory controls.

INSIDER'S EDGE   *Superb supply chain management and precision inventory control are absolute essentials for any firm that aspires to attain excellence in manufacturing.*

Even though advanced technology in the form of the automation of assembly lines and the installation of computer-controlled machines were important parts of this evolution, they were not sufficient by themselves to reduce costs and increase profits. Smart workers and managers were required to realize the potential of the technology. Thus, decisions such as moving away from batch production and Caterpillar's disciplined supply chain and inventory-control activities were essential elements of the company's success.

Words of Caution

Those who follow American industry and pay attention to management theory know well that every year produces a new management model or theory that is advertised as the best thing since sliced bread. Their names and labels should sound familiar: TQM, TPM, TOC, lean manufacturing, Six Sigma quality, reengineering, *kaizens*, and the like. Each has been bandied about as the solution du jour to corporate and organizational challenges, but most (e.g., TQM) have followed the trajectory of a shooting star: a brilliant ascent followed by disappointment and a flameout.

The relevant point and one that is well understood inside Caterpillar is that there must be traceable, quantifiable results connected to newly adopted managerial or production models. It's not enough to trumpet a seductive new nostrum that will cure the world's problems. There must be objective results that will have a positive impact on the company's bottom line.

It is here that Caterpillar's focus on the rate of return on its invested capital comes to the fore. If CAT invests in a modernization project, there must be a measureable, positive rate of return on the capital and resources used there. An illustration is its 2011 announcement of a $200 million investment in the modernization of its historic East Peoria, Illinois, plants that produce the undercarriages for its largest tractors. Company managers advocating these expenditures committed to specific revenue and cost models to justify the investment. The reality is that if the advocates are wrong, their careers will suffer and they may lose their jobs. Caterpillar is not a touchy-feely firm in which the deployment of its invested capital is concerned. Bottom line accountability exists in every business unit as well as for the company overall. No one doubts this.

> **INSIDER'S EDGE** *Management techniques such as TQM, Six Sigma, and reengineering will never be anything more than fads unless they are accompanied by weekly review, objective measurement of results, and constant formal updates.*

Summing It Up

In the 1980s and 1990s, Caterpillar was faced with a series of existential crises. It responded to those crises by taking vigorous, path-breaking actions in a variety of areas. It fundamentally changed the company's organization by (1) reconfiguring the floors of its factories to increase employee involvement, reduce errors, diminish production downtime, and increase production, (2) creating 17 semiautonomous business units, each of which had its own profit and loss statement, (3) increasing the efficiency of its internal resource use by means of transfer prices, (4) relying on Six Sigma methods to increase product quality, (5) diminishing required inventory by improving its supply chain management, and, (6) measuring business unit and employee success by specific measures of profitability, product quality, and return on invested capital.

Make no mistake. This was not an overnight turnaround. It was a three-decade turnaround accomplished even as the company was going to the mat time after time with its major labor union, the United Auto Workers. Efficiency improved on a continuous basis, employment levels fell, some plants were closed, and many careers were disrupted. Nevertheless, as a longtime CAT assembly line worker told us, "It's better to have a tough decade than a terrible century." Even three tough decades.

It took 30 years of tough sledding, and many employees had to make sacrifices. Nevertheless, Caterpillar firmly demonstrated that it had what it took to survive, then prosper, and finally scale to its position of global leadership. The future is bright. The twenty-first century may see CAT outperform all other American manufacturing companies.

A GLOBAL FIRM HEADQUARTERED IN THE UNITED STATES

"It's in Caterpillar's DNA," insists Thomas J. Bluth, the company's vice president for earthmoving, when talking about Caterpillar's sustained thrust into international markets. In 2011, for the first time, more than 70 percent of Caterpillar's consolidated sales and revenues came from outside the United States.

Caterpillar is hardly a newbie where international trade is concerned. Shortly after the Holt-Best merger that created the Caterpillar Tractor Company in 1925, the company established dealerships in Australia, East Africa, the Netherlands, and Tunisia. Early on, one of Caterpillar's guiding notions, if not the company's dream, was that expanding populations and rising incomes outside the United States would result in increasing urbanization. This would drive demand for the tractors, backhoe loaders, graders, and trucks needed to construct required urban infrastructure.

Caterpillar's high-energy chairman/CEO, Doug Oberhelman, who is fond of pointing out that 95 percent of the world's consumers live outside the United States, reiterated this long-standing vision in the company's 2011 annual report:

By 2020 the world population is expected to be 7.6 billion people. What are all those people going to need? They are going to need food, water, energy, housing, roads, schools—everything you and I have today and probably some new things we haven't even thought of yet. That means infrastructure, construction, mining and power systems are growing industries. Demand for our products is strong, and we think the big macroeconomic trends will mean good global growth for our industries for the next 25 to 30 years. 2011 was about getting us ready to capitalize on all of that growth.

Although about 70 percent of Caterpillar's 2011 sales and revenues came from outside the United States, almost 50 years ago, in 1963, international customers accounted for only 43 percent of the company's consolidated sales and revenues. Caterpillar's growing reliance on international sales and revenues has been slow but relatively steady through the years. By 1983, 46 percent of the company's consolidated sales and revenues were derived from international customers. By 2003, that number had climbed to 56 percent. Figure 3.1 shows the unmistakable growing impor-

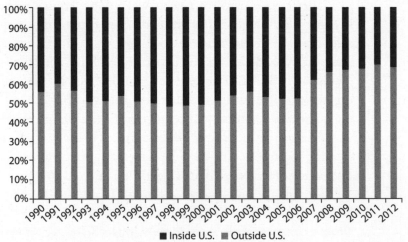

Figure 3.1 *The upsurge in Caterpillar's international sales.*
Source: Caterpillar annual reports.

tance of international customers to the company as the years have passed.

> **INSIDER'S EDGE**   *Doug Oberhelman is correct; 95 percent of the world's consumers live outside the United States. In manufacturing, high volume and scale are critical. It's much more difficult to achieve available economies of scale if you don't sell outside the United States. When properly developed, international operations also have the potential to reduce procurement costs and foreign exchange risks.*

WHERE DOES CATERPILLAR EARN ITS SALES AND REVENUES TODAY?

What areas of the world are most important to Caterpillar in terms of its sales? Table 3.1 shows that 25.9 percent of the company's total 2012 consolidated sales and revenues came from the Asia-Pacific region, 24.0 percent from EAME (Europe, Africa, and the Middle East), and 13.6 percent from Latin America.

Table 3.1   *Sources of Caterpillar Consolidated Sales and Revenue by Type and Location, 2012 ($ Billions)*

Type of Use or Sale	North America	Latin America	EAME	Asia/ Pacific	Percent
Construction Industries	$7.10	$2.65	$4.63	$4.95	29.3
Resources Industries	6.04	3.67	4.37	7.09	32.1
Energy/Power Systems	8.72	2.19	6.04	4.17	32.1
Financial Products	1.68	0.40	0.41	0.61	4.7
All Other	0.55	0.04	0.37	0.22	1.8
Totals	24.1	8.95	15.82	17.04	
Percent	36.6%	13.6%	24.0%	25.9%	

Source: Caterpillar Year in Review, 2012.

Table 3.1 also reveals that sales to the construction and resource industries are relatively more important in terms of generating sales and revenues in Asia, EAME, and Latin America than they are in North America. This sales pattern is consistent with Doug Oberhelman's hypothesis that growing populations and incomes in developing countries will drive urbanization and thus stimulate the demand for additional infrastructure that Caterpillar will help satisfy.

Globalization and the Caterpillar Culture

Caterpillar's increasing reliance on international customers is much more than a simple statistical phenomenon. The company's progressive globalization has changed the nature of its culture and in the process has had visible effects on its Peoria, Illinois, headquarters city. One sees this in the global economic coverage of the dominant *Peoria Journal-Star* newspaper, increased interest in foreign language study, and the fervent support of the region's congressman, Aaron Schock, for free-trade legislation. One also encounters this enhanced international awareness in Caterpillar facilities, where photos of the products of the company's competitors and sometimes of their CEOs are posted on the walls. There is a thin line between competition and war, and Caterpillar recognizes this. Make no mistake—Caterpillar's American employees are vitally aware that they are engaged in an international economic competition.

The globalization of Caterpillar vibrates through virtually everything the company does today. In 2011 Caterpillar had more than 70,000 employees "outside of North America," representing about 56 percent of the company's total employment. The "outside of North America" terminology is revealing because of what it says about Caterpillar's orientation. "North America" includes the company's facilities in the United States and Canada; reliance on this grouping enables the company both to broaden the focus of analysts and investors beyond the United States and subtly to make it a bit more difficult for critics to compute CAT's employment levels inside the United States proper. "Shipping jobs overseas" remains a sensitive political topic and could have collective bargaining implications for Caterpillar and many other corporations.

Caterpillar no longer is a conventional American company that sells to foreign customers. It has mutated and now is a global company that happens to be headquartered in the United States.

A Bit of History: Caterpillar and the Bolsheviks

Only four years after the merger that created the Caterpillar Tractor Company, the firm faced the challenge of the Great Depression. Caterpillar's sales plunged from $45.4 million in 1930 to $13.3 million in 1932. Salaries and costs were cut, four-day workweeks were imposed, significant employee layoffs rattled through the company, and dealers suffered. We now know that Caterpillar's ability to survive in this deteriorating arena depended in no small part on its ability to sell its machines and parts to the industrializing Soviet Union (USSR).

Selling to the Soviet Union was a far more daring proposition than it might seem today when the Russian Federation hosts the offices of most of the world's largest corporations. In 1929, the U.S. government did not recognize the USSR (it would not until November 1933). It was unclear how western capitalist companies would be treated in the USSR or what contracts Joseph Stalin and the Bolsheviks ultimately would honor. This much seemed certain: no private Soviet company similar to Caterpillar could exist in the early 1930s in the Soviet Union. Thus, it was questionable whether any profitable Caterpillar arrangement in the USSR was possible.

Caterpillar's dealings with the former Soviet Union provide a fine illustration of a basic economic principle: Every successful trading relationship is predicated on both parties believing that a trade will make them better off. And in the absence of dishonesty or coercion, both parties, at least initially, do end up better off in their own eyes. Otherwise they wouldn't make trades. This "trade makes both parties better off" relationship applies to virtually any transaction: buying and selling cars, houses, shoes, ice cream cones, and bulldozers.

In the case at hand, the USSR badly needed Caterpillar machines to support its drive to industrialize its economy as well as to enable it to impose what was to prove to be a brutally counterproductive collectivization regime on Soviet agriculture and begin to connect the far-flung 3,000-mile Soviet empire. In short, the Soviets needed and wanted Caterpillar products. Because Caterpillar was in the middle of a 71 percent decline in sales, Soviet sales might determine whether the company survived or went belly up. There was an obvious coincidence of interests that led to Caterpillar selling the Soviet agriculture sector alone 1,300 tractors and 750 harvesters.

Of course, Caterpillar not only survived the Great Depression but also turned a profit every year between 1929 and 1941 except 1932. In retrospect, it is apparent that the company's Soviet experience helped establish rough principles that Caterpillar still largely honors. With few exceptions, the company does not decide whether it should sell to a customer on the basis of that customer's ideology, the state of diplomatic relations between the United States and that customer's home country, or the customer's perceived love (or lack thereof) of capitalism. This attitude is exemplified by Caterpillar opening an office in Beijing in 1978 even though official documents in the People's Republic at that time still were derisive about "capitalist roaders" and denounced notions such as profit.

> **Fast forward to December 2012**, *when the U.S. Senate followed the U.S. House of Representatives in voting to end long-standing trade restrictions imposed on Russia. Caterpillar, which lobbied actively in favor of that change, will be a major beneficiary.*

Caterpillar's demonstrative lesson was not lost on other large American firms, which also began to do business with the Soviets and the Chinese. Today, except for international pariahs such as Burma (Myanmar), Cuba, Libya, North Korea, the Sudan, and Syria, Caterpillar does business in nearly every country. The company strictly adheres to the rulings of the Office of Foreign Assets Control in the U.S. Department of the Treasury and any Department of State and Department of the Treasury rulings concerning sanctions on specific countries.

This principle has wider application. Consider automobile manufacturers such as General Motors and Ford. They maintain production and distribution facilities around the world, sometimes in countries with autocratic regimes. If GMC and Ford are interested in the political or religious leanings of such customers, it is not apparent. They sell automobiles wherever they are able to sell them if those sales do not violate U.S. law or regulations.

Except in unusual circumstances and unless the Office of Foreign Assets Control or another relevant body has issued a ruling or imposed sanctions, modern businesses tend to sell to whoever wishes to buy their products, and they do so without regard either to their customers' politics and religion or to the economic system in the countries in which they reside.

The major difference in this regard between the Caterpillar and other companies is that Caterpillar evinces a strong interest in sustainable business models. First, the company actively strives to increase the efficiency of its core businesses in ways that will reduce its impact on the environment. Second, it attempts to help its customers do the same thing. Although Caterpillar typically cannot control how a customer ultimately decides to use one of its products, it does not wish to sell to customers that do not have environmentally sustainable business models.

> **INSIDER'S EDGE**   *The customer is king. From there, it can get complicated. Great companies don't have to like their customers or agree with their views. They do have to serve them well.*

Needless to say, nonjudgmental selling has not always been a popular stance with critics of modern American businesses, some of whom see it as an amoral or even immoral approach to economic life. Still, determining a sale on the basis of a customer's religious beliefs or political persuasion or the identity of the head of state in a country has never appealed to many American businesses. Nevertheless, this view of economic life sometimes can lead to complicated situations, as Caterpillar can attest.

Bulldozers and Palestine

On occasion, the salient issue for the company's critics is not the identity of the customers to whom Caterpillar sells its products but what those customers do with those products after they have purchased them. Some seek to hold Caterpillar responsible for the way its products are used after sale in the same manner that tobacco companies have been held liable for health problems among those who purchase cigarettes and then smoke them. The theory that Caterpillar should be held responsible for the way its products are utilized by its customers has never gained legal footing, but on occasion, discussions surrounding this notion have generated controversy.

To the disappointment of a few, Caterpillar sells products inside and outside the United States to those who cut down forests and to those who utilize fracking in their search for natural gas and oil. Outside the United States, Caterpillar has become notable (infamous to some) for selling bulldozers to the U.S. government, knowing that these machines are likely to be transferred to Israel. The bulldozers have been employed on occasion by the Israeli military to knock down Palestinian barricades and homes on the West Bank and in the Gaza Strip.

Caterpillar's indirect provision of bulldozers to the Israeli government has made the company a target for criticism from pro-Arab and pro-Palestinian groups and made the company the focus of a variety of somewhat amorphous human rights and peace groups in the United States and Europe. Caterpillar has been urged by groups such as Human Rights Watch and the U.N. Commission on Human Rights to find ways to stop the use of its bulldozers by the Israeli Defense Forces.

Criticism of Caterpillar on the Palestinian issue accelerated when an American activist, Rachel Corrie, was killed in 2003 after she apparently placed herself in the direct path of an armored D9R bulldozer made by Caterpillar but operated by the Israeli Defense Forces in the Gaza Strip. Corrie's estate subsequently sued the state of Israel over her death, but that suit was dismissed in 2012. Caterpillar previously had been sued inside the United States, but that action was dismissed in 2005.

Regardless, some large stockholders, such as TIAA-CREF's Social Choice Equity Fund, have used this situation as a reason to divest themselves of Caterpillar stock. Such actions usually reflect more than the Palestinian issue, though that is the hot button. There is a tendency on the part of some of Caterpillar's detractors to pile on by adding to the Palestinian indictment their distaste for the company's tough labor relations stances and the alleged degrading of the environment by Caterpillar production facilities and machines.

The Palestinian issue is frustrating to most Caterpillar executives and board members because the company does not actually sell bulldozers to the Israelis. Beyond that, however, they do not believe the company can or should be held responsible for the manner in which its products are used once they have been sold. Caterpillar's products, they argue, are designed for good and lawful purposes. Should General Motors be held responsible for the use of all the automobiles it has ever produced? Should Dell be held liable for how all the PCs it produces and sells are used? Can firms really restrict the right of a customer to resell a lawfully purchased product to another individual? With some exceptions, courts have answered no to all questions of this type.

At the end of the day, Caterpillar seldom has been deterred by the controversy that may accompany the sale of a tractor, an engine, or parts to customers that ultimately employ those products in ways some critics do not like. The company ordinarily does not reduce the size of its market by making moral judgments about its customers. Nevertheless, it consistently asserts that any and all of its activities must fit within the strictures of the company's Worldwide Code of Conduct. The Code asserts that Caterpillar employees must uphold its reputation "for acting with the highest values and principles." Integrity, says the Code, "is the foundation of all we do." The Code demands honesty and accuracy, prohibits discrimination and intimidation, and commits the company to supporting environmental responsibility and sustainable development throughout the world.

It's worth noting that after World War II ended, it came to light that Ford and General Motors not only had some facilities that had produced war goods for Nazi Germany but also that those facilities had used forced labor. No such skeletons exist in Caterpillar's closets; its Worldwide Code of Conduct and company culture are important reasons why. Caterpillar is a strong, resilient, and highly disciplined competitor in global markets, yet its success has not resulted from its being an immoral, dishonest rule breaker.

Globalization as a Vehicle for Peace and Understanding

To the surprise and delight of some, Caterpillar does listen to its critics. However, the company vigorously defends itself against international trade criticisms it believes are not well founded (the Palestinian issue is an illustration). At the same time, in our view, the company goes briskly about its business, which it sees as producing and selling excellent products that will make its customers better off. It appears to us that CAT's position is that in the long run, international trade has a liberating, peaceful influence on social, political, and economic affairs. Hence, we perceive that Caterpillar believes this dynamic is in play in China and that it would be a mistake for the United States to overreact to Chinese trade restrictions or China's periodic episodes of political repression and muscle flexing in the Pacific.

> **INSIDER'S EDGE**   *Although this is easier said than done, if your competitors are bending or breaking the rules, don't match them. Customers and suppliers will see it and feel it if you do. In the long run, good moral fiber wins more customers than it loses.*

Of course, Caterpillar's "we can make the world better via international trade" stance suits the profit-making interests of the company even as it has the virtue of liberalizing and improving international relations. At a minimum, however, this perspective represents a rather long-run view of the world and hence can discomfort those with more abbreviated time horizons. On occasion, critics disparage Caterpillar's expansion of activities into China and Russia as well as its willingness to do business with and inside politically repressive countries ranging from Saudi Arabia and Belarus to Libya (before the Arab Spring).

Even so, for those familiar with the company's history, such sales relationships are not surprising. Caterpillar's willingness to do business with "the Communists" (the former Soviet Union) in the 1930s set the tone. In fact, countries that have strong trading relationships with each other seldom go to war with each other. International business relationships provide strong incentives for otherwise disparate individuals to get to know each other, learn each other's languages and cultures, eat each other's food, and understand each other's point of view.

> **INSIDER'S EDGE** *Great companies can do well for themselves and do good at the same time. Globalization and international trade provide matchless opportunities for generating excellent people-to-people interactions that promote understanding.*

Caterpillar undoubtedly does more "getting to know you and respect you" work than most corporations because of its laser-like focus on the customer. In our interviews, we obtained a strong impression that CAT's sales executives push their staff and the dealers to walk in the metaphorical shoes of their customers. This means tromping around construction sites, playing golf during the day or mah-jongg at night, remembering the birthdays of wives and children, and believing that any customer's problem is Caterpillar's problem. This bonding with customers is subtle but very deliberate on the part of CAT, and the goal is to make the company, the dealers, and the customers part of one family that lives on through multiple generations. Such contacts represent a vintage quality "people-to-people" exchange because they occur under depoliticized conditions and frequently are outside the gaze of political minders and government agents. Caterpillar argues that this promotes both peace and prosperity and serves as highly productive informal diplomacy. This is a part of Caterpillar that the company's critics often miss.

The Komatsu Challenge

In 1967, Japan's Komatsu entered the American market and began to compete head to head with Caterpillar. Borrowing from the board game Go, Komatsu adopted the slogan *"Maru-C,"* which roughly translates to "Encircle Caterpillar," just as one captures an opponent's territory in Go by encircling it. Then and now, Komatsu was the second largest producer of items quite similar to those sold by Caterpillar, and today it employs about 44,000 individuals, of whom 2,000 work in North America.

The magnitude of Komatsu's challenge was a surprise to many Caterpillar executives. Gerald Flaherty, who would become a Caterpillar vice president, noted, "In 1981, some of us couldn't even spell Komatsu." Nevertheless, Komatsu had a reputation for producing quality items at competitive prices, and Caterpillar's leaders quickly came to understand that it represented an existential threat to CAT. Aided by early 1980s dollar/yen exchange rates that Caterpillar leaders such as CEO Lee Morgan (1977–1985) believed seriously undervalued the yen, Komatsu expanded aggressively and eventually opened up a 700-employee joint venture mining equipment manufacturing plant two miles away from CAT's headquarters in Peoria.

Caterpillar's responses were several, and as CFO and group president Ed Rapp comments, "Komatsu forced us to raise our game. The best way to be a great U.S. manufacturer is to be a great global manufacturer. We are a better company today because we have been going toe to toe with Komatsu in Japan since 1963." First, Caterpillar made the decision to do battle with Komatsu all around the globe and even in Komatsu's home territory in Japan. In 1963, Caterpillar had developed a partnership with Japan's Mitsubishi and concluded that it had to demonstrate that it could compete with Komatsu all across Asia as well as in Komatsu's backyard. Caterpillar opened several Japanese production facilities. By 1989 its Akashi plant had produced more than 100,000 hydraulic excavators, and by 2002 its Sagami plant had produced 300,000 units of various lines of construction equipment.

> **INSIDER'S EDGE** *"My opponents lifted my spirits, and, in doing so, reminded me of something I had spent twenty-two years learning: that opponents and I were really one. My strength and skills were only half of the equation. The other half was theirs." So said Sadaharu Oh, who hit 868 career home runs for the Yomiuri Giants in Japan—more than Babe Ruth, Henry Aaron, or Barry Bonds.*

During lean economic times, Caterpillar consciously accepted lower profit margins to maintain its market share in Japan and Asia and provide financial sustenance to some of the dealers in its invaluable network. Although it could not have been forecast at the time, the long-term appreciation of the Japanese yen relative to the dollar eventually made those movements much easier.

> **INSIDER'S EDGE** *Great companies recognize that their salespeople and dealers are their frontline troops. When they do well, the company does well. Nurture them, reward them, cajole them. Light the fires that will push them to succeed.*

While dancing with its main rival Komatsu, Caterpillar plunged enthusiastically into Latin America and sub-Saharan Africa, sensing that these were the areas where the ultimate future of the company resided. The company's 1963 annual report listed nine production or parts facilities outside the United States, including ones in Australia, Belgium, Brazil, Canada, France, England, India, Mexico, and South Africa that were owned outright or partly owned by Caterpillar. By 1983, England, Indonesia, Japan, and Scotland had been added to the list, and the company had training and sales centers in Hong Kong, Singapore, Spain, and Switzerland. Today, CAT has approximately 60 production facilities outside the United States plus about 50 inside the United States.

The Vital Dollar/Yen Relationship

Even as geographic diversification brought Caterpillar closer to its customers, it helped insulate the company from the impact of changes in the value of foreign currencies. Many U.S. manufacturers have struggled whenever the value of the U.S. dollar has increased relative to other major currencies. Caterpillar, however, avoids some of this problem because it already produces significant portions of its products in locations such as Japan and Europe. Hence, if the euro appreciates, this does not hurt Caterpillar as much as it may damage many other American manufacturers because many of CAT's transactions in Europe and elsewhere already are denominated in euros.

The dollar/yen relationship, however, has been of particular interest not only because Caterpillar has production facilities in Japan but also because Japan is the home base of Komatsu. For the last 50 years, the unmistakable trend in the dollar/yen relationship has been a decline in the value of the U.S. dollar relative to the yen. In 1970, the exchange rate between the two currencies was 360 yen per dollar. By September 2012, that rate had fallen to only 78 yen per dollar (Figure 3.2), a 79 percent decline in the relative value of the dollar relative to the yen. Even so, there have been periods of time such as 1980–1985 and 2013, when the yen fell in value and the dollar appreciated significantly. This constitutes more than a bump in the road and has an impact on Caterpillar's sales and costs. The appreciation of the dollar makes it more difficult for Caterpillar to sell its products in Japan because each appreciated dollar carries a higher price in yen to the Japanese. The dollar's appreciation with respect to most other currencies places Caterpillar at a disadvantage in competing against the likes of Komatsu in countries around the world.

However, a stronger dollar also enables Caterpillar to buy needed inputs such as labor and metals less expensively abroad. This means that Caterpillar does not have to supply as many dollars to hire workers or make such purchases. The strength of the dol-

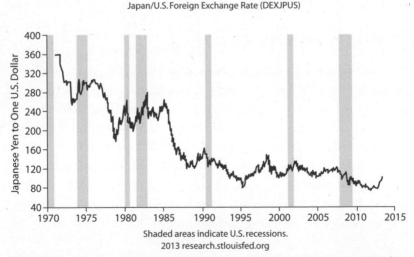

Japan/U.S. Foreign Exchange Rate (DEXJPUS)

Shaded areas indicate U.S. recessions.
2013 research.stlouisfed.org

Figure 3.2   *The long-term trend: the yen has strengthened with respect to the dollar (though recently it has weakened).*

Source: FRED, the St. Louis Federal Reserve Bank, May 18, 2013.

lar mitigates the significant price disadvantage that can exist with respect to Komatsu and other competitors.

Exchange rate difficulties facing Caterpillar in the early 1980s were one of several reasons the company lost money in 1982, 1983, and 1984. Indeed, in 1984 Caterpillar lost an average of $1.17 million *every day*. For the first time since the Great Depression, the company's future was in doubt, and bankruptcy was a whispered possibility. In retrospect, we know that many similarly situated firms did fail. The fact that Caterpillar was able to buck this trend, survive, and prosper is one of most compelling stories in American manufacturing in the twentieth century.

Caterpillar's 1981 annual report presaged the trials it was about to face when it stated, "Wage differences among countries—especially between the United States and Japan—are a major handicap to Caterpillar and other U.S. companies. In 1981, the average U.S. production worker was paid seventy-six percent more than a Japanese counterpart. . . ." This wide gap in wages was to be a recurring theme for Caterpillar as it struggled to dig itself out of the competitive hole in which it found itself.

The response of most American manufacturing firms facing similar circumstances at that time was to ask the U.S. government to intervene on their behalf. They requested trade restrictions such as tariffs and import quotas, tax preferences, and even outright subsidies. Most conspicuous among the supplicants for governmental interference were the automobile and steel industries, though numerous other industries and firms sought competitive protection from the Japanese.

> **INSIDER'S EDGE** *Great companies realize that if the only times they can succeed in international trade are when exchange rates are favorable, they're probably not doing things right. Exchange rates rise and fall. International success must be carefully constructed on the basis of factors such as quality, efficiency, life-cycle costs, and service.*

Caterpillar's reaction was very different. The company turned that argument on its head by demanding that trade restrictions be eliminated, not increased. It pointed out that the General Agreement on Tariffs and Trade (GATT) had identified 800 forms of trade barriers that circumvented GATT's free-trade rules. The company unabashedly declared, "We oppose governmental interventions that distort trade and investment," and, "U.S. international economic policy should support an open, competitive economic atmosphere. . . ."

Caterpillar's position on free trade has not changed over time. In its 2011 annual report, Chairman/CEO Doug Oberhelman noted, "Time and again, free trade is a proven winner for both sides. At Caterpillar, we promote freer trade wherever we can get it, but we also recognize that expanding global free-trade agreements through the World Trade Organization is a once in a generation opportunity to open markets and increase worldwide economic growth."

Caterpillar's free-trade advocacy placed it at odds with both of the 2012 presidential candidates. If elected, Governor Romney promised to brand China a "currency manipulator" on the first day of his term, and President Obama's administration filed formal complaints against China with the World Trade Organization during the peak of the campaign season, alleging illegal subsidies by the Chinese for internationally traded goods. Caterpillar, perhaps viewing these statements as campaign rhetoric, did not support either of those approaches.

Caterpillar often has walked a lonely road on trade issues when one compares the positions it has taken with those of other manufacturers. It is notable that in the 1980s, even though Caterpillar was under competitive siege, it did not ask the U.S. government for tariff protection.

> **Caterpillar's leaders** *have not been shy in prodding elected officials and American presidents of both parties to promote freer trade. When President Barack Obama visited Caterpillar's home turf in Peoria in February 2009, he received an unapologetic brief from Chairman/CEO Jim Owens on the importance of free-trade principles to the company's prosperity. The president also listened to CAT explain why the company believed that the president's*

"Buy American" initiative would result in retaliation by other countries that would backfire on trade-intensive firms such as Caterpillar.

Instead, it tightened its proverbial chinstrap and proceeded to undertake actions that within several decades would make it the envy of manufacturing firms around the world. It retooled its factories, cut costs, developed new products, opened new production and distribution facilities in countries around the world, and improved its supply chain management.

INSIDER'S EDGE   *Great companies understand that ultimately the only way they can be successful in any market is by becoming as efficient as their competitors. Trade and tariff restrictions seldom turn out to be anything more than temporary solutions and too often become a crutch that encourages inefficiency.*

One cannot help thinking how different the histories of the American automobile and steel industries might have been if those industries had followed Caterpillar's example. Senior management and board members at Caterpillar were wise enough to realize that ultimately the only viable solution to the company's economic challenges lay within the corporation. Bluntly, the company had to improve its performance across the board in order to survive. The fact that this book is being written reveals that it did so, and with remarkably great success as time passed.

Fortunately for Caterpillar, in 1985, the dollar/yen relationship began to reverse and the yen began to appreciate dramatically. Between September 1985 and December 1988, the yen appreciated slightly more than 50 percent relative to the dollar. This was precisely the tonic the company needed, and perhaps it saved the corporation. Caterpillar now could stand toe to toe with foreign competitors and battle them on the basis of both price and quality. Whereas Caterpillar's sales outside the United States had fallen from 57 percent of all sales and revenues in 1980 to only 42 percent in 1984, by 1990 the company was back to 55 percent of all its sales and revenues coming from outside the United States.

During the first decade of this century, the yen appreciated a further one-third relative to the dollar, and by November 2012 it stood at only 81 per dollar. By July 11, 2013, however, the yen had declined in value to 98.64 per dollar. Caterpillar's economic sweet spot may be disappearing. One of the company's fundamental value propositions is that the quality of its machines is very high and that they exhibit superior performance and have attractively lower life-cycle costs. This makes Caterpillar products very enticing purchases for customers who intend to use the machines intensively or who will keep the machines in service for long periods. This quality weapon has been supplemented by Caterpillar's ability to price aggressively because of the competitive cushion provided by the strength of the Japanese yen. The recent decline in the value of the yen relative to the dollar will temper this advantage.

Hence, it is no surprise that Caterpillar's non-U.S. activities now account for about 70 percent of its consolidated sales and revenues. The company is well positioned to project itself around the world and take advantage of growing world populations, urbanization, and the resulting demands for equipment that will support the construction of vital infrastructure.

The really interesting question surrounding Caterpillar's success focuses on the extent to which that success is a function of the weakness of the U.S. dollar and its mirror image, the strength of the Japanese yen. Without doubt, the spectacular long-term appreciation of the yen (it moved from 276 per dollar in November 1982 to 98 in July 2013) has had a very positive influence on Caterpillar.

Still, attributing all of Caterpillar's success to the dollar/yen relationship would constitute a gross error. Let's not forget that Caterpillar has done the following:

- Modernized its factories

- Streamlined its supply chains

- Initiated significant cost controls

- Negotiated labor contracts that are competitive in a global context

- Opened numerous facilities in strategic locations around the world

- Cultivated and supported its highly regarded dealership network

- Provided itself with flexibility by moving some of its production into states that are in a better position it to reach customers

- Acquired a series of firms that provide it with enviable positions in strategic industries

- Developed a strong, internationally experienced management team

- Brought to market a continuing series of highly regarded products

By any reasonable standard, any one of these achievements would by itself deserve kudos because each has contributed to Caterpillar's outstanding performance. All things considered, an even-handed analysis of Caterpillar's remarkable economic resurrection over the last 25 years can hardly avoid the conclusion that although the weakening dollar (strengthening yen) has been an important contributing factor to Caterpillar's sterling accomplishments, it is not the only factor and perhaps not even the major factor.

In fact, in recent years, the dollar has weakened with respect to nearly every major world currency. For example, even taking into account recent economic problems in Europe, the euro appreciated more than 35 percent relative to the dollar between 2001 and 2012. The Swedish krona, used by Caterpillar competitor Volvo, appreciated more than 42 percent relative to the dollar between 2003 and 2012.

Taken together, these currency rate changes have endowed Caterpillar with vastly improved price flexibility with respect to its customers. The company now has the ability to cut the effective price it offers its international customers when it wishes to do so, and it has room to increase prices on its products without necessarily making its prices noncompetitive with those of Komatsu and Volvo.

It is unusual for a company to be able to offer customers what many regard as the highest-quality products in its market space and at the same time possess substantial pricing flexibility. This is the essence of the economic sweet spot that Caterpillar occupies today in international markets. No sweet spot lasts forever, however, and sooner or later the company once again will have to rely on more traditional tools such as cost controls, the Caterpillar distributor network, and its supply chain management to excel. It is important to understand that it has been these factors rather than foreign exchange rates that historically have propelled Caterpillar to success.

> **Price Increases**: On September 28, 2012, Caterpillar announced that it would be raising prices on most of its machines by up to 3 percent in January 2013 and that prices would increase 7 percent on select models because of emission requirements. This was the "sweet spot" in action.

CHAPTER 4

CHINA: A METAPHOR FOR CATERPILLAR'S FUTURE?

When the words *China* and *PRC* are spoken by Caterpillar's leaders, nearly always they are accompanied by phrases such as "our future," "huge potential," "great opportunity," and "market size." Caterpillar sees the strength of the company being tied to its ability to produce and sell in the BRIC countries (Brazil, Russia, India, and China). However, its activities in China have assumed the status of a marker for these efforts. Paraphrasing the slogan of New York City, Caterpillar thinks that if it can make it in China, it can make it anywhere.

Some up and coming managers privately acknowledge that experience in Asia in general and China in particular may become a sine qua non for advancement to the highest ranks of Caterpillar management. It is taken as an article of faith that Caterpillar is going to invest major resources in developing production and sales in China even though in the first quarter of 2012 only about 3 percent of the company's consolidated revenues and sales came from that country. Caterpillar personnel are unfazed by the deceleration of the Chinese economy that became apparent in 2012 because their eyes are on future prizes.

By the end of 2013, Caterpillar will have more than 30 production and distribution facilities in the People's Republic of China (PRC), and in January 2013 it employed approximately 15,000 individuals in the PRC. Therefore, its activities in that rapidly growing country receive rapt attention from investors, analysts, labor leaders, and elected officials. China is, after all, the most populous nation in the world, with approximately 1.4 billion residents. By comparison, India, which has the second largest population in the world with approximately 1.2 billion residents, hosts only seven Caterpillar facilities.

Many non-Caterpillar individuals view the company's Chinese expansion as a transparent attempt to capitalize on the lower wage rates there. CAT executives, however, insist that this has not been the major factor. Frank Crespo, Caterpillar's vice president for global purchasing, says, "We put manufacturing plants in China not for labor arbitrage, but to be close to our markets." He and other company leaders told us that labor costs account for no more than 10 to 20 percent of the total cost of a typical product; other cost factors are far more important to Caterpillar. Therefore, they assert that it would be foolish to establish a production facility primarily on the basis of wage rates, which in any case are subject to change.

> **China consumes** *53 percent of all of the world's cement, 48 percent of all iron ore, 47 percent of all coal, 45 percent of all steel, and 41 percent of all aluminum. In short, it is an economic force to be reckoned with, and Doug Oberhelman is attempting to place Caterpillar in a position of being able to take advantage of this burgeoning market.*

Doug Oberhelman Plants the Flag

Caterpillar has a long history in China. It opened an office in Beijing in 1978 and in the 1980s signed a series of technology transfer agreements with Chinese manufacturers that allowed them to produce licensed Caterpillar products. In the 1990s, Caterpillar made the seminal decision to open local production facilities in

China and has vastly accelerated the rollout of its present there since that time. Doug Oberhelman, Caterpillar's chairman/CEO, pulls no punches when he observes that China may evolve into the company's most important market and that CAT's goal is nothing less than to "be number one in China by 2015." To do so, it must pass its ever present rival, Komatsu, which currently has the largest market share in China for most large earthmovers and excavators, as well as Sany, Doosan, and Hitachi. In the bulldozer market, CAT trails Shantui, HBXG, and Zoomlion in China and has a market share of only about 1 percent.

Oberhelman's attitude underpins Caterpillar's significant long-term investments in China (and indeed in many other parts of the world. A May 2013, Caterpillar publication, "Caterpillar in China," identified almost three dozen distinct production, distribution, finance, and joint ventures the company was operating in China. Stephen Volkmann, a Jefferies & Co. analyst in New York, averred that if Caterpillar is right, "they're going to make gobs of money." However, Volkmann also cautioned that "many investors were edgy" about Caterpillar's prospects. His comment underscores the reality that there was considerable risk in the company's activities over the last several decades. Caterpillar's consistent success is, however, an indication that its business plan has been executed intelligently. It is a lesson many other manufacturing firms could have, or should have, learned.

> **INSIDER'S EDGE** *Within the next five years, the risk-adjusted cost of manufacturing in the Yangtze River delta will be roughly equivalent to the cost of manufacturing in U.S. southern "right-to-work" states. When this occurs, it will be clear that the major reason to manufacture in China is to sell in China.*

Figure 4.1 shows how large a player China has become in the global market for construction equipment. Caterpillar is determined not simply to play in the Chinese market but to lead it. In light of the price-cutting abilities of Chinese competitors, the always difficult to quantify state subsidies that native firms receive from the Chinese government, and the influence of *guanxi* (connections) in Chinese

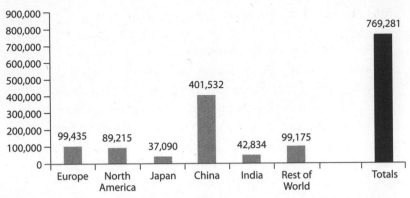

Figure 4.1 *China's share of global construction equipment sales is growing.*

Source: Adapted from Offhighway Research Global Volume and Service Report, www
.offhighway.co.uk/samples/The_Global_Volume_and_Value_Service_April_2011.pdf.

business dealings, it is apparent that Caterpillar is flying into headwinds. It remains to be seen how fierce those headwinds are.

Is the Yuan Undervalued?—Caterpillar's Take on the Issue

Many American manufacturing firms and elected officials long
have contended that the value of the yuan, the currency unit of the
People's Republic of China, has been deliberately manipulated by
the Chinese and that the yuan is undervalued relative to the dollar and most other major world currencies. An August 2012 report
from the Economic Policy Institute argued that "Currency manipulation is a major cause of the trade deficit," and the *New York Times*
asserted in May 2012 that despite recent strengthening, the yuan
remained undervalued relative to the dollar by 5 to 20 percent.
Treasury Secretary Timothy Geithner already was on the record say-
ing the yuan was substantially undervalued. Voluble political economist Paul Krugman averred that the United States should impose
a temporary 25 percent surcharge on the yuan to balance the scales.
Meanwhile, both presidential candidates in 2012 competed to show
who would be toughest in dealing with the Chinese on trade issues.

Figure 4.2 reports the value of the yuan per dollar between 1980
and 2013. One can discern three distinct stages in the yuan/dollar
relationship. The first, from 1980 to 1995, is the period when the

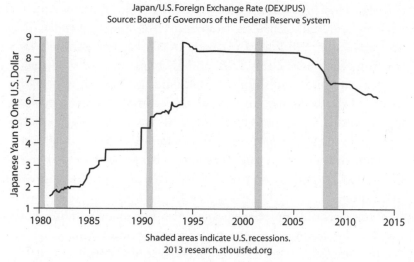

Japan/U.S. Foreign Exchange Rate (DEXJPUS)
Source: Board of Governors of the Federal Reserve System

Shaded areas indicate U.S. recessions.
2013 research.stlouisfed.org

Figure 4.2 *The value of the yuan in terms of U.S. dollars, 1980–2013.*
Source: FRED, Federal Reserve Bank of St. Louis (May 18, 2013), www.stlouisfed.org.

yuan depreciated relative to the dollar. This deliberate policy by the Chinese government reduced the prices of Chinese goods for foreign customers and stimulated Chinese exports to the United States. China began to accumulate significant foreign exchange reserves.

The second stage, between 1995 and 2006, saw the Chinese hold the value of yuan almost constant at about 8.3 to the dollar. The third stage began in 2006 and has seen the Chinese gradually allow the yuan to appreciate relative to the dollar. Because the Chinese government is relatively opaque on economic issues such as the value of the yuan, it is not clear precisely why China has allowed the yuan to appreciate relative to the dollar. We can speculate that external political pressure by the United States and others may well have had an effect, but historically the Chinese have been loath to respond to foreign demands in virtually any area. Perhaps the Chinese now view an appreciating yuan as a way to raise the standard of living of Chinese workers (because a more valuable yuan will make their labor worth more) and in the process stimulate domestic consumption in an economy that has long been excessively investment-driven.

In any case, taking inflation into account, the value of the yuan relative to the dollar has been increasing approximately 10 percent per year. How has this affected Caterpillar? Not quite as much as one might initially surmise. It remains true that Caterpillar does not produce its full line of products in China. For example, large machines such as the D9, D10, and D11 tractors are produced in the United States and shipped worldwide. It does not appear that this is likely to change because of the exorbitant cost of replicating in China the capital-intensive factories, technological know-how, and highly qualified labor forces found in the United States. The appreciation of the yuan has made these machines and any of Caterpillar's exports from the United States more price-competitive in China.

However, the appreciating yuan also has made it more expensive for the company to purchase inputs inside China when the funding source is dollars. Nevertheless, one of Caterpillar's goals in its vigorous move into China and other markets has been to insulate the company against swings in foreign exchange rates. Because it produces output and locally sources inputs in China, Caterpillar need not worry excessively about exchange rate swings because its activities there are denominated in yuan.

The slowdown in the growth of China's economy in fall 2012 and Caterpillar's need to bring down inventory levels saw the company begin to export products from China to other countries in Asia. Previously, the company had asserted that its Chinese production facilities were serving only Chinese customers.

> **Coca-Cola** *is an example of a firm that has encountered difficulties operating in the PRC. Its sales have disappointed analysts, and it has had to apologize to the Chinese government for having excess chlorine content in some of its drinks. "This is not the best moment for Coca-Cola in its 126-years' history," commented David Brooks, president of the company's China and South Korea operations.*

The posturing of political candidates aside, by fall 2012, some analysts had evolved to the point of arguing that the upward trend in the value of the yuan had brought the yuan/dollar exchange rate much closer to what they believe it would be in a freely operating, nonmanipulated market. In this vein, C. Fred Bergsten, director of the highly regarded Peterson Institute for International Economics, concluded that China no longer was a "major perpetrator" of currency "aggression." Bergsten previously had inveighed against the Chinese for undervaluing their currency. He and others noted that China no longer was accumulating foreign exchange reserves at the same rate and that China's balance of trade with the rest of the world was not excessive.

The Challenges Associated with Doing Business In China

State capitalism as practiced in China involves significant government subsidies to many Chinese firms. Those subsidies are problematic for Caterpillar, which would like to compete with the Chinese on a level playing field. Rich Lavin, Caterpillar's group president for construction industries and growth markets until he retired in fall 2012, reminded us that CAT has been in China more than 35 years. Hence, it can legitimately present itself to the Chinese government as a Chinese company deserving of a level playing field.

Caterpillar does lean on the Chinese government when it believes the government is supporting regulations that give unwarranted preference to Chinese companies. In light of the state of Chinese accounting and lack of company transparency, it often is difficult to tell if the government is providing subsidies to Chinese firms. However, the *Financial Times* reported in November 2012 that the revenues of state-owned enterprises in China had increased from 3.4 trillion yuan in 2002 to 20.2 trillion yuan in 2011, indicating a 21.9 percent compound annual rate of growth. If the numbers are trustworthy, that is a hefty rate of increase.

Since it is difficult to determine precisely what the Chinese government subsidizes and how, Caterpillar tends to focus less on subsidies and more on trade restrictions and rules that prevent it from competing at any level of subsidies. This is consistent with the company's stance inside the United States, where it consistently advocates the elimination of trade barriers, a point of view that sometimes antagonizes other American manufacturers.

Caterpillar knows well the sometimes complex nature of doing business in China. In November 2011, it announced that it would acquire the 4,000-employee Chinese firm ERA Mining Machinery, which produced hydraulic roof supports used in underground mining. CAT closed the deal in June 2012 but by fall 2012 became aware of "deliberate, multiyear coordinated accounting misconduct," some of which involved significant discrepancies between actual inventories and reported inventories and exaggerated profit reports.

The ERA purchase, though strategically sound and one that could prove to be productive in the future because the size of the Chinese machinery market already was $64 billion in 2012 and a higher-risk initiative at the time. ERA had been listed on the Growth Enterprise Market stock exchange in Hong Kong, which is "designed to accommodate companies to which a higher investment risk may be attached" (Caterpillar's language according to Reuters).

Caterpillar paid $653.4 million for ERA and its wholly owned subsidiary, Siwei, which was the product of an interesting reverse merger with ERA Holdings Global, self-described as a supplier of "corporate secretarial services." Disclosure standards in China typically are lower for reverse mergers than for other acquisitions, and some analysts have suggested that these lower standards have been the source of several accounting scandals involving American firms and small Chinese companies that went public by means of reverse mergers.

There is little dispute that Caterpillar stubbed its toe and perhaps even broke its foot in China with its ERA/Siwei failures. To address the accounting fraud at ERA, CAT announced a large $580 million noncash impairment charge equivalent to about one-half of its reported profit in fourth quarter 2012. It subsequently recovered $135 million of that write-off in May 2013 when it renegotiated some of the terms of the deal.

Multiple lessons were learned. First, we believe that the company acquired a new appreciation for the sharp variations in accounting standards and transparency that exist around the globe. Assumptions commonly made and terms easily understood on Wall

Street (or on Adams Street in Peoria, Illinois) do not necessarily apply around the world. Observers such as the *Wall Street Journal*'s Duncan Mavin have alleged that Caterpillar should have seen "red flags" related to ERA's accounts receivable and inventory and use of its cash.

Second, even though CAT has asserted that its due diligence procedures in examining potential acquisitions are "rigorous and robust" and that it completed many dozens of complicated international deals in an amazing variety of venues, we believe it now has renewed awareness of the difficulties that can hinder the performance of due diligence in some locations around the world. It is possible that the attention of the board, the CEO, and senior executives was diverted because of the company's $8.8 billion acquisition of Bucyrus (which closed on July 11, 2011). That merger immediately generated a flurry of activities designed to integrate Bucyrus into the Caterpillar family.

Finally, although it always is wise to have astute "locals" in senior management roles in international operations, if those locals aren't Caterpillar people who have been and will be dedicated to Caterpillar values and standards, difficulties can arise. Although Caterpillar always attempts to transplant its culture as quickly as possible, even if that culture had been transplanted in a microsecond at ERA, that would not have eliminated the extended financial malfeasances that CAT inherited from the existing ERA managers. Nevertheless, one hears almost no complaining from Caterpillar executives about the sometimes murky nature of doing business in China despite the fact that *TIME* magazine noted in September 2012 that non-Chinese firms face "a new Great Wall, one composed not of stone and earth but of regulations and restrictions, manned by an army of protective bureaucrats."

A China veteran writing in *Bloomberg Businessweek* in September 2012 cautioned Western businesses, "[D]o not expect to operate with the same opportunities as Chinese. It is not an even playing field and never will be." International firms that operate in high-profile industries that the government considers crucial often face the toughest bureaucratic resistance. This description would appear to fit Caterpillar to the proverbial T.

Investors have largely *been comfortable with Caterpillar's handling of the ERA situation. CAT's stock closed at $95.58 per share on Friday, January 25, 2013. On Monday, January 28, 2013, CAT held its quarterly earnings and guidance call, and Doug Oberhelman specifically addressed the ERA circumstance. CAT closed at $97.45 per share that day (up 1.96 percent) even though the S&P 500 index fell by 0.185 percent.*

Chinese authorities reportedly have placed considerable pressure on foreign automobile manufacturers to undertake joint ventures with Chinese partners. Although Caterpillar also has joint ventures in China and faces several Chinese competitors of growing significance, if its employees are being pummeled by Chinese officialdom, CAT diplomatically declines to say so. Grin and bear it may be the order of the day for Caterpillar in the People's Republic because Chairman/CEO Oberhelman and the company see China as a vital cog in Caterpillar's future.

INSIDER'S EDGE   *To conduct business successfully in China, one must become Chinese. This means many things, but here are a few key concepts: (1) operate at the scale of your Chinese competitors (small usually is a bad idea), (2) understand the motivation of Chinese political leaders, which is first to feed the people, (3) digest China's five-year plan and build into it because it really does provide a road map, (4) make sure you have senior employees who are also senior members of the local Communist Party and have guanxi, (5) develop an internal culture that understands and respects the Foreign Corrupt Practices Act, and (6) understand that your intellectual property could come under assault.*

Caterpillar's Long-Run View

Caterpillar's approach to China indisputably is long-run in nature, and the 2012 decline in sales in China did not alter the corporation's determination to assume a leadership position there within this decade. "I'm looking at China not quarter to quarter, or year to year, but as a market that ten or fifteen years from now will serve us very nicely," says Oberhelman. He adds, "I am not going to be in a position in China of catching up on supply and capacity as we have been for the last ten years." This is consistent with the company business model "Seed, Grow, Harvest," which means seed the business with great products, grow the field population, and harvest the parts and service business. Although China currently does not account for a large proportion of Caterpillar's consolidated sales and revenues, Oberhelman believes that that country, with its 1.4 billion people, has the potential to become the largest and most lucrative market in the world for Caterpillar products.

> **INSIDER'S EDGE** *Budgeting is about quarterly and annual financial goals. Don't confuse this with a strategic plan, which deals with ways to scale—either organically or via acquisitions—to larger markets and higher profits. Less successful companies often confuse these management tools and are unable to scale their operations effectively.*

Globalization Has Transformed Caterpillar

Doug Oberhelman is an aggressive leader with high standards and expansive goals. When he notes that 95 percent of the world's consumers reside outside the United States, he is attempting to focus the attention of Caterpillar employees beyond their local environments. This means that facilities must be located outside the United States so that Caterpillar can be close to its ultimate consumers. International sales have become an important factor in the company's prosperity. Subtly but undeniably, Caterpillar has transitioned from being an American firm that used to sell some product overseas into being a thoroughly global firm that happens to be headquartered in the United States.

The recognition that Caterpillar must be able to compete legitimately in each country it enters has infiltrated every aspect of the company's strategy and behavior. When Caterpillar engages in labor negotiations, it understands the need to negotiate agreements that will ensure that it is globally competitive in the long run rather than pacts that might fit within local U.S. norms or agreements that are based primarily on the corporation's most recent economic performance.

Much of Caterpillar's American focus now is on export activity rather than domestic U.S. markets. There's no mystery why that is the case. In 2011, the company exported $19.44 billion worth of products from the United States. When Caterpillar locates new production and distribution facilities in the United States, it places substantial weight on the access of a facility to a port because exporting has become second nature to the company. Although many different factors came into play when Caterpillar decided in 2012 to open a new production facility in Oconee County, Georgia, that location's access to the Port of Savannah (the second largest on the East Coast) was vitally important.

When Caterpillar weighs which of its management-level personnel to promote, it pays explicit attention to their international experience and ability to function in other cultures. Company executives will not be able to function effectively if they haven't had considerable experience abroad. This is an interesting juxtaposition for a company that takes pride in its Midwestern roots and heritage. Caterpillar board member David Goode, the former CEO of Norfolk Southern Corporation, confirmed to us that even though there is something very distinctive about the Midwestern culture and values that permeate the company and many of its employees, it also is true that Caterpillar now places a very high value on global perspectives and experience.

In our interview, Goode moved to the topic of future board governance in the coming era of being a truly global enterprise. He opined that Caterpillar (and its board) must avoid becoming "U.S.-centric." He believes that the time is not far away when Caterpillar will have a chairman/CEO who was not born in the United States. The board must work to maintain the corporation's cohesion and ability to communicate effectively. After all, its employees and customers are already spread around the world. For several years, the company has been utilizing electronic meetings as a means to bring together geographically dispersed employees. Board members know that out of sight, out of mind is a danger to which the board must not fall victim.

Understanding, cooperation, and mutual respect for diverse individuals and cultures will be necessary for Caterpillar to continue its globalization. This cannot be taken for granted. Nor can Caterpillar's future leaders assume that what former presiding board member Eugene Fife, previously a general partner at Goldman Sachs, calls "Caterpillar's core values" will be sustained as time passes. The challenge is to find a way to balance the requirements of Caterpillar's progressive globalization with a respect for those traditional core values.

Caterpillar's culture encourages the view that the company can retain its traditional values (many of which are evinced in its nonnegotiable Code of Conduct) as the locus of its prosperity moves outside the United States. Caterpillar leaders are determined to make this evolution succeed. Yet it is undeniable that numerous large American firms have encountered problems overseas. Walmart, for example, not only ran afoul of the law in Mexico but also had to withdraw from Germany when it found that its successful American model did not translate to the German retail space.

Caterpillar continues to press down on the accelerator with respect to globalization. The company's *2011 Year in Review* contained a revealing world map that shows where and how Caterpillar invested its funds to construct, expand, and retool its production facilities in 2011 (Figure 4.3). Caterpillar made investments in six facilities in China, five elsewhere in Asia, and three in Latin America.

Chairman/CEO Oberhelman is insistent that the company develop the diverse international employee experience set that he believes will characterize every successful global firm in the future. In the long run (and that's the horizon that Cat personnel mention repeatedly rather than this quarter's results), they believe extensive international investments of assets and people will position CAT for success whether measured by market share or by profitability. This is part of the transition of Caterpillar from an American firm that does business outside the United States to a global firm that happens to be headquartered in the United States.

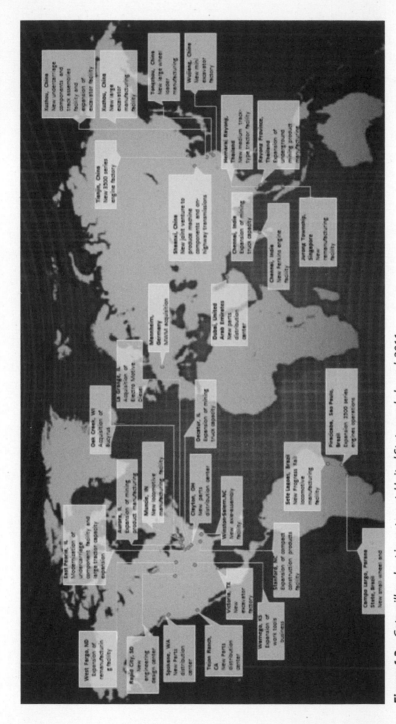

Figure 4.3 *Caterpillar plant investment: United States and abroad, 2011.*

Source: Caterpillar annual report, 2011.

INSIDER'S EDGE *Globalization means much more than simply selling products overseas. It demands culture change within the company such that all the employees understand what is at stake for them and how they fit into the company's globalization. Employees must begin to view issues and people differently.*

CHAPTER 5

CATERPILLAR AND THE INTERNATIONALIZATION OF OUTPUT

During the fall 2012 U.S. election campaign, it was almost obligatory for candidates for statewide and national offices to deplore the "offshoring" of American jobs. The candidates might have had Caterpillar in mind because a clear and increasing majority of CAT's workers now reside outside the United States. In 1960, 87.42 percent of Caterpillar's employees resided in the United States, but that number had fallen to 69.97 percent by 1990. By 2011, only 42.56 percent of CAT's employees were in the United States.

Thus if offshoring (a word with an emotional connotation) and related internationalization are wrongheaded, Caterpillar can be classified as one of the major American malefactors because it has rapidly increased the number of individuals it employs outside the United States. Nevertheless, a dispassionate analysis of both internationalization in general and Caterpillar's situation in particular leads to a far more favorable assessment of the company's activities. In fact, though the accounting is complicated, internationalization may create more jobs in the United States than it loses, and the incremental jobs created in the

United States include thousands in unionized Caterpillar production locations in snow belt states.

It is important at the outset to recognize that international capital flows seldom move only in one direction. Capital and production flow to where the most attractive opportunities exist, and frequently those opportunities are in the United States today. Companies headquartered in Europe or Asia also outsource and frequently establish production and distribution sites in the United States. This constitutes "inshoring." Witness the profusion of production and distribution facilities in the United States owned by companies such as Mercedes, Toyota, Canon, SONY, Stihl, Glaxo, Ahold, and BP. The list is long and impressive, and these and other foreign-owned firms employed 5.4 million workers in the United States in 2011 (about 6 percent of total private sector employment). California alone hosted 616,000 insourced jobs in 2011.

> **One of the most** intriguing economic trends today is the growing tendency of American firms to inshore production that they previously had outshored to locations such as China. In November 2011, Caterpillar announced that it would shift some construction machinery production activity from Japan back to the United States.

Table 5.1 shows the volume of direct foreign investment in the United States by country or area between January 2009 and June 2012. It is notable that virtually every major trading partner of the United States except China has been sending significant amounts of capital into the United States, and China is beginning to do so. Both the weakness of the American dollar and the attractiveness of investment opportunities in the United States are responsible for these large capital flows.

In 2008, 4.7 percent of all U.S. jobs were provided by insourced firms such as Siemens and Toyota. Delaware led all states with 8.2 percent of of its jobs provided by foreign employers, and Connecticut followed with 7.1 percent. Interestingly, more than half of all insourced jobs that result from such investments are subject to collective bargaining agreements. Further, a series of studies by Professor

Table 5.1   *Foreign Direct Investment in the United States,*
January 2009–June 2012

Country or Area	Direct Foreign Investment (in $ billions)
United Kingdom	89.1
Switzerland	72.8
Luxembourg	67.3
Canada	54.5
Germany	43.6
Japan	42.8
France	38.9
Netherlands	32.6
Belgium	30.9
Caribbean	21.5

Source: Bureau of Economic Analysis, U.S. Department of Commerce, "Direct Investment Positions," www.bea.gov.

Matthew J. Slaughter at Dartmouth found that on average the insourced companies paid their workers 24 percent more than the average wage for similar work in the American private sector.

The bottom line is that the United States often is a beneficiary of international flows of capital and expertise, not a victim. When American firms such as Caterpillar internationalize production, the usual reason is that it is an attractive investment that promises high rates of return. It is by no means an accident that Caterpillar has established production and distribution facilities in countries such as Brazil, China, India, and Russia. Those locations represent superb opportunities for Caterpillar to sell its products, and when it sells those products, that creates additional jobs in the United States or defends those already here.

The critical view of this process is that these investments could have been made in the United States, and undoubtedly in many instances this is true. However, if 95 percent of the world's consumers are outside the United States, frequently the most efficient way to serve those consumers is to locate production and distribution facilities close to them. All companies, great or otherwise, must consider whether locating such facilities in the United States would impose transportation and other costs on them of a magnitude that would make them unable to compete.

Caterpillar produces dozens of products, including rail products, engines, and turbines, in only the United States. These broad product ranges include huge tractors such as the D11 and pipe layers made only in East Peoria, Illinois; soil compactors, wheel loaders, and hydraulic excavators made only in Aurora, Illinois; engines made only in Lafayette, Indiana; paving products made only in Minneapolis, Minnesota; hydraulic shovels and draglines made only in South Milwaukee, Wisconsin; high wall miners made only in Beckley, West Virginia; freight locomotives in Muncie, Indiana; and locomotive engines made only in LaGrange, Illinois.

Why are these products manufactured exclusively in the United States? The reasons are many, but most often they relate to the high cost of replicating capital-intensive facilities in another country, the availability of skilled labor, port access, quality maintenance concerns, and the ability to price so that high margins can be maintained. These are among the factors that global firms must take into consideration if they want to survive and prosper.

Internationalization and American Jobs: A Closer Look

The internationalization of jobs issue is a sensitive one for Caterpillar and other global firms. Does internationalization ultimately result in more jobs and higher incomes in the United States? In general, the answer is yes, but this conclusion does not hold for every firm in every industry. International trade does destroy jobs in certain industries, but it does not destroy jobs overall. Internationalization usually results in American firms employing more individuals in the United States than they would otherwise.

In some industries, the American job creation connected to internationalization is truly significant. A frequently cited study by the Information Technology Association of America found that the internationalization of information technology jobs was associated with 337,000 new jobs in the United States between 2006 and 2010. An important reason internationalization tends to produce more American jobs is that it makes the offshoring firms more efficient in a variety of ways, especially by reducing their costs. McKinsey found that the typical firm saved $0.58 for every $1.00 it spent overseas. Earlier, McKinsey concluded that every $1.00 spent by an American firm in internationalization ventures generated $1.14 in value in the American economy.

Ultimately, the benefits of internationalization collectively exceed the costs of that offshoring. One of the reasons this is true is that the negative employment effects associated with offshoring actually are much smaller than offshoring critics typically assert. Consider Table 5.2, which is based on Bureau of Labor Statistics (BLS) data relating to mass layoffs of workers between 1996 and 2008. International trade overall was responsible for only 2.5 percent of total job loss during that 13-year period, and only 1.1 percent of that total job loss was due to American firms locating overseas.

Table 5.2   *Worker Layoffs Caused by Import Competition and Overseas Relocation*

Year	Total Number of Workers Laid Off for All Reasons	Number Due to Import Competition	Number Due to Overseas Relocation	Percent Due to Imports and Relocation
1996	948,122	13,476	4,326	1.9
1997	847,843	12,019	10,439	2.4
1998	991,245	18,473	8,797	2.8
1999	901,451	26,234	5,683	3.5
2000	915,962	13,416	9,054	2.5
2001	1,524,832	27,946	15,693	2.9
2002	1,272,331	15,350	17,075	2.5
2003	1,216,886	23,734	13,205	3.0
2004	993,909	8,064	16,197	2.4
2005	884,661	11,112	12,030	2.6
2006	935,805	10,458	13,367	2.5
2007	965,935	11,589	11,526	2.3
2008	1,383,553	9,592	11,147	1.5
	Percent Averages	1.5	1.1	2.5

Source: U.S. Department of Labor, Bureau of Labor Statistics, www.bls.gov/mls/#tables.

A more recent BLS study for 2010 disclosed that only 6 of 229 mass layoff events (2.6 percent) in that year were due to import competition. Thus, traceable job losses caused by globalization are rather small and certainly are much smaller than vote-hungry political candidates and organized labor leaders suggest.

> **INSIDER'S EDGE**   *The internationalization of American jobs may have a bad reputation in some quarters, but the truth is that in the aggregate internationalization usually creates more jobs in the United States or defends jobs already here. Less than 3 percent of all job losses in the United States in recent years have been due either to competition from imports in the United States or to the relocation of American jobs to other countries.*

The Caterpillar Global Job Experience

In addition to the job gains and losses that accompany internationalization, the economic value created in the United States by international activities must be considered. The truth is that a rigorous analysis of the jobs balance sheet for Caterpillar's internationalization has never been performed. However, Caterpillar's aggregate employment data suggest that notable increases in company employees outside the United States always are accompanied by significant increases in North American employees. Table 5.3 illustrates this phenomenon in eight years after 2000 when Caterpillar expanded its total year-end employment by at least 3,000 employees. On average, 37.21 percent of Caterpillar's expanded employment occurred inside the United States in those eight years even as international employment was climbing.

Indeed, between 2004 and 2005, when Caterpillar's overall employment increased by 8,196, the company's employment inside the United States increased by 5,750 (70.16 percent of the total). Hence, additional international jobs at Caterpillar brought with them additional jobs in the United States. The lesson is straightforward: when Caterpillar taps into dynamic, growing international markets, this always increases employment inside the United States.

Table 5.3 *Expanded International Employment at Caterpillar Leads to More Employment in the United States, 2000–2011*

Eight Years in Which Major Employment Changes Occurred at Caterpillar	Overall Increase in Year-End Caterpillar Employment	Increase in Caterpillar Employment in the United States	Percent Increase in Caterpillar Employment in the United States
2000 to 2001	3,564	1,004	28.17
2003 to 2004	7,751	2,868	37.00
2004 to 2005	8,196	5,750	70.16
2005 to 2006	9,477	4,831	50.98
2006 to 2007	6,740	1,836	49.88
2007 to 2008	11,554	2,964	25.65
2009 to 2010	10,677	4,068	38.10
2010 to 2011	20,609	5,917	28.71
Totals	78,586	29,238	37.21 Avg.

Sources: Caterpillar annual reports and Rachel Potts, Caterpillar Public Affairs

Some might quibble with Caterpillar's performance in this area; after all, more than 62 percent of all net new company jobs in those years were created outside the United States. This is true, but the size of Caterpillar's workforce inside the United States is tightly tied to the company's worldwide expansion. We've already noted that all of CAT's D9, D10, and D11 bulldozers are made in the United States and then exported. The majority of the company's research and development activity and information technology planning and development occur inside the United States even though the effects are felt around the globe. Caterpillar's international headquarters is in Peoria, Illinois, and the company has signaled that it has no plans to move.

United Auto Workers leaders clearly would prefer that Caterpillar concentrate more of its production inside the United States and in unionized plants, and so would many elected officials and ordinary Americans. Nevertheless, the battle over these issues was fought in the 1990s and won by Caterpillar. In the 1990s, the company gained substantial freedom to locate its plants, move its production, hire or lay off its workers, and deploy its capital in the way that its managers and board determined was in the best interests of the company and its stockholders. It is difficult to argue with the results. Caterpillar now employs more individuals in the United States than it has since 1981. The company is thriving, and so are its stockholders. Local, state, and federal governments in the United States are collecting significant tax revenues from the corporation.

It is difficult to argue that this does not constitute an outcome distinctly superior to the agony that many American manufacturing firms and their surrounding communities experienced when the production of manufacturing companies contracted and those companies shuttered numerous plants as they headed for bankruptcy. That process has resulted in devastated cities, ruined housing markets, disappearing pensions, and shattered lives.

It is instructive to compare Caterpillar with firms such as Allis-Chalmers (which no longer produces any equipment inside the United States and in essence has become an oil field service company), Wheeling-Pittsburgh Steel (which has gone out of business), and Eastman Kodak (which filed for bankruptcy protection in January 2012). Even organized labor leaders acknowledge privately that "the Caterpillar way" often is better than the alternative, which may be no jobs at all.

Caterpillar and Tradable Goods

The issues surrounding the internationalization activities of multinational firms are complex, and only a confirmed trade ideologist would argue otherwise. The truth is that both benefits and costs are associated with the increasing globalization of the markets. Although the benefits overall clearly appear to exceed the costs, this assessment should not be taken to imply that the benefits will exceed the costs in every industry or for every firm.

One of the fashionable ways to look at globalization issues today is to focus on which goods and services are *tradable* in an international context. Tradable goods and services are those for which the prevailing market price is determined globally. Oil provides an illustration. The price of oil, whether the oil is produced on the Northern Slope in Alaska or in Saudi Arabia, is determined by the interaction of the forces of global supply and demand. However, contrast oil with haircuts, which are supplied and consumed locally. The prices of haircuts in New Delhi or Buenos Aires have almost nothing to do with the prices of haircuts in Dallas or Philadelphia.

Haircuts are not an internationally tradable service. Bulldozers, along with most of the things Caterpillar produces, are. This means that their production, distribution, prices, and sales are subject to international competitive influences. Hence, a company such as Caterpillar must carefully weigh decisions about where to produce, what prices to charge, how to interact with its dealers, and what level of compensation it pays its employees in the context of international markets rather than local markets.

The greater the tradability of a good or service, the greater the influence of international supply and demand on that good or service. Further, the greater the tradability of a good or service, the greater the likelihood that companies will not respect international borders when they decide where to produce. Their survival virtually requires this.

Nevertheless, high levels of tradability do not spell doom. The notion that internationalization is laying waste to the American economy is substantially false. As Matthew J. Slaughter, the premier researcher on these issues, has concluded, "The idea that global expansion tends to 'hollow out' U.S. operations is incorrect." Caterpillar provides an example in support of this judgment.

INSIDERS' EDGE *The prices of internationally tradable goods such as oil and bulldozers are set by the interaction of supply and demand in international markets. That's not true for haircuts. Both companies and nations must recognize the difference when making policy.*

The Foreign Corrupt Practices Act

The Foreign Corrupt Practices Act specifically forbids bribery of local business and governmental officials regardless of local custom and practice. Caterpillar's widely praised Worldwide Code of Conduct contains the same prohibitions, and this is a charge that CAT employees both in the United States and elsewhere take seriously. They are determined that the company will not be dragged down by the actions of employees inside or outside the United States.

The lessons attached to the unfortunate experience of Walmart in Mexico were not lost on Caterpillar's leaders. The *New York Times* concluded both that there was "credible evidence that bribery played a persistent and significant role in Wal-Mart's rapid growth in Mexico" and that senior Walmart executives had attempted to shut down the company's internal investigations of that behavior. Subsequently, the *Times* reported that Walmart's practices "extended beyond Mexico to China, India, and Brazil."

Caterpillar Chairman/CEO Doug Oberhelman reacted quickly to the initial Walmart disclosure and dispatched a message to all Caterpillar employees, calling their attention once again to the company's Worldwide Code of Conduct.

He reiterated that the Code explicitly bans payments of the sort Walmart is alleged to have made.

> **IBM paid** *a $10 million penalty in 2011 to settle a Securities and Exchange Commission charge that it had bribed officials in the PRC and Korea.*

When Caterpillar confronted its own crisis in China in November 2012 relating to accounting fraud in its acquisition of ERA Mining Machinery, it acted swiftly and transparently. It acknowledged its problem, announced a write-off, dismissed personnel, and unambiguously restated the standards of the Code. Chairman/CEO Doug Oberhelman declared that the behavior of its former managers at ERA was "offensive and completely unacceptable" and stated, "This conduct does not represent in any way, shape, or form the way Caterpillar does business, or how we expect our employees to work."

Obviously, Caterpillar cannot say that it never has encountered violations of its Code. However, in contrast to Walmart and others, it has not swept such matters under the proverbial rug. Further, it did not escape notice that all the discovered violations were committed by "new" ERA managers and employees rather than "old" Caterpillar managers and employees who had been with the firm when the acquisition occurred. At the end of the day, however, the ERA experience once again underlines the reality that many challenges can accompany corporate internationalization.

In light of Caterpillar's far-flung operations, it is not an easy task to ensure that its Worldwide Code of Conduct is honored worldwide by all of its approximately 125,000 employees. In a country such as Mexico, where *gestores* ("facilitators") are commonplace, "Nobody is exempted" from demands for bribes, says Mexico City security consultant Max Morales, who advises companies on Mexican-specific topics such as construction projects and security against kidnappings. In the opinion of Morales, "Even the big American companies are subject to extortion."

> **Back in the 1950s**, *Caterpillar Chairman Louis Neumiller set the tone when he said, "There is but one Caterpillar and wherever it is, you will find it reaching for the highest levels of integrity."*

Caterpillar, however, has never been tainted by such accusations because it requires all employees (and board members) to review its Worldwide Code of Conduct annually and also because senior management has made it clear that the company would rather lose a sale than violate its Code and/or break the law. Caterpillar's reputation in this regard is reasonably well known, and so it may no longer be subject to quite as many illicit approaches as are companies that on occasion may have bowed to bribery pressures. Practically speaking, Caterpillar also benefits from the fact that it produces and sells high-quality products that are highly valued by customers, many of whom have been patronizing the company for many years. They know the rules of the road, place high value on the service and attention they receive from Caterpillar and its dealers, and prefer the solidity of that relationship to the shadowy world of gestores and bribes. Caterpillar does not contend that it never has encountered violations of its Code but does assert that it takes vigorous action, up to and including termination, when violations are discovered.

Caterpillar's competitors are for the most part envious of the principled environment that the company has constructed worldwide and realize that such a situation cannot be created overnight. Some privately query whether Caterpillar really is able to maintain its high ethical standards and venture that some of the company's dealers worldwide may stray from time to time. Nevertheless, there is no evidence that "Caterpillar has to play the game too" (the speculation of a competitor). Former presiding director Eugene V. Fife's observation that "Caterpillar is an unbelievably ethical company" remains salient. Caterpillar places a very high value on adherence to its Worldwide Code of Conduct and never has viewed non-U.S. locations as constituting exceptions to those rules. This, too, is a lesson that many American corporations should take to heart.

CHAPTER 6

CATERPILLAR AND ITS EMPLOYEES

Notwithstanding Caterpillar's sterling performance as a global manufacturer, some individuals know of the company primarily because of its difficult history in the area of labor relations. This is despite the fact that the company's current relationship with its largest union, the United Auto Workers (UAW), is rather pacific and, from our conversations with UAW members, surprisingly low-key.

Wall Street Journal reporters James R. Hagerty and Bob Tita noted in May 2012 that Caterpillar often plays hardball in labor relations. The company, they said, "is known for crushing union opposition." Caterpillar has earned a reputation as a tough, durable, and skillful adversary in labor relations. It is this reputation that draws corporate labor negotiators from around the country to Peoria "to learn the Caterpillar model" (comment made by an executive at another Fortune 500 corporation).

Caterpillar's corporate stance in labor relations today typically emphasizes two points. First, the company prefers not to have third parties or unions stand between it and its employees. Nevertheless, approximately 20 percent of Caterpillar employees in the United States are unionized. Unionized or not, Caterpillar is insistent on its right to communicate directly with its employees, manage them, and address their concerns. It does not believe it must communicate with its employees through union stewards and argues that such a practice would put distance between the company and its employees. The real story of CAT and labor begins with this very simple—and nonnegotiable—foundation of the collective bargaining process.

> **INSIDER'S EDGE**   *Collective bargaining agreements (CBAs) can be 10 pages or 300 pages long. Their length usually is inversely related to how good they are for management.*

Second, Caterpillar asserts that every one of its plants must be cost competitive on a global basis whether or not a plant is unionized. The implication is that facilities that do not enable the company to compete globally with all comers will be repurposed, closed, or sold. In the case of Caterpillar's London, Ontario, plant, the company locked out Canadian Auto Workers (CAW) members on January 1, 2012, and then announced its decision to shutter the plant on February 3, 2012. This came after the company and the CAW had reached a negotiating impasse. Newspaper reports suggested that CAT wanted CAW employees to agree to "concessions" (a term Caterpillar was careful not to use) that involved a 50 percent wage cut for some employees and material reductions in employee pensions and benefits.

Caterpillar, however, maintained throughout the negotiations that the salient issue was global competitiveness. (This has been its position for at least two decades.) To the company, the question was simple: What would it take to enable the locomotives produced at the London location to be sold at a competitive price worldwide? The *Wall Street Journal* reported that Caterpillar officials maintained that wages and benefits were twice as high at the London plant as they were at the company's EMD locomotive plant in LaGrange, Illinois. CAT argued that the London plant, a former General Motors operation, had a cost structure that simply "was not sustainable."

Subsequently, in August 2012, the *New York Times* reported that the 780 striking employees represented by the International

Association of Machinists and Aerospace Employees at CAT's hydraulic parts plant in Joliet, Illinois, had voted to ratify a contract "that contained almost all of the concessions the company had demanded." This ended a three-and-a half-month strike. Caterpillar was reported to have driven a "hard bargain," and *Washington Post* business columnist Steven Pearlstein said the message was, "Caterpillar to Unions: Drop Dead." The Joliet outcome occurred despite the support Governor Pat Quinn offered the machinists in the form of a $10,000 check to their union's food fund, a position that was unlikely to have endeared him to Caterpillar's management.

Some Important History

The first Caterpillar union to be certified by the National Labor Relations Board was the United Farm Equipment Workers in 1942. Politically radical, this union refused to comply with provisions of the Taft-Hartley Act passed in 1947 and subsequently was decertified. Several unions competed to take its place, and the United Auto Workers (UAW) prevailed in 1948.

Between 1948 and 1980, UAW-represented employees at CAT went out on strike a not insignificant eight times. In 1982, the union and the company went to the mat in a bitter strike that lasted 205 days. The length of the strike severely damaged the Peoria-area economy and resulted in a wave of bankruptcies and store closings. Although the UAW claimed victory after the contract was signed and emerged with a profit-sharing plan and job security guarantees, Caterpillar avoided a significant cost increase, gained some flexibility in assigning tasks to employees, and preserved its right to move production where it saw fit. It was this flexibility in work rules and production that provided the foundation for the strategy Caterpillar would follow. A modicum of labor peace ensued as new UAW contracts were negotiated in 1986 and 1988 without strikes. By 1991, however, Caterpillar's senior managers and board of directors had concluded that it had become absolutely essential for the company to break out of the pattern bargain model that the UAW had imposed on CAT and competitors such as Deere. In essence, the UAW would negotiate a labor agreement with one of the Big Three automobile companies and impose the substance of that agreement on many others. Pattern bargaining enabled the UAW to whipsaw individual firms into submission because a company could not afford to be idled by a strike while all its competitors continued production and increased market share to the detriment of the company being struck. The United Autoworkers and United Steel Workers are famous for having used this strategy in their respective industries. Caterpillar's urgency to put an end to pattern bargaining increased when the company once again began to lose money.

It would lose $404 million in 1991 and a further $2,435 million in 1992. The company estimated that its Japanese competitor, Komatsu, had labor costs that were 30 percent below those of CAT. Hence, Caterpillar found itself in a difficult competitive position and reduced its dividend payment per share by 50 percent to shore up its cash reserves.

In 1991, the pattern bargain that the UAW sought to impose on Caterpillar was very similar to one that had been agreed to by Deere. It called for a 3 percent raise in the first year of the contract and a 3 percent lump-sum payment in the next two years. Caterpillar's counter essentially offered UAW-represented employees cost-of-living wage increases above their $16.89 per hour average wage.

> **How things have changed.** *When we interviewed current Caterpillar employees and discussed the 1990s strike with them, most expressed amazement at the high levels of wages that existed in 1991. Today the company's employees often start for less than that $16.89 per hour. In February 2012 in Muncie, Indiana, CAT reopened a long-closed ABB manufacturing facility to produce locomotives and offered wage rates as low as $12 per hour for assemblers. Nevertheless, hundreds of prospective employees showed up to bid for the jobs.*

Caterpillar had been consistent in its opposition to pattern bargaining but had never been willing to endure a strike over the issue. The company's argument was straightforward. It believed that its economic situation was distinctive and not comparable to that of the Big Three automobile manufacturers. For example, the company argued that its strong dependence on export sales put it at odds with the likes of General Motors, for which export sales were small. Thus, whereas global cost competitiveness was critical to Caterpillar, it was less important to General Motors. Therefore, the desire of the UAW to transplant to CAT the wage, benefit, and work contractual rules developed at General Motors were off base in Caterpillar's view.

A consensus gradually arose within Caterpillar's management and board that the company had to end pattern bargaining to ensure its future existence. If this produced a lengthy strike, the company would have to find a way to live through it. Hence, Caterpillar began to plan actively for how it would continue to operate if UAW-represented employees walked out.

It is easy to observe today that the gradual deterioration of the American automobile industry and its loss of cost competitiveness ultimately would validate the fears of CAT's leaders. However, in 1990, the company's executives and board members could only guess that pattern bargaining probably would lead to such problems. They believed they could read the handwriting on the wall. At the same time, they were buying into a long, hostile fight with uncertain prospects for success.

Interestingly, on the other side of the negotiating table, the UAW also was feeling threatened. Its overall number of dues-paying members at Caterpillar fell 60 percent between 1979 and 1991. UAW membership at Caterpillar in the Peoria area fell from 23,000 to 9,700 during that period even as CAT was able to produce the same output in 1991 as in 1979.

The UAW blamed Caterpillar's outsourcing of jobs from the Midwest to foreign countries for much of the decline in employment and vocally deplored the company's implicit threat to move production from Illinois locations such as Peoria, Decatur, and Aurora to the American South.

Not surprisingly, CAT executives saw things differently. They viewed the union's membership losses as self-inflicted because non-competitive wages, fringe benefits, and harmful work rules had increased costs and stymied labor productivity. This, they argued, made CAT less competitive and reduced its need for employees.

In any event, negotiations did not lead to a contract, and on November 4, 1991, the UAW declared a limited strike that involved 2,400 employees in Peoria and Decatur, Illinois. The UAW's goal was to punish Caterpillar's bottom line by idling two key facilities in CAT's home state of Illinois. At the same time, the union did not want to impose heavy costs on its members. Veteran UAW members still remembered the profoundly negative impact the 205-day 1982 strike had on their personal finances and families. To mitigate such damage to its members this time around, the UAW amassed an $800 million fund that would enable it to pay striking employees benefits that would begin at $100 per week and healthcare assistance plus a $2,000 bonus per employee. In retrospect, we know that the UAW believed that Caterpillar would be forced to fold under this pressure.

However, Caterpillar surprised the union on November 7, 1991, by locking out 5,650 employees: approximately 3,500 in Peoria and East Peoria and 2,150 in Aurora, Illinois. As the *Chicago Tribune* later noted, "This neutralized [the UAW's] attempt to limit the effects of the strike."

Never before had Caterpillar locked out its employees, and the *Chicago Tribune* reported that the workers were "stunned." The shock of the lockout for CAT employees increased when the company successfully convinced the Illinois Department of Employment Security that the locked-out employees should not receive unemployment benefits because the reason for their not working was a labor dispute, not a decline in economic conditions. This hard-hitting move represented a classic bargaining strategy: impose costs on your adversaries to make them more pliable.

INSIDER'S EDGE   *A worker lockout can be an effective first negotiation tool on the part of management. It should never be used as an emotional response to the threat of an employee walkout. Instead, it should be the result of thorough planning, both legal and operational.*

Early in the dispute, Caterpillar offered the UAW a contract that would have raised the salaries of top UAW-represented employees to $39,000 annually in 1994, only slightly less than the $40,000 being paid by its competitor Deere. The UAW rejected the offer and made a critical strategic mistake: in several cases, it refused to meet with Caterpillar to negotiate. The UAW did not respond to Caterpillar's offers with its own offers and in one case confirmed in writing that it did "not even open" the envelope in which a company offer was delivered. UAW President Owen Bieber reputedly boasted that he would "close down Caterpillar."

The UAW's failure to respond to the company's offers (however inadequate they were thought to be) enabled Caterpillar to declare that negotiations were at an "impasse." Although at the time the UAW's refusal to respond to Caterpillar offers appeared to be tough and satisfied many of its members, we believe this was one of the greatest gaffes ever committed by a major American union negotiation team. CAT pounced on the mistake. When a labor dispute is at impasse, management may hire replacement employees or use internal staff to fill union positions in the plant. CAT was ready. It hired replacement employees and put its managers on the line to continue production. Anticipating the possibility of a strike and a lockout—as well as an impasse—the company had trained many of its managers so that they could step in and take the place of UAW-represented employees on production lines. The CAT replacement employees, ranging from secretaries to general managers, surprised themselves and shocked the UAW with their ability to make machines and fill orders on time and to do so at a high level of quality.

Nonunion individuals at all levels pitched in on production lines. Ronald Bonati, vice president of CAT's North American Commercial Division, took a position on a line making tracks for tractors. A. J. Rassi, the Aurora, Illinois, plant manager at the time and later a vice president, occupied a spot on a production line assembling products. Secretaries ran machines. They were supplemented by temporary nonunion employees and eventually as many as 4,000 UAW members who would cross the picket lines (though this occurred only slowly). Caterpillar's ability to do these things was directly related to training programs that had been initiated in the company to prepare for such a strike. The company's Plant with a Future Program (PWAF) also was a key factor because it automated production, reduced manual labor, increased the ability of employees to do more than a single task, and gradually reduced the amount of labor required to produce most Caterpillar products.

When it became known that Caterpillar had jobs available, skilled employees from across the country traveled to Illinois seeking to work for the company. Caterpillar reported that it eventually received 100,000 telephone calls from prospective employees. The company dealt with a potential labor skills bottleneck by hiring a large group of welders from America's Gulf Coast who had been laid off because of a decline in shipbuilding. The *New York Times* opined that CAT's ability to hire replacement employees (a tactic President Ronald Reagan had used in 1981 to stop the air controllers' strike) had "decisively tipped" the balance of power toward companies such as CAT and away from unions.

In truth, it was the combination of strategy, preparation, training of internal staff, and hiring of replacement employees that won the fight. CAT had set a new standard in methodically planning the chess game.

> **"Thank God for the Plant with a Future,"** *reminisced Gerald Flaherty, a retired Caterpillar group president, in 2012. Automation lowered costs, reduced the need for employees, and enabled managers and temporary employees to step in and maintain production levels and quality.*

UAW personnel and some Caterpillar retirees who were around at the time insisted to us that Caterpillar found it difficult to maintain the quality of its output, and several regaled us with stories of machines that "the newbies" had produced that had to be junked because of production errors and quality control problems. These accusations may hold water, but even strong union supporters agree that the diverse group of personnel assembled by Caterpillar soon worked out the kinks and within a few months was making machines whose quality was up to prestrike standards. Longtime Caterpillar dealer Peter Holt of San Antonio told us that after a few months, he couldn't tell the difference and neither could his customers. However, it does appear that labor productivity declined—not as much was being produced each shift.

Donald Fites at the time stated, "We have not lost a single sale, as far as we can tell, as the result of this strike. Our problem isn't supply, it's demand." At an April 1992 meeting of stockholders, Fites also stated that as a result of the strike, Caterpillar managers learned they could operate their plants with 10 to 15 percent fewer employees. This was a somewhat raucous meeting because Bill Casstevens, secretary-treasurer of the UAW international union (he was the UAW's chief negotiator at Caterpillar and a CAT stockholder), showed up and demanded the floor to make the union's case. Casstevens and Fites sparred verbally, and Casstevens advised the stockholders that Fites had said "a lot of things that are false."

This may have been one of the more refined exchanges of views during the strike. This strike and related events between 1991 and 1998 were acrimonious and often nasty. Numerous insults, taunts, and threats were hurled during the lockout. Violent incidents occurred, shots were fired, intimidation of strikebreakers was common, and 443 unfair labor practices charges would be filed with the National Labor Relations Board (NLRB).

On April 14, 1992, the union surprised many by sending its striking employees back to work under the terms of Caterpillar's most recent offer, but it refused to sign a contract and said negotiations must continue. A series of work slowdowns followed as the UAW instructed its members to "work to the rules" and do nothing more. Production at CAT's three largest plants might have fallen as much as 40 percent.

Public opinion was a major weapon in the strike, and Caterpillar was more active than the UAW in presenting its case to the media. It took out advertisements in local newspapers such as the *Peoria Journal-Star* and the *Decatur Herald and Review* and sent communications directly to Caterpillar employees, bypassing the union. The company asserted that the UAW's proposal would increase its worker compensation costs by 46 percent over three years, something the union disputed but did not counter with its own numbers.

> **INSIDER'S EDGE** *Moving public opinion in one's favor is an important way to exert leverage during a strike. Further, both striking employees and their spouses have plenty of time to read newspapers and watch television. Caterpillar relished such opportunities to make its case.*

In 1993, Caterpillar and the UAW did not come close to reaching an agreement, and several short wildcat strikes occurred over local issues such as the suspension of union officials and activists. Local walkouts continued in 1994, highlighted by a nationwide walkout at all Caterpillar facilities with UAW-represented employees. CAT responded by again using as many as 5,000 managers and 2,500 temporary replacement employees to continue to produce output. Sensing deadlock or defeat, the strikers returned to work in December 1995, still without a contract after a fruitless series of negotiations and conciliation attempts. One striker lamented that "the company's in complete control. We have to accept defeat."

During the 1994 strike, the UAW asserted that it was all about Caterpillar's unfair labor practices. The company rejected that characterization and described the strike as "an economic dispute." This was more than a casual distinction. Federal law does not permit employees to be permanently replaced if an unfair labor practice is the cause, whereas employees can be permanently replaced if the strike is taking place for purely economic reasons. In a letter it sent on April 2, 1992, to all striking employees, Caterpillar already had upped the ante by warning the striking employees that it would replace them permanently if they did not return to work.

The years 1996 and 1997 were notable because of the way the National Labor Relations Board (NLRB) responded to some of the charges of unfair labor practices that had been levied by the UAW against Caterpillar. The NLRB added to this pile by alleging that the company had committed unfair labor practices in its treatment of UAW-represented employees.

Meanwhile, Caterpillar was thriving with record sales and profits, a reality that was not lost on the union. Finally, in February 1998, Caterpillar and the UAW reached a long-term, six-year agreement. The pact included wage increases and pension gains for the UAW members, and the company agreed to the reinstatement of 160 of the UAW-represented employees that the union said the company had fired illegally during the dispute. The union agreed to drop all the unfair labor practices charges it had filed with the NLRB and granted amnesty to the 4,000 of its members who had crossed picket lines during the strike. Thus ended one of the most contentious and lengthy labor disputes of the second half of the twentieth century.

A *Los Angeles Times* reporter suggested that this was a strike that seemed to be a "throwback to another era." However, this was a misperception of events because the strike actually was ushering in a new era that would alter the balance of negotiating power between management and labor. By any reasonable accounting, Caterpillar was a decisive winner of the dispute because it:

- Succeeded in shattering the pattern bargaining chain around its corporate neck

- Demonstrated that it did not need the UAW to increase both its sales and its profits

- Augmented its ability to move employees flexibly around its plants and into different time slots

- Initiated a two-tier wage structure by which new hires would receive lower compensation

- Solidified its prerogative to move production to any location it desired

Tony Green *was the president of UAW-974 between 1984 and 1990 but was defeated for reelection in 1990. Interviewed in 1994, he asserted that the new UAW-974 leadership had been*

> *outmaneuvered by Caterpillar, at least partially because it had adopted an excessively adversarial relationship with CAT management.*

As the Associated Press put it, "In the end, the United Auto Workers could not find much to boast about except survival."

Despite holding out for and winning these pivotal results, Donald Fites, Caterpillar's chairman/CEO, and Caterpillar board members consistently stated that the company was not out to break the union. Instead, they asserted that they had to have the ability to decide how CAT was operated and how it used its capital. At its most basic, said Fites, it was a question of "Who was going to run the plant?" Who would decide whether employees and assets could be moved from one location to another or how many employees were needed? Fites and other CAT leaders viewed restrictions on their managerial prerogatives and the constraints imposed by union work rules as issues at least as important to the company as wages and compensation.

The UAW, however, believed that Caterpillar was attempting to break the union and refused to retreat willingly from the pattern labor agreements that had been hammered out at other UAW locations and that contained the managerial restrictions that Fites and his board abhorred. As time passed, however, the UAW saw its bargaining position progressively weaken because CAT had demonstrated that it was able to function without the cooperation of the UAW. Further, UAW members and leaders perceived that the continuation of the strike would only encourage Caterpillar to move production to nonunionized sites in the American South and outside the United States.

Faced with these realities, the UAW in essence capitulated and agreed to a contract. This end result was widely viewed as a decisive rout of the UAW by Caterpillar.

CAT executives today downplay the ultimate significance of "defeating the UAW in the 1990s" (the language of a UAW member), and clearly it is true that many other factors are vitally important to CAT's prosperity. Among the most important have been the company's ability to scale its operations on a global basis, the development of business unit profit centers, CAT's dealer network, well-chosen acquisitions of complementary firms in growing industries, and skillful planning for bad times. Collectively, these factors have been more important to CAT's prosperity than its bitter labor strife with the UAW in the 1980s and 1990s.

Even so, the events of the 1990s decisively changed the way things were done at Caterpillar and supercharged the confidence of the company's leadership. The episodes of the 1990s involving CAT also sent strong vibrations throughout American industry. The company's example of toughness and resolve in labor negotiations had watershed significance. Like it or not, Caterpillar's labor victory in the 1990s soon accorded it iconic status in American industry.

> **INSIDER'S EDGE** *If you emerge victorious, don't rub the noses of the defeated into the dirt. Stick to the issues and avoid ad hominem attacks.*

This turnabout would not have occurred if Caterpillar's senior leadership and board members had not been ready to take the substantial though well-calculated risk that they could prevail and had not been willing to take immense personal heat and criticism, sometimes from friends and neighbors. The reality is that senior CAT executives were willing to sacrifice friendships—and possibly their reputations—to put the company in an economic position in which it could succeed in the long term. Leaders such as Chairman/CEO Donald Fites (1990–1999) placed the company ahead of their personal circumstances. However, as Fites later put it to us, "Anything you do in the CEO chair can be career jeopardizing." The record demonstrates that he was one who was willing to take such a risk and that he could take the condemnations he received in some quarters. This is the paramount reason he may be the most important chairman/CEO in the company's history.

As momentous as these events were, it is well to bear in mind once again that labor costs typically account for only 10 to 20 percent of Caterpillar's total production costs. Therefore, CAT's success hinges on many factors besides globally competitive labor costs.

The labor struggles of the 1980s and 1990s visibly symbolize the company's determination to find the means to become a competitive manufacturing firm in a global economy. Nevertheless, to Caterpillar's leadership, an appropriate labor contract was only one piece in a larger competitive puzzle.

In retrospect, we know that the Big Three automobile manufacturers repeatedly shied away from major confrontations with the UAW. Ultimately, their timidity was one of the factors that led to their actual or near bankruptcy. Caterpillar traveled a different path, and that was one of the reasons it became a great company.

It is fair to say that today's UAW-974 (the large Caterpillar-based UAW local in East Peoria, Illinois) recognizes that Caterpillar is a global manufacturer that necessarily will produce substantial output outside the United States. Caterpillar's contract with the UAW does not prevent the company from relocating production to other sites within the United States or to facilities outside the country. Knowing that it is unable to reverse this situation, UAW-974 now appears to focus more on the additional unionized jobs that profitable CAT globalization may produce in Illinois.

In any case, the current UAW-974 contract with Caterpillar runs through 2017, and UAW-974 leaders describe the current state of labor relations, while still adversarial, as "agreeable and about as good as they ever have been." Both the company and the UAW seem eager to move on to other matters.

Parsing Caterpillar's Negotiating Success

Caterpillar's skill and success at negotiating favorable labor agreements have put it on the radar screen of virtually every large unionized firm in the United States. As a consequence, many visitors travel to Peoria to meet with Chris Glynn, Caterpillar's somewhat legendary director of human relations, to "see how CAT has been doing it," in the words of an executive at another large corporation. Glynn is a 36-year Caterpillar veteran intimately familiar with the company's terrain. One of his assignments is to oversee the negotiation and daily implementation of CAT's numerous collective bargaining agreements. Incrementally, he has developed a negotiating strategy and environment that have placed Caterpillar in an envious position in the eyes of most large industrial firms.

The company's proficiency, however, is not something that most other firms can easily replicate immediately. It's worth exploring what we discovered in this regard during our visits to Caterpillar.

First, Caterpillar energetically strives to head off and deal with employee gripes and problems long before they get to the collective bargaining table. Caterpillar actively surveys its employees to find out what may be bothering them and is insistent that its supervisors talk with their employees constantly. Glynn says, "We try to manage in such a way that employees should not feel a need for third parties. But if they have third parties, then we will deal with them in a professional way. We should manage the same way whether or not someone has a union card in their pocket."

CAT's strategy is to manage so well that its employees either won't feel the need for a union or will find it easy to vent any frustrations to their supervisors or company officials and obtain a productive response. Glynn underlines the idea that Caterpillar's policy is to treat all employees the same whether or not they are represented by a union. In fact, a large majority of Caterpillar's American employees are not union members.

> **Caterpillar also deals** with labor unions in China, but those unions function primarily as a Communist Party control mechanism. This has made it difficult at times for CAT to decipher who is in control and what is possible.

Employee satisfaction surveys and the company's low attrition rates compared with similar firms suggest that most CAT employees are reasonably happy with their work environment. The profusion of CAT hats and T-shirts one sees Caterpillar employees wearing is casual evidence of this. Our interviews with Caterpillar employees revealed that the hard feelings associated with the labor strife of the 1990s largely have disappeared and constitute nothing more than ancient history to employees hired since then. Representative was a 15-year CAT line employee who, when we asked him if he "bled yellow," replied, "Damn betcha!"

Every year, Caterpillar undertakes independent assessments of work conditions at each of its plants in an attempt to uncover concerns before they fester and become major problems. As Glynn told us, "There's no magic here." Instead, the company simply tries to know what is happening in its facilities so that it can manage more effectively.

Second, Caterpillar may be a tough negotiator, but it has demonstrated its concern for the health and welfare of its employees, whatever their level. An illustration is the popular health maintenance programs it offers, many under the title "Healthy Balance." These initiatives have been visibly successful in improving employee health and reducing employee downtime. Annually, each employee, up to and including Doug Oberhelman, must complete a health questionnaire or pay $100. Employee responses are utilized to suggest more healthy lifestyles and alert employees to potential problems. "This saves lives," Oberhelman says.

Caterpillar self-insures more than 150,000 individuals and is proud that in recent years the increase in its healthcare costs has trailed the rise in the consumer price index. Oberhelman says that because employees must pay a portion of their health costs, they have become more careful shoppers and users of healthcare. According to Oberhelman, Caterpillar pays approximately 70 percent of employee health costs, and the employees pay the remaining 30 percent.

Another concrete means for Caterpillar to slow the trajectory of healthcare increases was its 2008 decision to ban smoking in all of its U.S. facilities. The UAW responded to that initiative by filing an unfair labor practices charge with the NLRB, contending that smoking had been a contractual privilege for 60 years. Caterpillar's smoking-cessation program (free for employees) now is regarded as a model.

Don't be shy about asking your employees to pay a meaningful part of the cost of their health insurance. This helps eliminate unnecessary care and controls costs. Everyone needs to have skin in the game. Self-insuring your employee base can save 10 to 15 percent per year on average if a firm has a large and diversified base of employees. Great companies spend resources to ensure healthy lifestyles for their employees. This vitally important point often is given short shrift.

Third, Caterpillar has earned a reputation that it does not bluff. When the company puts on the negotiating table what it labels its "last, best, and final offer," it is time to pay attention because it signals that the company has calculated the limit of what it believes it can do in an agreement and still remain locally and globally competitive. The company's past successes in such situations increase its power these days when push comes to shove. CAT's long lockout of UAW-represented employees in the 1990s ended with the union accepting the company's offer and going back to work. The more recent closing of the London, Ontario, locomotive plant and the Joliet machinist settlement added to this aura of power, determination, and negotiating prowess.

By contrast, many of the firms that would like to replicate Caterpillar's negotiating success have very different histories. Their negotiating teams are less skillful, and their managements are more eager to avoid strikes and lockouts. Hence, they have acceded to contracts that in the long run not only inflated their current operating costs but also set difficult precedents for future negotiations (we are speaking primarily about the American automobile and steel industries throughout the second half of the twentieth century). The point is that over time companies build reputations. It does not matter whether one agrees with Caterpillar's labor negotiating stances and results. CAT has constructed an effective, usable reputation in the collective bargaining arena that would take other companies years and multiple negotiations to duplicate.

> **INSIDER'S EDGE**   *In a CBA negotiation, the foundation of success is being better prepared than your adversary. If you are, say what you mean and mean what you say.*

Fourth, a very important reason for Caterpillar's effectiveness at the negotiating table is that it has consciously developed many alternative sources of supply and locations for production. The company deliberately has ensured multiple sources of supply for the inputs it needs so that a strike or disruption that affects a single input supplier will not damage the company as a whole. This also applies to production. Caterpillar usually has multiple locations where it can produce a product. Witness the London, Ontario, situation. Caterpillar had the ability to shift Canadian production to Muncie, Indiana, or Mexico. It's difficult to negotiate successfully when you know that in the last analysis, the person on the other side of the table really doesn't need you. Once again, firms that have not developed the input and production flexibility of Caterpillar should not expect to have CAT's level of negotiating leverage.

> **INSIDER'S EDGE**   *Great companies prize and develop flexibility in their supply chains and in how and where they produce output.*

Fifth, Caterpillar approaches collective bargaining as an evolving, long-term process. Chris Glynn already has plans and priorities for several contract negotiations into the future. Thus, Caterpillar may focus on fringe benefits during this contract negotiation, work rules in the next negotiation, and wages in another negotiation farther into the future. The company does not like to include multiple classes of major issues in a single contract negotiation. It wants the focus of negotiations to be clear. Thus, if the major contract issue in a negotiation is going to be wages and salaries, CAT does not want to confuse the publicity and discussion around the negotiations by also including significant revisions in work rules.

> **INSIDER'S EDGE**   *Collective bargaining cannot be approached on an ad hoc basis. It requires serious, long-term strategizing and*

a recognition that every negotiating session is a captive of past negotiating history.

Sixth, Caterpillar knows what its bottom line is and what things it cannot give up. Although the company is not about to disclose its list of "we'll never negotiate this away" items, its statements and behavior suggest that it will not negotiate over its ability to allocate its own capital when and where it sees fit or its ability to assign flexible working hours; it also will not agree to labor union card check provisions. In fact, CAT has coded all of its anticipated collective bargaining issues P1 through P5. P1 issues are those over which the company is prepared to endure a strike to maintain its position. We believe that the list of P1 issues almost certainly includes neutrality, successorship, input and output sourcing, and card check. P5 issues are those in which there may be considerable flexibility. The moral to the story, however, is this: Caterpillar spends great time and energy strategizing its collective bargaining position and consistently adopts a long-term horizon. It takes pains not to enter contract negotiations with hazy goals and unclear priorities.

INSIDER'S EDGE *If you don't know precisely what you want and what you are willing to sacrifice to get what you want, you are likely to fare badly in collective bargaining negotiations.*

Caterpillar and the National Labor Relations Board

Boeing, Inc., the world's largest manufacturer of passenger airplanes, encountered significant problems with the National Labor Relations Board in March 2011. The company was accused of shifting work on its new Dreamliner passenger plane from a unionized plant in Seattle to a nonunionized plant in South Carolina as a means of retaliating against its unionized workforce in Seattle. The Seattle workers had gone on strike multiple times, and the NLRB hypothesized that Boeing was retaliating against the union and therefore moved to stop Boeing from shifting production to its South Carolina plant. Less than elegant public statements by

Boeing executives put the company in a hole and clearly revealed that Boeing believed that it could avoid work-disrupting strikes by housing production in South Carolina.

The Boeing case was of significant interest to Caterpillar because CAT has often moved production from unionized states such as Illinois to right-to-work states in the American South. Although Caterpillar executives always have been judicious in avoiding statements that could be interpreted as antiunion, they were alarmed that the NLRB might begin to tell the company when and where it could invest its capital. This possibility was blunted when the 31,000-member union that represented Boeing asked the NLRB to drop the case after Boeing agreed to increase production in Seattle and raise wage rates. The NLRB soon dropped the case, which the *New York Times* appropriately labeled "politically charged," but many critics considered the NLRB's actions in the case to represent regulatory overreach.

Since Caterpillar has made its ability to allocate its capital as it sees fit an almost existential issue, it is fair to conclude that its executives had a very dim view of the NLRB's apparent presumption that the regulatory body might assume such a responsibility. It's important to note, however, that although in recent years Caterpillar's leaders have not shrunk from fiercely advocating the company's position on issues such as free trade and worker compensation costs, they have been careful not to utter statements that would paint the company as antiunion or provide fodder either for union negotiators or for regulators such as the NLRB.

Caterpillar also has been careful to negotiate contract language that is exhaustive in underlining that the company has the right to move production and jobs to the locations it deems best as well as to obtain its inputs when and where it sees fit. Historically, the NLRB has not interfered in situations in which the movement of production and jobs clearly is permitted by negotiated contract language.

Thus, the NLRB has had no grounds in recent years to charge Caterpillar with antiunion retaliation. Once again, things have changed since the 1990s, when the regulatory agency swarmed the company with charges. That is no longer the case because the company and the UAW have reached a modus vivendi that is civilized, businesslike, and sometimes even amicable. Further, the UAW also may have concluded that attempts on its part to constrain Caterpillar's ability to shift production and employment ultimately will fail because CAT has such a great ability to move production, assets, and employment around the world. In fact, the UAW gains dues-paying members if the company is prosperous and growing. Restricting CAT's management flexibility could reduce that prosperity and growth.

> **INSIDER'S EDGE** *Good (or bad) relationships with the National Labor Relations Board seldom are accidents, the political makeup of the NLRB notwithstanding.*

Summing It Up

There is no shortage of individuals critical of Caterpillar's labor relations practices. They censure the company for its tough labor relations stance and its proclivity to shutter plants that it deems unprofitable. Thus, the company's closure of its London, Ontario, plant not only offended union supporters but also was a bone in the throat of Canadian nationalists. Newspaper columnists talked of CAT invoking a "Hobbesian scenario" and setting "dangerous precedents" and fulminated that "Caterpillar is the culmination of globalization run amok."

Caterpillar is anything but a cream puff in labor negotiations, yet its approach is not antiunion but procompany. Our interviews with dozens of Caterpillar employees revealed that the overriding concern of the company in labor negotiations is to ensure that CAT is globally competitive. Employee compensation is only one part of this equation but is perhaps the most visible and eye-catching variable that the company can influence to achieve cost competitiveness in the global markets in which it earns 70 percent of its sales revenues. After all, supply chain management (another very important determinant of global cost-effectiveness) isn't nearly as visible as labor negotiations or closed plants.

Nevertheless, Caterpillar leaders (current and former), even though they have been targets for abundant criticism, are remarkably serene in light of the volume of disparagement that has been directed at them over the years. This is the case because they believe they are doing the right things for the corporation, its employees, and the citizens of the many different countries in which the company is located. They see the slow, tortuous decline of the original U.S. automobile industry and the failure of firms such as Kodak as the proof of the pudding. Hence, rather than destroying jobs, most people at CAT are genuine in the belief that they are saving them.

Taking a longer view, one can observe that the historical job creation record of great companies supports Caterpillar's point of view. Great companies do not destroy jobs in the long run; they create them. This is true even though they often utilize new technologies that are labor-saving in nature.

CHAPTER 7

CATERPILLAR'S PRICELESS NETWORK OF DEALERS

There isn't much doubt in the minds of Caterpillar's competitors: CAT's most important competitive edge is its network of dealers. A Cummins power systems dealer put it simply: "Those CAT dealers make a huge difference. We can compete with their products, but it is awfully difficult to match the entrenched dealers they have. They supply parts and service as well as anybody in the industry, and they are so *#$% committed."

One of the spinoff benefits of Caterpillar's visits to other companies during the 1980s was that those visits underlined the key role of CAT's well-established global network of local and regional dealers. Except for the U.S. military and some select products, Caterpillar seldom sells directly to end users. Instead, the company's dealer network distributes all products to the end users. The dealers (189 in number in 2012) also supply parts to customers and service the products they sell. In addition, the dealers rent and lease Caterpillar equipment to customers. The dealers in many cases control the contact with the company's customer base.

Because Caterpillar's dealers are not in competition with CAT in terms of selling to customers, the dealers have become strategic and tactical partners. Donald Fites might not have been exaggerating when he proclaimed, "We'd rather cut off our right arm than sell directly to customers and bypass our dealers."

Except in rare instances, Caterpillar's dealerships never have been owned by CAT and to this day often involve highly proficient third- and fourth-generation owners who have strong loyalty to the company. Typically, they are well capitalized, and this is one of the reasons the network constitutes a major barrier to the entry of competitors into CAT's markets. During times of economic recession, the rental, service, and parts activities of the company's dealers sustain both the dealers and CAT even when the dealers are not selling many new machines. Their capital base allows them to ride through such storms without being destroyed. We believe the maintenance, repair, and overhaul (MRO) component of CAT's revenue has also bolstered its stock price, because equity markets place a premium on consistency of revenue. Throughout the industrial sector, stock multiples tend to be higher for firms that lead their sectors in the MRO category.

Hence, in the 1980s, Caterpillar's leaders concluded that the dealer network provided the corporation with a competitive advantage that was very difficult to replicate. They resolved to find more ways to take advantage of this superiority. One important way this came to fruition has been Caterpillar's willingness during rough times to reduce its profit stream to support the viability and profitability of its dealers. The company also earned plaudits from its dealers during the recession when it gave some dealers favorable inventory, payment, and credit terms to ensure their viability.

The benefits of the company-dealer relationship, however, flow in both directions. Donald Fites has an interesting take on this. He considers the sale of a Caterpillar machine to a customer to be analogous to an annuity that continues to pay dividends over time. Machines must be serviced and will require parts, both of which will generate business for CAT and its dealers over time. During the Great Recession of 2008–2009, this enduring source of revenue was vitally important to both CAT and its dealers because sales of some machines plummeted as much as 62 percent.

Contrary to what some may believe, it is not always advantageous to sell directly to one's customers. In scaling to a national and global business playing field, the risk-adjusted cost of building a customer base can be reduced by not selling directly. Dealer networks multiply the effective number of employees a company has without the company having to pay for them. Compensation plans in the company are simplified, hiring mistakes are reduced, and customer service is less politicized within the company.

Caterpillar Dealers and Their Capitalization

It is no exaggeration to say that Caterpillar dealers are located all around the world. Figure 7.1 shows the locations of CAT's main dealers, distributorships, offices, and dealerships for non-CAT-branded products within the Caterpillar family. Non-CAT branded companies within the CAT family include Perkins, one of the leading suppliers of smaller diesel and gas engines in the 4- to 2,000-kW (5- to 2,800-horsepower) market, and Solar Turbines, which

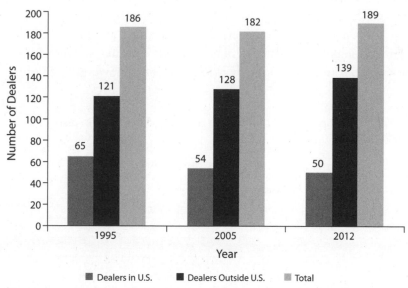

Figure 7.1   *Caterpillar dealers inside and outside of the United States.*

produces larger gas turbines (1,590 to 30,000 horsepower), gas compressors, gas-turbine-powered compressor sets, mechanical-drive packages, and generators.

The theme underpinning Caterpillar's global footprint is straightforward: locate production, distribution, and dealer facilities where the customers are and in so doing pay attention to input sources, worker availability, and transportation logistics. In the case of partnering with dealers, be patient and select only those which have outstanding reputations, good connections, and strong balance sheets.

More than 74 percent of Caterpillar's 189 dealers in 2012 (Table 7.1) were outside the United States. This represents a significant change from 1980, when only 62 percent of the company's dealers were outside the United States. This fact reflects where Caterpillar now harvests its sales.

It's not clear why the number of Caterpillar dealers has fallen over the last decade. Caterpillar says that the Great Recession that began in fall 2008 had very little to do with the decline in dealer numbers and also asserts that the company has not consciously attempted to pare the number of dealers. Nonetheless, the number has fallen about 10 percent since 2000. It is fair to conclude that the current roster is even more secure, stable, and reliable than has traditionally been the case.

Only a handful of Caterpillar dealerships are publicly held, and this makes it difficult to obtain precise information about their activities. Among the publicly held dealerships, however, is Finning

Table 7.1 Changes in the Number and Location of Caterpillar Dealers, 1980–2012

Year	Number and Percent Inside U.S.	Number and Percent Outside U.S.	Total
1980	91 (41.0%)	131 (59.0%)	222
1990	67 (35.3%)	123 (64.7%)	190
2005	54 (29.7%)	128 (70.3%)	182
2012	49 (25.9%)	140 (74.1%)	189

Source: Rachel Potts, Caterpillar Public Affairs

International, thought to be the largest CAT dealership in terms of annual sales (an estimated $6.785 billion in 2012). Finning serves a variety of burgeoning markets, including many shale oil and gas firms in western Canada, and also is extensively involved in Latin America, the United Kingdom, and Ireland. It sells, rents, finances, and provides customer support for Caterpillar equipment and engines. Its October 2012 market cap was $3.948 billion.

Another publicly held Caterpillar dealership is Toromont, whose Equipment Group consists of Tormont CAT, one of the largest Caterpillar dealerships, and Battlefield, which operates CAT rental stores. Toromont operates in Ontario, Manitoba, and portions of Newfoundland, Labrador, and Nunavut. Its estimated 2012 revenues were $1.536 billion, and its October 2012 market cap was $1.528 billion. Since 2000, its annual dividend per share has increased at a compound annual rate of more than 16 percent. Its October 2012 market cap was $1.528 billion. By virtually any standard, Toromont is a healthy, prosperous company.

Toromont's EBIT margin (its earnings before interest and taxes divided by its total revenue) was 13.7 percent in late 2012. Figure 7.2 shows EBIT margins for four publicly traded Caterpillar dealers. Finning International, though the largest dealer in size, has the lowest EBIT margin.

Finning International and Toromont are large and well capitalized, but so are most Caterpillar dealers. Figure 7.3 reveals that the net worth of CAT dealers surged from about $4.0 billion in 1990 to $21.3 billion in 2012, a healthy 7.9 percent compounded annual rate of growth. Caterpillar's prosperity has been good for its dealers and vice versa.

Table 7.2 provides additional information about Caterpillar dealers worldwide. The average dealership is more than 40 years old in terms of its relationship with the company, and these dealers have outposts in 182 countries. As of year end 2011, they operated an amazing 1,981 dealer branches and 1,332 dealer rental outlets. This means that the typical dealer has more than 17 branches and outlets in addition to his or her home base. Their annual sales volumes ranged between $1.5 million and $5.8 billion in 2011.

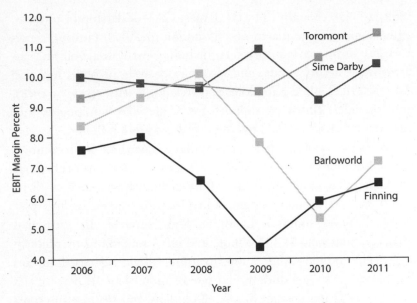

Figure 7.2 *EBIT margins for four publicly traded Caterpillar dealers, 2006–2011.*

Source: Adapted from Canaccord Genuity, "Toromont Industries, Ltd.," October 14, 2012, www.canaccordgenuity.com.

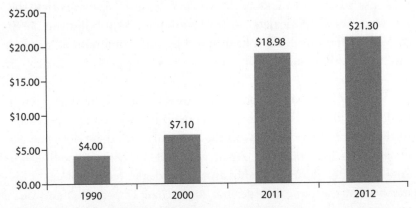

Figure 7.3 *Net worth of Caterpillar dealers ($ billions).*

Source: Caterpillar annual reports.

Table 7.2   *The Amazing Reach of Caterpillar Dealers (Year-End 2011 Data)*

• The average Caterpillar dealer has been with the company more than 40 years.
• Independent Caterpillar dealerships numbered 191, and they operated in 182 countries.
• There were 1,981 dealer branch stores.
• There were 1,332 dealer rental outlets.
• Caterpillar dealers employed more than 140,000 people.
• Caterpillar dealers had a net worth of $18.98 billion.
• Annual dealer sales volume ranged between $1.5 million and $5.8 billion.

Source: Rachel Potts, Caterpillar Public Affairs

Long-Standing Relationships, Handshakes, and Trust

Many Caterpillar dealerships have been owned and operated by families for several generations. We interviewed Peter Holt of Holt CAT in San Antonio. He is the fourth generation of his family to operate a Caterpillar dealership, and it was his ancestors who agreed to the merger of the Holt Manufacturing Company with the C.L. Best Tractor Company in 1925 to create Caterpillar.

Caterpillar's dealers are notable for their strong, nearly unbreakable sense of loyalty. Why? Because they make money. It's business, after all. Interestingly, when it comes to CAT, we also observed softer, more difficult-to-measure answers. "Relationship" is certainly one of them. Peter Holt notes, "My great-grandfather was Benjamin Holt. He's the guy who put the tracks on the tractor back in 1904. He and Best Tractor Company both had dealer systems before CAT was incorporated. Those systems were based upon mutual respect and integrity between the manufacturers and their distributors. Honesty, integrity, respect, the desire for mutual success—that's always been at the core of the relationship." Blake Quinn of the Quinn Group, which owns the Caterpillar dealership in central and southern California, is a third-generation CAT dealer: "My grandfather was a Holt dealer. One of my dad's greatest ambitions was to perpetuate the business to the next generation."

If all this might be mistaken for an arrangement one might find in Voltaire's *Candide* and its "best of all possible worlds," it is because Caterpillar dealers actually are a very satisfied bunch. They bleed yellow very much as the people in Peoria do.

In contrast to the many manufacturer-dealer relationships that exist throughout the world, the Caterpillar-dealer association is not one-sided and usually reflects a genuine partnership. Caterpillar dealer Jim Parker of Carter Machinery in Virginia and West Virginia, a former Caterpillar vice president, told us that his relationship with the company is "more of a handshake than a huge set of rules." The company's dealers and Caterpillar are mutually dependent on one another. CAT can't sell its products or service those products without the dealers. However, the dealers are dependent on CAT for products, parts, and technology, and in lean economic times some depend on Caterpillar for financial help and understanding. Donald Fites observed in 1996, "The kind of trust that exists between Caterpillar and its dealers is something that could be built up only over generations."

This trust, which is an intangible that is difficult to monetize directly but clearly is a spur to profitability, is the source of an important advantage for Caterpillar relative to its competitors. Such trust cannot easily be replicated and constitutes a real barrier to entry by competitors both for specific products and for specific geographic locations. If a competitor such as Komatsu decided to imitate CAT's dealer network, it would take years, if not decades, for it to assemble the right group of dealers, establish them in their market areas, and cultivate the required levels of trust.

INSIDER'S EDGE *The handshake nature of Caterpillar's agreements with its dealers should not be overemphasized. A more litigious society and the onset of Sarbanes-Oxley have brought with them an era of greater board oversight and a host of legal, external, and internal audit controls. However, when unusual levels of trust exist, the handshake still plays a role in business, creating profits above and beyond normal expectations.*

What Caterpillar Expects from Its Dealers

Caterpillar is critically dependent on its dealers to advertise and sell, rent, and lease its products, service those products, and sell parts. Because the dealers are the company's frontline troops, they are vitally involved in establishing, defending, and enhancing CAT's brand reputation. CAT understands this and supports both its dealers and its customers by deploying more "on the ground" representatives than do any of its competitors. These reps listen to consumers, liaison with the dealers, help smooth the flow of machines and parts, and provide the home office with intelligence on what is happening in the field.

Edward Rust, the CEO of State Farm Insurance Company and the presiding member of Caterpillar's board, told us that the dealer network provides the company with a "superb feedback loop." When problems arise, CAT dealers repeatedly have demonstrated that they will not hesitate to relay those problems to the home office because they have a positive incentive (their own profitability) to do so. In fact, the company expects and encourages dealers to let them know what is happening in the field even if the news is not good. If Caterpillar sold even small amounts directly to the same customer base, this level of trust would not be possible. As a consequence of these rules and the handshake atmosphere, CAT receives a steady stream of vital feedback from its dealers concerning product design, product durability, life-cycle costs, pricing strategy, financial market conditions, and what the competition is doing.

Gerald Flaherty, a retired Caterpillar group president, told us about meeting a Caterpillar customer who told him what "we" (meaning Caterpillar but including his dealer and himself) needed to do to compete with Komatsu. The customer was totally invested in Caterpillar. One cannot buy such commitment and devotion. "First and last look" is the nirvana of every salesperson in the world. CAT looks to its dealers to create a first and last look environment.

Dealers are expected to avoid selling the products of competitors and also to stay clear of affiliation relationships with their customers to avoid charges of favoritism. They are expected to embrace

CAT's vision, perform at a very high level, serve customers fully and effectively, maintain and emphasize quality, act as CAT's eyes and ears, and be flexible and adaptable in response to changing conditions.

There are few secrets between Caterpillar and its dealers. The company requires the dealers to provide it with their financial and performance data. In turn, the dealers have instant access to Caterpillar's data system and can easily track product availability and shipments, customer satisfaction, and other vital signs.

Regardless of where its dealers are located, Caterpillar fully expects them to honor its Worldwide Code of Conduct. Tom Gales, now a retired vice president, was president and general manager of Caterpillar Mexico and Caterpillar France and also had responsibility for CAT's Latin American division. He asserts, "There are no cultural problems with our values. They are essentially boundaryless. Dealers all over the world embrace them."

INSIDER'S EDGE *It's better to lose a sale than compromise core values. Such values help create the foundation for a sustained competitive advantage and set apart industry leaders from also-rans.*

Ultimately, Caterpillar's insistence that its Code be followed usually engenders a grudging respect even in countries where standards such as the Code are unusual. "People appreciate our iron, but our Code of Conduct—the way we do business—that is why we are admired," observed a Brazilian dealer, Pedro Esteva.

What Dealers Expect from Caterpillar

Caterpillar dealers expect the company to provide them with a steady supply of highly capable, technologically advanced machines that will perform at least as well as those of competitors such as Komatsu, Deere, Cummins, and Joy. The dealers are the first to hear when CAT's products fall short, and in such situations they demand prompt attention from the home company. They have built long-standing relationships with their customers and don't want to poison those relationships by supplying products that don't work as advertised.

Dealers also expect the company to be able to supply them with the parts customers need and do so almost immediately. On this score, dealers are an impatient lot. "We want those parts yesterday," said one Caterpillar dealer. CAT dealer Peter Holt told us he can handle about 90 percent of all customer requests for parts immediately at his expansive San Antonio location and further states that he can satisfy 98 percent of all parts needs within one day even though CAT has more than 500,000 distinctive parts in its system. Holt says his dealership holds about $600 million in inventory. This financial commitment sets an imposing standard that discourages competitors.

Caterpillar dealers also expect to be kept informed. Indeed, they do much of this on their own by accessing the company's data system. There, they can find out what is selling, what products (if any) are encountering problems, how much inventory is available, and so forth.

Why Don't Caterpillar's Competitors Do the Same Thing?

The notable success of Caterpillar's dealer network leads naturally to an obvious question: If it's such a good thing, why don't CAT's competitors replicate its essentials? This is a question we addressed both to the company's executives and to its competitors. The answer (from both parties): it would take lots of time and resources to do so. Figure 7.3 revealed that the net worth of Caterpillar dealers had risen to $21.3 billion by 2012. Although not all CAT dealers have deep financial pockets, many do; this, along with their established reputations and loyalty to Caterpillar, makes them a tough nut to crack. One of Caterpillar's competitors (who does not wish to be named for obvious reasons) told us, "It will take us twenty years to be able to assemble a dealer network like Caterpillar's." It is difficult to avoid the conclusion that the risk-adjusted present value of the discounted profit stream associated with attempting to replicate CAT's dealer network simply isn't high enough to move its competitors to large-scale action.

Thus in simple economic terms, the Caterpillar dealer network and its approximately 140,000 employees provide a strong competitive advantage for Caterpillar (only Deere among its competitors has anything similar). This drives sales, customer loyalty, and an attractive stream of profits. At the same time, the dealer network constitutes a major barrier to the entry of new competitors. Firms such as Komatsu and Sany must think carefully about when and where they will do battle with Caterpillar, knowing that CAT is entrenched in major markets worldwide with reputable, well-established, well-capitalized dealers. Sany, however, seems ready to take on the challenge. It has taken out full-page advertisements in the *Wall Street Journal* and states that it now has 12 dealerships in the United States, though many of them appear to be at early stages of development.

> **INSIDER'S EDGE** *Products can be duplicated, customers and employees wooed away, governmental favors wiped out, and intellectual property stolen. However, the long-term commitment and loyalty of highly reputable, well-capitalized dealers are not easy to replicate and constitute a significant competitive advantage and barrier to entry.*

Final Thoughts

In 1926, a team of Caterpillar managers addressed the company-dealer relationship in a short volume titled *Across the Table.* They described a relationship based on "mutual respect," stating, "As the dealer profits—so do we." Our personal observations of Caterpillar and its dealers reveal that these still are accurate observations. We found almost none of the "the company is trying to stick it to us" conflicts that seem to characterize so many company-franchisee or company-dealer relationships today. The company and the dealers genuinely appear to respect each other and understand that the welfare of each depends on the other. They simply can't go it alone.

At the end of the day, Caterpillar's global dealer network arguably is the greatest single advantage it has over current and future competitors, some of whom are likely to come from China. Most of the company's other advantages (e.g., the technology embedded in its machines) can be duplicated by competitors in the space of a few years. This is not true for the dealer network, which might take decades to replicate. Hence, CAT's careful choices in the 1980s and 1990s to cultivate that network and even to reduce its own profits in order to nurture it were in retrospect very wise.

CHAPTER 8

PRODUCT QUALITY, PRICING, AND BRANDING

C aterpillar should provide cautionary food for thought for those who have strong opinions about the precise characteristics required of a successful chief executive officer. Beginning with George Schaefer and extending through Doug Oberhelman, the company has been guided by successful CEOs with very different personalities and strengths. George Schaefer, Donald Fites, Glen Barton, James Owens, and Doug Oberhelman each had distinctive personalities and leadership styles. Further, each took a different path and acquired many different experiences as he moved up the ranks at CAT. Virtually the only common denominator among these successful leaders is that there is no doubt that each of them "bled yellow."

"Each brought something different to the table," board member David Goode told us. "Each was the right guy at the right time." As we've seen, Don Fites was the right leader to deal with the restructuring challenges and labor difficulties of the 1990s, whereas an individual such as Jim Owens, a PhD in economics, had a strong international bent and an eye for the future and accelerated Caterpillar's push into growing markets outside the United States.

Doug Oberhelman, today's chairman/CEO, is a vigorous, enthusiastic leader who has brought a sense of urgency to Caterpillar's business. "Second place" is not in his lexicon. He knows individual employees, customers, and dealers and consistently walks shop floors. At the same time, he is not hesitant to make Caterpillar's case forcefully with elected officials up to and including President Barack Obama.

Glen Barton, who led Caterpillar from 1999 to 2004, was "a product man" (a description given by a CEO in a related industry) who was strongly interested in the menu and quality of the company's products. Barton is a University of Missouri engineering graduate who joined CAT in 1961 and accumulated extensive international experience. He and subsequent CEOs broadened the company's product offerings and services, developed new dealer-rental stores, firmly nudged CAT into e-business, and, in particular, emphasized cost-reducing, quality-enhancing process improvements.

Retrospectively, it appears that Caterpillar's board of directors instinctively understood what the company needed at a given point in time and then selected the individual who could bring the leadership talents to the table to move CAT in the necessary direction. In 1999, coming off a very difficult decade, they chose the product man, Glen Barton.

A Digression on Leadership Selection

Caterpillar's board of directors is on a winning streak insofar as its selections of chairmen/CEOs are concerned. Without exception, they have selected high-level performers, each of whom has become a vital part of the company's history of success. This sterling record of selection, however, leads to an obvious question: Has the board been lucky, or has it been good? How much do the board's excellent leadership selections over the last 30 years reflect simple good fortune and how much do they reflect carefully calibrated, accurate decisions designed to meet what the board identified as the pressing needs of the company at the time?

Let's give luck its due. No individual or board is omniscient. Boards of directors can neither anticipate everything in a company's future nor precisely predict a leader's behavior. With regard to the latter point, witness the sudden fall from grace of General David Petraeus because of indiscretions and the way the ripples from that episode spread to other individuals. More than a few of our idols turn out to have feet of clay.

No board can purchase an insurance policy against such eventualities. What boards can do, however, is observe prospective leaders under fire for long periods. Caterpillar presiding board member Ward Rust told us that at board meetings, group presidents and vice presidents make the most presentations. Thus, board members can see what makes executives tick, the things they value, the way they react to challenges and criticism, the ways in which they react to the unexpected, how comfortable they are with data, their skill in making public presentations, how they deal with the media, the ways in which they interact with their peers and those below them in the hierarchy, what vision they have for the organization, and other qualities. These are among the benefits associated with choosing an insider to become an organization's next leader. Boards tend to know what they are getting when they appoint an insider.

The most obvious danger connected to the insider approach to choosing a leader is that the organization's culture may become stale, confining, and self-confirming. Just as there is a "Caterpillar Way," there also was a "Kodak Way," but the Kodak variation did not fare well because it was resistant to change and loath to confront reality. Or consider Motorola, a pioneer in cellular telephones that was ranked number 24 on the Fortune 500 list in 1995. Motorola's insiders ignored the competitive threat provided by the likes of Nokia, and by 1999 Motorola had to declare bankruptcy. In 2012, it became a property of Google. Joseph Schumpeter's waves of creative destruction live on in American industry.

These examples should inspire caution as we contemplate and applaud the distinctive company culture that powers Caterpillar. That culture is tinged with pride and a "we can do it" attitude that at times almost appears to mock the financial titans on the two coasts, thousands of miles away from Peoria, Illinois.

Our interviews allow us to credit the Caterpillar board with conscientious, careful, thoughtful, long-term deliberation about the issue of insider leadership. In the view of the board, the primary candidates for the position of chairman/CEO audition for the spot for many years in a row. The board is able to observe and evaluate each potential candidate's modus operandi firsthand. Further, Caterpillar's meticulous employee evaluation system and "everybody owns their own numbers" approach to business unit and leadership assessment provide board members with essential empirical evidence that lends a strong dose of reality to discussions about leadership.

There is some empirical evidence in favor of the insider approach to CEO selection in for-profit firms. In a recent comprehensive study, Ang and Nagel reported the total financial performance of all publicly traded U.S. firms between 1985 and 2005 and then examined whether those firms were led by internally hired CEOs or CEOs brought in from the outside. They found that internally promoted CEOs outperformed external hires substantially and that this advantage increased over time. It is interesting that the empirical evidence on the selection and performance of college presidents tends to point in the opposite direction.

Regardless, Caterpillar's former presiding board member Eugene Fife told us, "It is not our job to be the best buddy of the management." Good board members respectfully challenge and question the company's managers (long-term insiders or not) and force those managers to articulate and justify their courses of action. As we point out in Chapter 10, an excellent example of this occurred when Caterpillar acquired Bucyrus, a well-regarded but expensively priced mining firm. Gene Fife told us that it was "three or four meetings before we waved the green flag and said go ahead." This careful, structured, civilized approach to board-leader relationships has yielded many positive results; one of the most important is that it enables board members to assess the strengths and weaknesses of prospective CEOs and ultimately to make intelligent leadership decisions.

Thus it was no accident that Glen Barton succeeded Don Fites as chairman/CEO in 1999. The board sensed that his distinctive mix of talents and personality was especially well suited to the times even though Caterpillar boasted a deep bench of other CEO possibilities. Challenges relating to the company's menu of products and the quality of those products were one of the company's paramount concerns, and Barton was the right man to address them. They also expected him to speed the healing of labor-management relationships, which had frayed seriously in the 1990s.

> **INSIDER'S EDGE**   *Unless your company is in trouble and requires a shake-up or lacks managerial bench strength, you should select your next CEO from inside the firm. Well-executed succession planning by the board allows the assessment of candidates under fire and enhances the board's ability to find the right person for the times. Also, assuming that your company has developed a productive culture, this approach extends that culture. Succession planning for the next CEO must be one of the highest priorities of an independent board of directors. Done well, it will eliminate the element of surprise and lower the risk of the board hiring a lemon.*

Caterpillar's Product Mix

Great companies know that the breadth and quality of their product line are crucial to their prosperity. In manufacturing, it's not easy to earn significant revenue from anything you don't sell, rent, lease, or service. In some corporations, this understanding generates a bias in favor of a large product line because, at least on the surface, a large product line appears to allow the company to earn more revenue and profits. "You can't sell something you don't have," asserted the CEO of a midsized manufacturing company we interviewed.

Nevertheless, as Caterpillar learned when it reorganized and established business units in the early 1990s, not all of its products were profitable, and some of them were being produced and serviced at less than the highest levels of quality. Consequently, in recent years, Caterpillar always has understood that a larger product line is not necessarily a good idea because both costs and benefits are entailed with larger product lines. This applies not only to manufacturers but also to the dealers and distributors who sell, rent, lease, and service those products.

Since its reorganization in the 1990s, Caterpillar has been better able to track accurately the revenues and costs associated with its products. This means being able to determine how much each product actually contributes to the company's bottom line. Although this may seem to be something any large company should be able to do, most do this critical accounting poorly. A company such as Caterpillar has hundreds of thousands of inputs into its manufacturing processes. There are tens of thousands of indirect costs to be measured and then attributed to the correct revenue streams. And of course, corporate overhead (the "GO") must be allocated to the appropriate revenue stream.

When divisional or group bonuses are determined by EBITDA or profit metrics, there is a natural tendency on the part of those affected to attempt to avoid having indirect charges applied to their particular units. In a company as large as Caterpillar, there are thousands of managers with an incentive to find ways for some other unit to take responsibility for a particular cost. Almost needless to say, the internal politics of cost allocation processes can become quite complicated and lead to a degree of disunity of purpose. Nevertheless, the stakes are so high that it is essential that accurate cost accounting occur. Unless costs are allocated correctly, managers respond to false signals and companies end up making unwise decisions because they are flying blind.

A very important foundation for an accurate, operational accounting system is a user-friendly information technology (IT) organization. High-quality IT organizations gather and generate information in forms that enable companies to measure what they are doing and then interpret the results in ways that permit more intelligent, informed decision making. Caterpillar shines in this arena. It has wisely invested the resources necessary to produce a top-flight IT system that attracts visitors from other companies because it is known to be one of the best in the business. CAT locations throughout the world utilize high-speed T1 communications lines that enable them to track what they are doing and then make astute evidence-based decisions. The company's productive IT system has been a significant contributor to profit and growth and supports CAT's logistics, its entire supply chain, inventories, its financial system, production activities on shop floors, and even its customers. The payoff is evident. CAT has been to scale upward from a $20 billion company to $40 billion and then to $60 billion without hitting a wall.

CAT introduces new products sparingly and only when they enhance the "core" of the company; that means that a new product will complement and strengthen the existing product line. No one would ever mistake Caterpillar for a go-go conglomerate like Ling-Temco-Vought, Textron, or Litton. When CAT produces a new product, this reflects its judgment that it will strengthen its existing product line and thus help its dealers and will enable the company to make a profit.

> **Contrast Caterpillar's product strategy** with that of Apple, which derives more than 70 percent of its revenues from only two products: the iPhone and the iPad. Although no one is predicting Apple's demise, its market share in both of these product areas has declined significantly, and this has placed it in an exposed position. On July 12, 2013, Apple's share price was down 38 percent from its September 2012 high.

Especially after 2000, Caterpillar leaders came to view the company's market position and product line as unproductively narrow. Although they were well aware of the problems associated with excessive conglomerate diversification, CAT's leadership also concluded that they could improve corporate performance if CAT moved into markets and companies closely allied to its core excavation and earthmoving activities. The motivation was threefold. First, they sought to increase the company's penetration of growing markets such as mining and energy. Second, by offering a somewhat larger product line, they hoped to reduce some of the sensitivity of CAT's sales and earnings to the business cycle. Third, they believed that there were potential economies of scope (in addition to scale) at the dealer level and that dealers would seize on the opportunity to broaden their product lines.

Caterpillar added a variety of items to its product line between 2000 and 2012. The company acquired Progress Rail Services, which put it into the locomotive, railcar, and rail service and repair business. Progress Rail in turn acquired Electro-Motive Diesel, which, along with General Electric, is one of only two original equipment manufacturers of diesel-electric locomotives in the United States.

Table 8.1 shows Caterpillar's most important acquisitions between 2000 and 2012. It is apparent that the company has relied on acquisitions to expand its product line and plant its production flag in markets outside the United States. This expansion has been deliberate and calculated though on occasion also opportunistic. The Electro-Motive Diesel (EMD) acquisition was both. CAT originally attempted to buy EMD in 2005 but lost out to the Greenbriar Equity Group. Greenbriar, knowing Caterpillar's continuing interest in a product line closely related to CAT's Progress Rail activities, sold to CAT in 2010.

At the same time, however, Caterpillar was generating a series of other new, non-merger-related products such as towed scrapers and a first of its kind electric drive, track-type tractor, the D7E, and the company's first hybrid machine: the 336E hybrid hydraulic excavator (this was in 2012).

Product improvement was also an important part of the story. In 2001, Caterpillar dramatically improved its engines with its ACERT technology, which reduced emissions at the point of combustion. By 2003, all of CAT's on-highway truck and bus engines were equipped with ACERT, which satisfied increasingly rigorous U.S. Environmental Protection Agency requirements.

In 2004, the company vastly increased its commitment to remanufacturing both its own and other manufacturers' products. The remanufacture of existing equipment and engines appeals to many customers during tough economic times. In essence, it involves the refurbishing, repair, and replacement of worn-out parts and equipment. The goal is to produce a product that may not be as good as new but might well last as long as a new product. This was an excellent management decision. Maintenance, repair, and parts revenues are highly valued on Wall Street and constitute a source of support for Caterpillar's stock price because of the stability they provide to the company's income stream throughout the business cycle.

Table 8.1   *Product and Market Extension Acquisitions by Caterpillar,*
2000–2011

Year	Acquisition	Product/Market Entry
2000	Bitelli, S.p.a.	Italian manufacturer of paving equipment
2000	Sabre Engines, Ltd.	Handles Perkins engine line in the United Kingdom
2000	CAT Elphinstone Joint Venture	Handles Caterpillar products in Australia
2000	Hindustan Motors, Earthmoving Division	Earthmoving equipment in India
2004	Turbomach S.A.	Natural gas and liquid fuel turbines manufactured in Europe and Asia
2006	Progress Rail Services	Railroad and transit system equipment and service
2007	Eurenov S.A.S.	Remanufacturing engines, gearboxes, injection pumps, subassemblies, and injectors in France and Poland
2007	Blount International Inc., Forestry Division	Forestry equipment and parts
2008	Lovat, Inc.	Tunnel boring production based in Canada
2008	Shandong SEM Machinery Company, Ltd.	Soil compactors and wheel loaders in the PRC
2008	Shin Caterpillar Mitsubishi, Ltd.	Increased activity in construction equipment in Asia
2008	MGE Equipamentos & Serviços Ferroviários, Ltda.	Traction motors and electric traction generators for locomotives, and commuter and underground trains in Brazil
2010	Electro-Motive Diesel	Diesel-electric locomotives and diesel power engines in Canada and Illinois
2011	Bucyrus International, Inc.	Surface and underground mining equipment in Wisconsin and numerous locations outside of the United States
2011	MWM Holding GmbH	Leading global supplier of sustainable natural gas and alternative fuel engines, headquartered in Germany
2012	ERA/Siwei	Manufacturer of underground mining equipment in China

The year 2004, incidentally, was the hundredth anniversary of the first track-type tractor, which has been Caterpillar's bread and butter product through most of its history. Although track-type tractors used in construction still feature prominently in CAT's product line and revenue generation, financial analysts increasingly see the company becoming more identified with mining and energy activities around the world in addition to construction.

The Quality Challenge

We already have touched on Caterpillar's commitment to Six Sigma levels of quality. Caterpillar's chairman/CEO Glen Barton took this on "as if driven by God" (an observation by a former CAT executive). Barton described Six Sigma as "a relentless quest for perfection through the disciplined use of fact-based, data-driven, decision-making methodology." This was much more than a passing fad with him and the company. Six Sigma was the tool that would enable CAT to beat back foreign competition, set premium prices, retain satisfied customers, and clearly delineate the company as the industry leader. It also is credited with shaving approximately $1 billion from Caterpillar's operating costs in the space of five years.

Without Six Sigma or a similar commitment to product quality, Caterpillar could not become a great company. It would instead be just another producer in a set of highly competitive markets. Six Sigma quality standards were Caterpillar's way of putting distance between itself and its competitors. It was a brand-enhancing development that has paid many dividends to the company in the twenty-first century. However, as we shall see, the commitment to Six Sigma levels of quality also introduced an interesting set of new challenges.

INSIDER'S EDGE *Although there are companies that deliberately decide not to produce or sell the highest-quality products in their markets, such companies usually are good at nearly everything else they do. Costco provides an excellent example. It is an acknowledged master at the art of selling ordinary products. The most imposing companies, however, combine very high levels of quality with very proficient production, sales, and service. Caterpillar is one of the very few firms that has been able to do all these things.*

The logical precursor to Caterpillar's emphasis on Six Sigma quality standards was the Plant with a Future (PWAF) initiative of the 1980s and 1990s, during which the company retooled its factories and girded itself to compete head to head with its competitors, both domestic and foreign. The combination of PWAF and Six Sigma enabled CAT to produce a quality dividend that has served the company well over the last two decades. It has burnished Caterpillar's reputation and enabled it to engage in premium pricing.

Caterpillar's hefty spending on new plants and equipment in recent years suggests that its leaders believe that another PWAF-like thrust is merited to maintain CAT's leadership position. Caterpillar's competitors have not been standing still and "have closed much of the quality distance between CAT and them in recent years," according to Rob Wertheimer of Vertical Research Partners. Thus, "Caterpillar's quality is excellent, but Komatsu's machines now may be just as good as CAT's," suggests Wertheimer.

> **Boeing, one of the "Big Ten" companies** *identified in Chapter 1, could learn from Caterpillar. Boeing had a terrific year in 2012 in terms of sales but not in terms of product quality. The company's 787 Dreamliner passenger airplanes have been beset by problems large and small, including electrical malfunctions, fires, and fuel leaks. The FAA grounded all Dreamliners worldwide in January 2013.*

Product quality, of course, is not a static concept, and our notions of what constitutes acceptable quality change over time. Unless one collects vintage automobiles, it would be nonsensical to trade any new automobile for a 1950 Ford or even a 2000 Chevrolet. Automobile performance and quality have increased dramatically. So it is in the markets for Caterpillar's products and services. Standing still is a time-tested recipe for deceleration and eventual failure. Great companies such as Caterpillar understand this and know they must improve their game on a continuous basis. We interpret CAT's generous capital expenditures in recent years as a signal that it does not intend to be caught with its hands in its pockets.

The Brand Challenge

For as long as anyone can remember, Caterpillar's product strategy has involved selling a high-quality product at a premium price. A Harvard Business School case reported that between 1973 and 1983, CAT increased its prices at an average annual rate of 10 percent, a pace that may have been unwise. CAT acknowledges that the initial price of its equipment (e.g., a D11 tractor) usually exceeds that of its competitors but asserts that the life-cycle cost of operating the company's equipment is lower and that the eventual residual value of its equipment is higher. CAT states that 80 percent of the equipment that it sells comes back to it in the form of a trade-in for a new CAT product. CAT executives frequently talk of their "value proposition" and argue (backed by a variety of statistical studies generated by the company's Value Estimating Tool) that a customer who wants a highly durable, reliable piece of equipment with minimum downtime should buy a CAT product because in the long term it will involve lower costs with higher reliability.

> **In contrast to Caterpillar, IBM's** *service units have been struggling to maintain growth and quality as smaller, quicker rivals such as Accenture have invaded its turf and are gaining market share. This is a major challenge for IBM because 50 percent of its revenues now come from services. The company's iconic status has not been sufficient to protect it from such nimble competitors. Lou Gerstner's time at IBM has long passed, and the dancing of the elephant once again needs to improve.*

Caterpillar estimates that about three-quarters of the customers in its markets are interested in buying, renting, or leasing equipment that fits the CAT value proposition (high quality, capable of being used intensively, low life-cycle costs). By the same token, it recognizes that some customers, especially outside the United States, may be interested in different kinds of equipment because they do not intend to use the equipment so intensively or plan to use it for longer periods.

One measure of Caterpillar's resolve to produce the highest-quality products in its industries is the fact that it spends approximately 4 percent of its annual revenues on research and development, a percentage larger than that of most of its competitors. It's true that a significant proportion of these expenditures have been driven by mandatory environmental standards that CAT's products must satisfy. Even so, Tana Utley, CAT's former chief technology officer and a vice president, points out that there are about 10,000 engineers and technologists throughout the company. Hence, its commitment to product improvement cannot be doubted, and it has 6,500 active patents in its portfolio to demonstrate this.

Although Caterpillar has jealously defended its CAT brand, it has consciously chosen not to forfeit the lower-end segment of the potential market to its competitors. Consequently, it has bifurcated its branding approach. The Caterpillar brand remains the premium high-quality product, and Caterpillar products are sold at premium prices. However, the company now offers many other brands, some of which focus on the growing international markets, where product requirements differ from those in North America and Western Europe. For example, in 2008, CAT acquired China's Shandong SEM Machinery, now a wholly owned Caterpillar subsidiary that makes construction equipment such as wheel loaders. Shandong SEM produces equipment that is less durable and is priced 30 to 50 percent lower than conventional CAT equipment. Further, SEM machines may not satisfy the more rigorous environmental rules CAT faces in North America and Europe. By November 2012, SEM was producing wheel loaders, motor graders, bulldozers, and paving machinery.

The company's approach to positioning Shandong SEM provides an instructive example of the tensions involved in determining "what is CAT and what is not" (in the words of a competitor).When searching the Internet for Shandong Machinery Company, Ltd., one reads that SEM is a Caterpillar brand and that many Caterpillar technologies have been incorporated into SEM products. The SEM site features the familiar Caterpillar logo. However, SEM's products are, for example, labeled SEM 8218 (a soil compactor) rather than CAT 8218. Caterpillar says that "SEM products meet or exceed regional industry requirements for quality and reliability that target customers who emphasize initial acquisition cost over long-term total cost of ownership." Thus, we perceive that Caterpillar subtly puts a bit of distance between itself and SEM insofar as product quality and durability are concerned.

> **Caterpillar group president Ed Rapp** *underlined the importance of China to Caterpillar when he said, "If you are going to be a good baseball team, you have to win on the road. Winning in China is us winning on the road."*

Caterpillar's deliberate decision has been to preserve, protect, and enhance its primary CAT brand while using brands such as Shangdong SEM to address differentiated markets. Caterpillar says that, "The CAT brand represents the industry-leading products and services made by Caterpillar. The CAT brand is Caterpillar's primary public-facing brand name, appearing on our world-class equipment and related services." Note the difference between this "world-class" description for explicitly Caterpillar products and the regional industry requirements standard applied to SEM.

In the estimation of Colum Murphy of the *Wall Street Journal,* the "low-price segment increasingly is critical for Caterpillar as its core business is pressured in China." Nevertheless, this is a delicate tap dance for Caterpillar. We believe that it wants to endow companies such as SEM with the patina of Caterpillar's sterling reputation yet not place itself in an upscale price/quality market position that would be untenable. Although conditions may change over time, Caterpillar executives understand that a top of the market, premium pricing approach is not likely to achieve great success in China today. Therefore, it has devised a strategy that recognizes market segmentation much the way a brewer such as Anheuser-Busch InBev produces and sells many different kinds of beers under many different labels.

Caterpillar maintains approximately 30 different brands around the world. Among them are well-known and highly regarded brands such as Perkins (gas and diesel engines), Solar Turbines (industrial gas turbines used in electric power generation, gas compression, and pumping systems), and MWM (environmentally friendly natural gas and diesel engine power plants). CAT's decision to maintain these brands has been based on the outstanding reputation these firms had when they were acquired and worries that placing CAT's name on them would disturb loyal customers.

Contrast the decision on branding Perkins, Solar, and MWM with the one made by the company when it acquired the mining equipment producer Bucyrus in 2011. Reversing its original inclination, it moved quickly to place the CAT label on that company's products. Caterpillar concluded that it would benefit from having only one name associated with its mining equipment and that Bucyrus was operating in much the same quality and price sphere as CAT. Hence, its products could be subsumed by CAT without endangering the brand. Almost from day 1 of this acquisition, Bucyrus employees began wearing CAT badges and hats and were integrated into the operational culture of Caterpillar.

We visited the former headquarters of Bucyrus in South Milwaukee, Wisconsin, expecting to find fearful workers who resented Caterpillar's acquisition and the abolition of the well-regarded Bucyrus name. However, that was not the case. Even though the typical Bucyrus workers were very proud of the mining equipment they had been producing, that feeling was coupled with a grudging respect and admiration for Caterpillar. They understood that CAT was an industry leader in every product area it had entered and that it would give the newly merged combination an imposing array of surface and underground mining equipment to sell and service. One Bucyrus worker put it this way: "These guys [CAT] are good. But we're good too. Both of us together are going to be even better. I think this will increase job security."

The Caterpillar-Bucyrus operation was led by Luis de Leon, who was the chief operating officer for Bucyrus and since has left the company. He noted that the mining industry has been consolidating for 25 years that and the Caterpillar-Bucyrus merger enabled

CAT to dominate the mining equipment market.Interestingly, Bucyrus had been in an acquisitive mode before being acquired by Caterpillar and had acquired mining equipment firms such as DBT and Terex. De Leon saw Caterpillar's highly proficient dealer network as one of the major positives emanating from the merger insofar as the former Bucyrus is concerned. However, integrating Bucyrus into that network will not be easy because Bucyrus had pursued a traditional direct sales model rather than working through dealers. De Leon also believed that Caterpillar would benefit from the highly entrepreneurial, quick-to-the-mark culture that characterized the much smaller Bucyrus. De Leon resigned in January 2013 after the discovery of Caterpillar's accounting problems with its Chinese subsidiary, ERA Mining Machinery.

The Value of the Caterpillar Brand

Caterpillar has reason to protect its brand, which Interbrand valued at $6.306 billion in 2011. This made it the sixty-first most valuable brand in the world. John Deere, the nearest American competitor of CAT in many markets, was ranked eighty-fifth at $4.221 billion. Komatsu was not ranked in the top 100 global brands but was ranked tenth in Japan with a brand value of $2.317 billion.

Fortune magazine's 2012 "most admired companies" edition ranked CAT the nineteenth most admired firm in the world and ranked it first in the industrial and farm equipment category. Deere ranked thirty-eighth overall and placed second in the industrial and farm equipment category. Komatsu did not finish in the top 50 overall but did rank eighth in the industrial and farm equipment category.

Even so, there is little value in having a recognizable brand or in being widely admired if a company cannot translate that recognition into sales and profitability. Caterpillar has been able to do this. The power of the Caterpillar brand and its status as a highly admired company constitute barriers to the entry of new competitors. Slowly and incrementally, Caterpillar has differentiated its products so that they now are regarded worldwide as reliable, durable, high-quality items worthy of premium prices.

INSIDER'S EDGE *It's difficult to find a great firm that does not have a significant, highly valued brand. Brand value is a thermometer that in the long run provides a measure of the totality of what a firm is doing. Brand value also can constitute a significant barrier to the entry of new competitors.*

Caterpillar did not achieve this enviable position by blowing smoke. Its leadership position is not the result of seductive television advertisements filled with Swedish blondes in bikinis or talking Australian lizards. Instead, it is the result of producing products that are demonstrably excellent, a worldwide dealership system that has no peer, a relentless drive to be globally competitive in terms of its costs, and astute decision making.

This does not mean that veteran competitors such as Deere, Komatsu, Joy, and Cummins are condemned perpetually to watch Caterpillar's proverbial taillights or that newer competitors such as China's Sany cannot make CAT squirm. After all, Komatsu's market share currently is larger than that of Caterpillar in both Japan and China.

The ultimate reality is that economically speaking, nothing is forever and competition never stops. Caterpillar absolutely must be on its toes. However, it's not a walk in the park for Caterpillar's major competitors, either. They privately confess that it's not easy for them to compete with a strong, resilient, driven company that has developed an excellent worldwide reputation. All things considered, our estimation is that barring major mistakes, Caterpillar should maintain its leadership position through the remainder of this decade.

CHAPTER 9

The Burning Platform

In 2000, Caterpillar earned $1.05 billion in profit on $20.18 billion of sales. "Fantastic!" you might say. Most business leaders would mortgage their kids to achieve sales and profit numbers of that magnitude. Well, maybe mortgage their houses. Glen Barton, however, saw things differently and sensed stagnation when he examined Caterpillar. Appointed chairman/CEO in 1999, Barton believed Caterpillar was "stuck on a plateau."

We've already described how Caterpillar completely reorganized itself in 1990 and how this provided one of the sparks for years of sterling performance. Annual revenues exploded from $10.18 billion in 1991 to $20.98 billion in just seven years (a 10.9 percent compound annual rate of growth), but then the company seemed to lose momentum. Consolidated sales and revenues hardly moved for the next four years.

Barton was aware that $20 billion in annual revenue often constituted a mysterious ceiling that appeared to constrain the growth of many previously dynamic companies—a sort of growth Twilight Zone where scaling to larger sizes suddenly became much more difficult. Now this appeared to be happening at Caterpillar, and he found it unacceptable.

Many large-company CEOs spend much of their time on global issues, board relations, corporate strategy, and Wall Street financial issues. Barton worried about those things but in addition focused on less sexy topics such as the warranty costs on equipment that CAT had sold and that now was being used in the field. Users' costs connected to CAT equipment were rising rapidly. This was a red flag to Barton because it soon could lead to consumer dissatisfaction with the company's products. In fact, Barton began to see a series of red flags, not the kind waved by matadors but the product quality and reliability red flags waved by customers and dealers.

Barton devoted time to reading employee surveys. (Most CEOs of Fortune 100 companies say they read these things, but few actually take the time to do so.) Caterpillar employee feedback suggested a blah feeling about things at the company. Too many employees no longer were bleeding Caterpillar yellow; their devotion and commitment to the company might be flagging. Thus, even though Barton was leading one of the world's most storied companies, the platform on which he and CAT were standing was beginning to burn. He concluded that Caterpillar had to change. The salient question was how.

Barton thought carefully about what he could and would demand of his troops to shake the company from its torpor. Like most CEOs of note, he decided to choose objectives for Caterpillar that might be viewed as "slightly unachievable." Easily achievable goals often send the wrong message about the need for action. By the same token, clearly unachievable goals often are discarded as unrealistic. However, slightly unachievable goals—ones that really make the organization stretch—are optimal. Barton decided he would insist that his team reach $30 billion in annual consolidated sales and revenue within five years. Further, CAT managers would be challenged to take 10 percent out of their costs even while consolidated sales and revenues were rising. If you are not familiar with large corporate financial statements but somewhat familiar with politics, imagine the U.S. Senate and House of Representatives lowering government expenditures by 10 percent while the economy is growing.

Nevertheless, Barton wasn't finished. He would also demand total commitment to improved product quality. Status quo with the customer base was unacceptable. Six Sigma levels of product quality, which we discuss in greater detail later in this chapter, would become Caterpillar's calling card.

Barton viewed his list of goals, including immediate attainment of Six Sigma quality, to be slightly unachievable though conceptually achievable. However, he wanted to introduce a sense of urgency into Caterpillar's operations. Announcing a list of goals like this took guts even at Caterpillar, where CEOs traditionally have been powerful leaders. In retrospect, Barton deserves immense credit for being willing to do this.

Barton would begin with the company's Strategic Review Committee (SRC), convince it first, and only then put his name and career on the line. In light of the company's devotion to "you own your own numbers," this meant that each executive reporting to Barton would be putting his or her career on the line as well.

> **INSIDERS EDGE** *As they approach $20 billion of revenue, many companies become their own worst enemies. They develop lazy cultures, and often this spawns a culture of arrogance. Continued success is viewed as inevitable. Such companies become resistant to change and improvement. They underestimate their competitors and in the process overestimate themselves. Here is how to avoid the arrogance trap: (1) Cull the ranks of management and infuse fresh, talented managers who both extend and disrupt and (2) reward productive behavior.*

The Origins of Six Sigma and Lean Production at Caterpillar

Kevin Giovenetto, a Caterpillar consultant, described the company's entry into the land of Six Sigma in an internal Caterpillar report/book titled *Giant Steps*. We paraphrase and summarize:

It was December 19, 2000. The senior executives had congregated at Caterpillar's headquarters in Peoria for a series of meetings that would turn out to be pivotal for the company, equaling in importance the impact of the fundamental reorganization a decade earlier. The attendees had been alerted that CEO/Chairman Glen Barton would make an all-hands-on-deck presentation focusing on

Six Sigma. General Electric (GE) had long since made news by initiating a Six Sigma quality improvement program. 3M and a growing list of other prominent firms had followed suit.

It already was late in the afternoon on this winter day, and perhaps many of the executives in the audience were ready to start the cocktail hour because they had already been in the room for six hours of strategic and operational presentations. To compound things, Barton was a bit late. Some people were beginning to pull out their cell phones—an innovation in December 2000—to check their messages.

> **"The devil is in the details.** *If you look long and hard, it's not that you will find something wrong, it's that you will find something that can be done better. The devil resides in not improving." These are the words of Jerome Hamilton, senior vice president and head of Six Sigma at 3M. In 2012, 3M went over the $1.0 billion mark in cost savings extracted by Six Sigma.*

Then a gong reverberated, and mouths dropped as Glen Barton, dressed in a black belt karate uniform, burst into the room. He was followed by four similarly clad men. One of the black belts proceeded to split a one-inch-thick piece of hard wood that was said to represent a breakthrough in Caterpillar product quality. A second black belt screamed and split a similar one-inch piece of hard wood representing a breakthrough in reducing Caterpillar's costs. The third black belt stared at three one-inch pieces of wood that were held together. Most people in the crowd probably were thinking, No way! This three-layer block was said to represent the $20 billion annual revenue ceiling that seemed to stymie so many companies, including Caterpillar. Barton was about to tell the crowd that Caterpillar *will* hit $30 billion inside five years *or else*. The third black belt took this advice to heart and proceeded to smash the thick block to smithereens with his elbow.

Geoff Turk, an employee who was soon to join Caterpillar's Six Sigma Champions Office (6SCO), described the moment: "There is utter shock. People in this room have been beat up before, but never physically. It is unbelievable." The room erupted in applause.

Barton now had their undivided attention. He informed the group that the fourth black belt was the father of the three other Black Belts and that all four were Caterpillar employees.

Then the sound of a train whistle filled the room. That was the signal for Barton to deliver a riveting ten-minute speech that would change the course of the company. Barton left no doubt; he informed the crowd that the company train was leaving the station and they should climb on board. This was not a decision that was going to a committee. Barton asserted: We *will* get to $30 billion of revenue. We *will* get 10 percent companywide cost savings, and this *will* translate to $1 billion in annual cost savings. Further, we *will* improve our product quality and reliability. Almost casually, he noted that the dealers and customers would be "asked" to participate. In Caterpillarese, this translated to "they *will* participate."

Astonishingly, Barton added that the entire company would begin a transition to new ways of doing business the *next* month and that the new approach would be rolled out over just 100 days. There would be no exceptions.

Further, Barton said that he expected the program to be "accretive." No one in the room knew exactly what that meant. He told them: this means that in year 1, Caterpillar *will* achieve sufficient hard cost reduction and revenue enhancement to pay for the large investment required to implement its companywide Six Sigma program.

Very few people in the room had any idea what the size of the investment in Six Sigma would be. Some sarcastically guessed that it would mean another few million dollars flowing out the door to PricewaterhouseCoopers and similar consultants. They did not know that each person in the room would soon be required to identify real cost and revenue projects designed to improve the company. Caterpillar soon would take on thousands of those projects. They also were unaware that consultants would not do most of the work. Instead, CAT employees trained to become Six Sigma black belts would quickly be trained to spearhead the effort.

After his speech, Barton surveyed the faces in the crowd, and Kevin Giavanetto records that most individuals were stunned. It was one of those defining moments that invariably confront a leader who is introducing significant change. Leaders are supremely challenged by such situations. The way they respond in those circumstances often makes or breaks their leadership. This was such a moment for Barton. He could see the faces of those who believed and the faces of those who didn't. This is Giovanetto's description of what Barton said at this key moment:

> It is very obvious to me, from where I'm standing as I look across this room, that there are some people who are not on board. This train is going to leave the station, and it's going to leave the station with all of you on board. I want each of you to come down and stand toe-to-toe with me and make a personal commitment to Six Sigma. I want each one of you to tell me how you are going to support our new way of doing business.

This might have been the most critical single moment in Glen Barton's five years of service as chairman/CEO. One by one, major Caterpillar officers came down and stood in front of Barton. He looked each one in the eye. He demanded their public commitment, and he received it. Reluctant or not, they had joined his team and had crossed Caterpillar's equivalent of the Rubicon.

Black belts soon were produced in waves to tackle the problems and/or opportunities identified across the company. The first wave hit Caterpillar's shore on February 19, 2001, when 290 employees began their black belt training. The second wave surged forward on May 21, 2001, with another 200 individuals. On July 23, 100 more began, and on September 10, another 125 people started down the path. In total, the company selected 715 of its best and brightest, trained them, and put them into new jobs designed to change the way CAT did business. Caterpillar was reinventing itself once again.

The black belts needed trained assistants to help move the cultural mountains. These persons were called green belts; 3,800 green belts were identified in the company and trained for the Six Sigma tsunami of change. In total, the company provided over 300,000 hours of training to the black belts and green belts. Barton never missed a black belt graduation ceremoney or sent one of his group presidents to take his place. He understood that recognition by the company's leaders was the key to being sure people did not think this was another "flavor of the day" program that soon would go away. He and his leadership team became frequent visitors at black belt–led storyboard presentations of Six Sigma projects and the identified savings or quality improvements that would result. This further energized the black belts and green belts by confirming that the work they were doing—the extra hours they were putting in each day—was important.

What Is Six Sigma, and How Is It Connected to Lean Manufacturing?

Six Sigma is a technique that focuses intently on product quality and the elimination of product defects. With Six Sigma, teams of people are created who work together to identify and implement opportunities to improve product quality and eradicate errors. The name is derived from the statistical notion of six sigmas from the mean. A sigma is a standard deviation; an outcome six sigmas away from the mean of a distribution reporting product errors is extremely rare. Specifically, the probability of an outcome that is six sigmas away from the mean of a normal distribution is less than 0.0000001. The guiding notion of Six Sigma, then, is essentially to cause product errors and defects to disappear. This is what a 0.0000001 probability implies.

> **Somewhat confusingly**, *a Six Sigma level of defect-free and error-free production has become associated with having only 3.4 defects per million possibilities. Statistically, however, this corresponds to only 4.5 standard deviations away from the mean in a normal distribution.*

How does Six Sigma relate to lean manufacturing programs? They are different. Lean manufacturing does not ignore product quality but instead focuses on cost reduction. Lean is a philosophy that pushes companies to make what customers want, when they want it, in the correct amounts, and to do so at the lowest possible total cost and the highest possible quality, even with minimal lead time. Put simply, lean manufacturing refers to production systems and processes that target waste. Lean engages the entire workforce to attack waste anywhere it is found.

Practically speaking, a lean production system is one that minimizes waste in the purchasing department (for example, bringing to a halt the practice of buying at high prices or poor quality from "old friends"), reduces waste in the handling of incoming material, and ensures that plant floors run like a clock both in how the workers move and in how materials are handled, manufactured, and packaged. Finally, lean production moves products smoothly off the floor and into the hands of the customer at the very moment they are needed. This requires robust IT/finance system controls that chart every step of the process accurately and (not to be forgotten) should allow customers to follow the movements of the products they have ordered as they are prepared and shipped.

Lean and Six Sigma work together to create an environment of cost savings combined with higher revenue potential. First, eliminate waste; second, eliminate errors and defects. When utilized together, lean production and Six Sigma form a powerful combination. When implemented successfully, they are synonymous with cost reductions and increased product quality. Glen Barton believed these two tools would supercharge Caterpillar so that it could break though the $20 billion annual revenue ceiling.

Caterpillar and Lean Production

Lean is about eliminating waste, but there is no acknowledged founder of the concept. Benjamin Franklin, Fredrick Winslow Taylor, W. Edward Deming, Henry Ford, and Genichi Taguchi are just a few of the people who made contributions in this area. The team most credited with pulling lean production ideas together into a usable form was composed of Sakichi Toyoda, the founder of Toyota; his son, Kiichiro; and a company engineer, Taiichi Ohno. Originally called just-in-time production, their philosophy became famous as the Toyota Production System (TPS), or simply the Toyota Way. The beauty of TPS was that it was so simple that virtually any committed manufacturing organization could implement portions of it. And many did. TPS became the most implemented lean system in the world, and Taiichi Ohno's book on the subject became the lean manufacturing bible.

> **The Japanese notion of a _kaizen_** (an improvement) _motivates and rewards any employee at any level for suggesting improvements that reduce costs or improve product quality. The Toyota Production System utilizes the_ kaizen _as a means to eliminate waste and enhance product quality._

Frank Crespo is Caterpillar's chief procurement officer and vice president of the global purchasing division. We have had two fascinating conversations with him about CAT's purchasing strategies and how lean techniques have changed the manner in which the company conducts its purchasing business. Before Crespo arrived, Glen Barton demanded a $1 billion reduction in CAT's costs. A significant proportion of this eventually was derived from price reductions from suppliers. Further, many of the company's suppliers were encouraged and in some cases pressured to adopt Six Sigma methods; sometimes their Six Sigma training was provided by Caterpillar. In the first year after Barton's call, 100 American and European suppliers became Six Sigma enabled. Soon afterward, a second list of 100 additional suppliers was identified. In the end, more than 1,600 employees of CAT suppliers participated in Six Sigma training.

Table 9.1 shows Bloomberg's estimate of Caterpillar's largest five suppliers and the percentage of Caterpillar's expenditures that each receives. One can see the influence of information technology (IT) on Caterpillar's expenditures. Oracle and SAP are its two largest suppliers by volume of purchases. A top-flight IT organization is critical to CAT's ability to manage efficiently.

Today, Crespo leads a large and efficient purchasing organization that he describes as being "on a journey" to building a continuously improving supply base. A stringent set of operational and financial criteria must be satisfied by any potential supplier before that company is eligible to do business with Caterpillar. On-site reviews are part of the exam. Supplier "score cards" are issued

Table 9.1 *Bloomberg's Estimate of Caterpillar's Largest Five Suppliers by Dollar Value of Caterpillar's Purchases, 2013*

Name of Supplier	Percent of Caterpillar's Input Purchases Spent with This Supplier
Oracle	1.30
SAP	1.10
Emerson Electric	0.99
Accenture	0.99
Walgreen	0.37

Source: Bloomberg (accessed May 6, 2013).

quarterly. CAT actively scores and in most cases helps its suppliers improve their QCLDM, an acronym that stands for the *q*uality, *c*ost, *l*ogistics, *d*evelopment, and *m*anagement score assigned by CAT. Suppliers are monitored closely and coached to improve in these categories. Each year, less than 10 percent of CAT's suppliers fail to meet the company's standards and end up being removed from its supply base. This comparatively low percentage is a direct result of the collaboration efforts made by Crespo's organization.

A $65.88 billion company (2012) such as Caterpillar is a huge buyer of commodities. The company maintains a team of people active in hedging physical and financial commodities to reduce the company's vulnerability to swings in input prices and exchange rates. Crespo's purchasing organization works with CAT's finance group to forecast the commodities markets. Relatively few corporations (even Wall Street banks) have such strong capabilities.

Of course, one can chatter the jargon of lean manufacturing endlessly, but executing a viable lean plan can be a struggle. Smaller companies sometimes encounter trouble adopting lean techniques because their managers must fulfill many different roles and therefore never acquire specialized lean training and expertise. Also, many small business owners are highly pragmatic and tend to manage their companies by following whatever idiosyncratic model worked well for them in the past. It is not a coincidence that many such firms perished in the Great Recession that began in 2008. The "old-fashioned way" may produce excellent results in more intimate workplaces, but it breaks down when revenues dry up and fixed costs become especially burdensome. Lean management techniques, unfortunately, are not for amateurs.

Many large companies also fail the lean test; this usually occurs because their scale works against them. Large companies often buy thousands of inputs in multiple locations, move the material to dozens of production locations, and then have to deliver finished output on a just-in-time basis to a large, distributed customer base. Sensible coordination of all this is an imposing task. It is a situation that often permits or even invites inefficiencies. Put simply, very large corporations are difficult to manage. The fact that we do not observe only one firm operating in each industry suggests that many firms begin to experience diseconomies of scale as they scale upward. The fact that such diseconomies have not descended upon Caterpillar to any great degree sets CAT apart from the typical manufacturing firm.

> **INSIDERS EDGE** *Ideally, companies should develop a lean manufacturing umbrella and then implement Six Sigma. It's difficult to get employees to take the reduction of product defects seriously if inefficiency and waste abound.*

Caterpillar was hardly the first large company to implement Six Sigma. Among companies in the Fortune 500, GE implemented Six Sigma well before CAT, and 3M began its Six Sigma program in 2001, nearly the same time as CAT. Interestingly, all three companies compared notes on their Six Sigma operations. GE shattered the $20 billion ceiling well before CAT, and 3M's operations hit that target a few years after CAT. Hence, they provide interesting models for benchmarking.

Jeffrey Immelt took the reins at GE during the terrible week of the September 11, 2001, attacks. He embraced Six Sigma to turn the massive GE ship toward a more profitable course. Six Sigma was one of the tools that helped Immelt manage the company through the Great Recession and the collapse of the financial markets after the Lehman fiasco. In 2012, GE amassed revenues of $146.78 billion and a total enterprise value (TEV) of $584 billion.

3M is now under the stewardship of new CEO and President Inge Thulin, a strong proponent of Six Sigma. Inge has a strategic mind and great customer awareness, the reasons why Six Sigma is important to him and to 3M. We visited 3M's Six Sigma war room in St. Paul, where its master black belts congregate to attack operating problems. It is a fascinating place where hundreds of millions of dollars have been saved. We expect 3M, with annual revenues of $29.90 billion and a TEV of $74 billion in 2012, to double these numbers in the next five years. Ten years after implementing Six Sigma, 3M can point to $1 billion of cost savings.

The Magnitude of Caterpillar's Commitment to Lean and Six Sigma

In December 2000, Glen Barton convinced, cajoled, and ordered his management team to do four things:

1. Reach $30 billion of sales and revenues within five years.

2. Cut costs by $1 billion.

3. Make dramatic improvements to product quality.

4. Be accretive in year 1.

To accomplish his goal, he put 4,500 Caterpillar employees into the Six Sigma black belt and green belt training programs during 1991. By 2005, 30,000 Caterpillar employees had participated on Six Sigma teams that were involved in 24,000 separate projects. This was an investment in people and processes that absolutely had to pay off or CAT's future would be in jeopardy.

> **"I think it was a bold move** to go with the global tsunami, but if we wanted action and immediate results, and to be accretive in year 1, this was the only way to do it." This is Group President Ed Rapp talking about Six Sigma's introduction at Caterpillar.

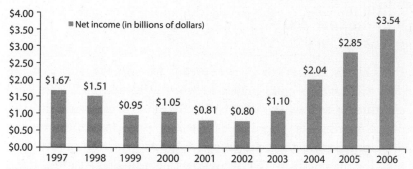

Figure 9.1   *Caterpillar's net income, 1997–2006.*
Source: Caterpillar annual reports

The reader already knows how this story ends. After implementing Six Sigma and later implementing lean production techniques, Caterpillar saw its net income leap upward. Figure 9.1 shows CAT's net income between 1997 and 2006. After falling 37.1 percent in 1999 and a further 15.8 percent by 2002, CAT's net income increased by 37.5 percent in 2003, an amazing 85.5 percent in 2004, and another 39.7 percent in 2005. This surge was capped by an increase in net income of 24.2 percent in 2006.

Meanwhile, Caterpillar's consolidated sales and revenues reached $30.31 billion in 2004, a year ahead of Barton's seemingly ambitious schedule. Even these goals soon could be seen only in Caterpillar's rearview mirror. By 2008, the company sprinted upward to $51.32 billion of consolidated sales and revenues. "Slightly unachievable" goals, indeed! Caterpillar's singular dedication to reinventing itself yet again had paid off handsomely.

Can we attribute all the improvement in net income at Caterpillar to its adoption of Six Sigma? Clearly not. The recovery of the U.S. economy from a recession was the most important influence. However, Six Sigma improved Caterpillar's margins and product quality even while demand was reviving. CAT's profit before tax (PBT) margin rose from 5.5 percent of total sales and revenues in 2002 to 10.7 percent in 2005. The company's relentless drive to reduce its costs and retard the growth of its overhead expenses yielded measurable results.

Why Are Lean and Six Sigma So Important to Caterpillar's Story?

In Chapters 12 through 14, we develop a financial model that predicts Caterpillar's performance between 2013 and 2020. We present three scenarios describing what is most likely to occur. Two of the scenarios develop a case for strong performance on the part of Caterpillar; in those scenarios we predict widening profit margins for the company. We recognize that this doesn't often occur where mature companies such as CAT are concerned. Why do we believe this is possible for CAT? In this chapter, we have sketched two of the more important visible reasons: Caterpillar's emphasis on lean manufacturing techniques and its devotion to Six Sigma quality. Even so, those closest to the company recognize that the most salient rationale for this view is that Caterpillar's intrinsic culture and its entire workforce are attuned to flushing unneeded costs down the toilet. The company has built a history of reorganizing, repositioning, and reinventing itself to generate increased margins and enhanced profitability. We expect this to continue.

CHAPTER 10

TWEAKING THE CATERPILLAR MODEL

aterpillar's prodigious success, as we have argued throughout this book, is primarily a function of the company's ability to scale its operations on a global basis, the development of its business unit profit centers, a terrific dealer network, its well-chosen acquisitions of complementary firms in growing industries, and its skillful planning for bad times. However, these factors are rather generic and don't provide specific guidance to someone interested in creating the next great firm. Lending substance to these general statements are many specific strategic choices that have contributed strongly to Caterpillar's surge ahead of similarly situated firms. We'll examine several of these choices, and this will provide a more operational view of the sources of the company's success.

Five of the most important strategic choices Caterpillar has made in recent decades are (1) savvy decisions about what products to produce and where to produce them, (2) an emphasis on promoting from within, especially at the level of group presidents and the chairman/CEO, (3) the development of Caterpillar Financial, (4) the implementation of a "Southern Strategy," a label routinely applied by outsiders to CAT's locational choices inside the United States but words neither used nor favored by the company, and (5) CAT's gradual move to smaller plant sizes.

We will consider each of these developments in turn, for each has been important in generating Caterpillar's comparative advantage over its competitors.

Choosing What to Do (and Not Do)

Every company must decide what businesses it should be in and then take pains to avoid the rest. But determining what businesses to be in is not an easy task because the answer changes over time. There always has been a certain romance attached to growth and expansion. Growth, whether by acquiring other firms or by broadening one's product line, tends to generate initially positive headlines. It conveys the impression that a firm is on the move. Further, even the most doltish executive is aware that there is a positive correlation between firm size and executive salaries.

There is an almost irresistible tendency for many firms to expand their product lines. Some have done so very successfully. McDonald's, for example, has broadened its American product line to include items such as McCafe, McEgg sandwiches, McNuggets, and the occasional McRib sandwich. Outside the United States, the company offers Lakse in Finland, Cheese Katsu sandwiches in China, and a Chicken McCurry in India.

The common denominator in McDonald's product expansions is that it has grown its menu within the context of its existing production and sales model. The company's new products have been marketed by its ubiquitous local franchises, which now number more than 33,000. The company did not need to acquire substantial new assets or expertise to support these new products.

> **McDonald's** *sold more than 300 billion hamburgers by 2013, but the 2012 return to its stockholders was –5 percent. It has not always been able to convince investors of the worth of its business model.*

At the same time, McDonald's concluded that other firms were better at growing and supplying the potatoes that are the foundation of its famous French fries. Therefore, it opted not to vertically integrate to acquire its potatoes and instead has developed a huge preferred supplier arrangement with three potato growers. The point is that McDonald's has assembled a record of carefully evaluating what it can do well and what it cannot do so well and has acted accordingly.

In another sphere, Canon successfully added office equipment to its basic line of cameras. Like McDonald's, Canon was able to utilize its existing production and sales expertise to produce office equipment that called upon many of the company's traditional skills and strengths.

Alas, it doesn't always work this way. National Semiconductor flopped when it attempted to produce electronic consumer products that contained its semiconductors. Northrup Grumman failed when it attempted to move into shipbuilding. Hewlett-Packard was taken aback when one of its acquisitions, the software maker Autonomy Corporation, allegedly made "outright misrepresentations" and forced H-P to take a stupendous $8.8 billion write-off.

Few CEOs and boards of directors possess a crystal ball, much less one that provides straight answers. Further, frequently it takes considerable time for large organizations to arrive at product and acquisition decisions and even longer to rectify mistakes when they take a false step. In the meantime, opportunities are lost and financials deteriorate. Simply put, it is not easy to scale a company upward from $20 billion to $40 billion to $60 billion as Caterpillar has done. Getting it right takes a large collection of good people making good decisions. The examples provided above demonstrate that many companies fail this test.

Product and business diversification can provide new sales opportunities, smooth earnings variability, and reduced risk. The most successful examples of diversification typically involve clearly related product line extensions or support for existing product lines, or they involve the acquisition of key suppliers. Additional instructive product extension examples include Coca-Cola stretching its offerings into diet colas and Toyota going upscale with new automobile models such as the Lexus. Not so good examples include Northrup Grumman's attempted move from building airplanes to building ships; only on the surface did this constitute a product line extension because building airplanes and building ships are fundamentally different enterprises. Exxon attained notoriety for taking a false detour into electronics production.

What do these examples have to do with Caterpillar? CAT has been diligent in avoiding dramatic changes in its product line. A proposed new product or service not only must promise to be profitable, but it also must be clearly related to the company's activities and strengthen what CAT already is doing. A classic example involves Caterpillar's 1981 acquisition of Solar, a producer of industrial gas turbines. This move positioned CAT to expand the horsepower/kilowatt range of the turbines available to its customers in a market that it knew well but in which it had minimal penetration. The acquisition also placed the company in a position to be able to supply marine, natural gas, and oil markets that promise to grow more rapidly than the overall economy. Solar now is a major cash generator for CAT because its compressor sets are widely used on natural gas pipelines, and analysts suggest that CAT enjoys very positive profit margins on those sales. The frenetic expansion of fracking in the United States in recent years has made the Solar acquisition even more prescient.

In a nutshell, CAT wants to produce goods and services that will enable it to grow faster than the world economy. It can do this, it believes, if it hitches its star to the elements of the world economy that are destined to grow most rapidly. In the areas of construction, mining, and engines, it has focused on products that capitalize on growing populations, increased urbanization, rising incomes, and environmentally friendly engine solutions. CAT aspires to become the world leader in supplying machines that will meet these needs. Further, following the insight of Don Fites that machines purchased by customers represent an annuity that continues to pay dividends over time, CAT and its dealer network want to supply the services and parts over the lifetime of these machines.

This emphasis on the MRO (maintenance, repair, and operations) component of the business, which Caterpillar describes as "Seed, Grow, Harvest," was a subtle but brilliant strategic decision by the company. It smoothed Caterpillar's revenue stream and helped lock in its customer base. Financial markets have noted these developments approvingly, and this has lowered the cost of Caterpillar's capital.

Many heavy industrial firms have pursued upstream vertical integration: they have acquired many of their input suppliers. Thus, steel firms have acquired iron ore mining firms, aluminum producers have bought bauxite suppliers, and oil companies have acquired oil deposits. More recently, in an attention-getting move, Delta Airlines purchased a petroleum refinery to protect it from rising jet fuel prices. The general goals of these and similar moves are to reduce uncertainty with respect to the supply of inputs and perhaps to lower the prices paid for those inputs. In some cases, there may be anticompetitive motives as well because control over input supplies may enable a firm to freeze out its competitors or charge them elevated prices for those inputs. Alcoa, for example, dominated the production of bauxite (essential for the production of aluminum) before World War II and wielded that dominance as a weapon to discipline its competitors.

In general, Caterpillar has eschewed upstream vertical integration. Like Apple, it does not own very many of its major input suppliers. Instead, as we have described, CAT has chosen to use futures markets to hedge the prices it pays for many inputs and has decided to become best pals with its major input suppliers by stationing CAT people on site at supplier plants. Further, the company maintains multiple sources of supply wherever possible and is absolutely insistent that its collective bargaining agreements not restrict its ability to source needed inputs however it chooses.

It's not that Caterpillar never has pursued upstream vertical integration (CAT's dealer network represents downstream vertical integration). An example is the company's acquisition of a remanufacturing business that had been a supplier. Nevertheless, it has been very judicious in acquiring suppliers. Instead, it prefers to cooperate closely with suppliers even to the point of stationing CAT personnel on site at those suppliers. This reflects four factors. First, CAT may be uncertain that it could do the job as well as the supplier does. Second, producing a wide range of inputs might distract the company from its core production activities. Third, to some extent, CAT is able to force its input suppliers to share some of the risk associated with their supply of inputs to CAT. Fourth, if CAT does produce the entire supply of a specific input that it needs (perhaps a generator), it effectively has replicated a single-source input supply, a situation it always has sought to avoid to retain its decision-making flexibility.

Caterpillar has constructed a record of choosing its battlefields carefully and then taking the steps necessary to dominate the competitors in those spaces. It seldom expends resources on tasks or functions that might be interesting but ultimately are extraneous to the mission it has defined for itself. As Kent Adams, who leads Caterpillar Financial, put it to us, "We don't do refrigerators!" This means that in recent years, mere profitability has never been a sufficient reason for CAT to enter an industry. More than that is required.

Over the last 20 years and especially in the last few years, Caterpillar has embarked on an aggressive program of acquiring firms that it believes satisfy three criteria: (1) The acquired firms are closely related to CAT's core businesses, (2) they position the company well to achieve significant market share, and (3) they will become profitable quickly. With respect to profitability, CAT's hurdle rate of profitability ordinarily is 17 percent pretax. Investments that do not promise this expected level of profit ordinarily are discarded.

In 2010–2011 alone, Caterpillar made eight acquisitions of consequence, including Electro-Motive Diesel (EMD) and MWM of Germany, a manufacturer of environmentally friendly engines and power sources. Its 2011 acquisitions were crowned by its acquisition of Bucyrus, a well-regarded producer of mining equipment. This gave Caterpillar customers one-stop shopping in the area of mining equipment either above or below ground. Further, in 2012, CAT received formal approval from the Chinese government for its acquisition of ERA Mining Machinery.

Although some observers initially blanched at the prices Caterpillar paid for its acquisitions (it paid a premium $8.8 billion for Bucyrus, and those assets probably aren't worth that much today), the corporation has received praise for the strategic character of those acquisitions, which have positioned it in growing market segments (mining, locomotive production, and sustainable engines and power sources). To fund the Bucyrus purchase, CAT had to take on significant new debt, but CEO Doug Oberhelman, who has his eye on the long run, believes that these strategic acquisitions will enable the company to generate consistent growth rates that exceed the global average. Besides, interest rates were so low that the company was able to borrow money at minimal cost to finance its acquisitions. It was a propitious opportunity that might not be replicated for a decade or more.

> **Before its acquisition by Caterpillar, Bucyrus** *might have been enjoying 30+ percent margins in its after-market parts and service business. Now this after-market business is being done by CAT dealers. It's not yet clear how this will change the profitability of these activities. This matters because about 45 percent of CAT's mining revenues are after-market.*

Our view is that Caterpillar did pay a premium when it acquired Bucyrus, probably much more than another unrelated firm would have been willing to pay. However, we believe the Bucyrus acquisition will come to be regarded as one the company's very best decisions because of the superb positioning it provides CAT in the mining industry. Sometimes solid strategic thinking overwhelms short-run financial X's and O's.

Wall Street investors and analysts generally have agreed with Caterpillar's approach, though some have expressed concern that CAT may have acquired these companies at the peak of an international economic cycle rather than in the cycle trough. Analyst Joel Tiss of BMO Capital Markets, who has covered the company for 15 years, is enthusiastic about CAT overall but worries that its rapid acquisition of additional production capacity in recent years may put it in the same position as the legendary Looney Tunes cartoon character Wile E. Coyote, sprinting off the cliff into mid-air as the global economy decelerates or even contracts. Other analysts, such as Rob Wertheimer of Vertical Research Partners, believe that as a consequence CAT's inventory levels may be somewhat inflated.

In the best of all worlds, companies accurately forecast the business cycle and plan and decide accordingly. In the past, Caterpillar has done this relatively well, but because its revenues and profit have been so sensitive to the business cycle, the company's performance sometimes has appeared to have been boom or bust in nature. The relevant consideration is not whether CAT's revenues and profits are sensitive to the business cycle; clearly they are. There is no doubt that CAT is a cyclical firm. Instead, the salient questions are twofold: (1) Can the company accurately forecast peaks and troughs so that it can take advantage of them? (2) Is it capable of bouncing upward quickly from trough conditions and promptly restoring its revenues and profits?

An unspoken goal of Caterpillar CEOs in recent decades has been to diversify the company's revenue and profit sources. Historically, revenues and profits have flowed primarily from construction markets, and as recently as 2006, Trefis estimated that up to 60 percent of CAT's profits were generated by its sales and activities in construction markets (CAT suggested a much lower percentage). By 2012, however, Trefis Stock Analysts reported that construction would account for only 20.9 percent of CAT's adjusted EBITDA, an estimate much closer to CAT's informal estimates.

Table 10.1 provides the 2012 financial and market share estimates for the four major segments of Caterpillar. One can see that resource industries and power systems account for about two-thirds of Caterpillar's estimated 2012 revenues and almost two-thirds of its estimated 2012 adjusted EBITDA. Further, CAT's margins and market shares are larger for resource industries and power systems than for construction industries. This reflects CAT's gradual diver-

Table 10.1 *Comparing the Major Segments of Caterpillar in Terms of Revenues, Market Share, EBITDA, Margins (Trefis Estimates for 2012; dollars in billions)*

	Revenues	Estimated Market EBITDA Share	Amount and Percent of CAT's Adjusted EBITDA
Resource Industries	$30.9	30%	$4.70 (36.1%)
Power Systems	$32.9	7.8%	$3.60 (27.6%)
Construction Industries	$31.9	15.6%	$2.72 (20.9%)
Financial Products	$ 2.8	—	$2.00 (15.4%)

Source: Trefis, Analysis for Caterpillar, October 10, 2012, www.trefis.com/company?hm= CAT.trefis#.

sification away from construction activities and into the supply of equipment and services for firms involved in mining and energy.

Among Caterpillar's four major areas of thrust, construction has declined the most in relative importance in recent years and may offer the least dynamic growth prospects internationally. Power generation, oil- and gas-related activities, and mining, in that order, may offer more attractive growth possibilities. An important reason for this is that the construction market is crowded with viable competitors, whereas the other three product areas contain smaller numbers of sizable experienced contenders. In construction, for example, there may be 20 or more viable competitors, whereas in power generation, the number of important players is much smaller: Caterpillar, Cummins, and Finland's Wärtsilä. Further, in China, perhaps the world's largest construction market, CAT trails Komatsu (Japan), Sany (China), and Zoomlion (China) in terms of market share. It will take a great effort on CAT's part to change this.

By contrast, according to Rob Wertheimer of Vertical Research Partners, Caterpillar's market share in oil- and gas-related activities and mining equipment may exceed 50 percent in the United States. *May* is the operative word here because traditionally Caterpillar has been very tightfisted with sales and market share data; hence, authors and analysts can only estimate because CAT is so reluctant to disclose such information.

Caterpillar Financial

Caterpillar operates Caterpillar Financial, a highly successful arm of the corporation that exists to provide financing to CAT dealers and customers throughout the world. Kent Adams, Caterpillar Financial's president, says that CAT Financial currently has $31.5 billion in assets related to financing and lease agreements around the world and that some 77 percent of this portfolio involves contracts for less than $100,000. It currently has approximately 115,000 active customers.

In some ways, Caterpillar Financial occupies a role analogous to that of CAT dealerships. Caterpillar Financial is in daily contact with the company's customers and helps meet their needs. Adams asserts that Caterpillar Financial touches CAT customers an estimated 10,000 times a day in terms of price and interest rate quotes, credit approvals, loan details and documentation, loan modifications, and the like.

Caterpillar Financial doesn't make CAT equipment and machines, but our conversations with customers clearly reveal that it helps make the sale. Ultimately, customers and dealers end up financing with Caterpillar Financial for a variety of reasons, including the recommendations of other customers, satisfactory past experiences, the ease of doing business, and the competitive financing terms that the company offers.

Any financing deal that Caterpillar Financial concludes with a customer or dealer faces explicit competition from rival financial institutions, including commercial banks. Caterpillar Financial works with CAT dealers to offer customers competitive financing options, allowing them to compare CAT's deal with those offered by Deere, Volvo, Case, Joy, and Komatsu. If customers already have decided to purchase a CAT product, they still can compare the terms offered by Caterpillar Financial with those put forward by commercial banks such as Wells Fargo, BNP, Credit Suisse, and Bank of America as well as large hybrid financial competitors such as GE Capital.

The emphasis of Caterpillar Financial focus has always been on servicing Caterpillar customers. CAT has not chosen to imitate organizations such as GE Capital, whose financial efforts have graduated far beyond the financing of GE customers. In Adams's words, "We've always stuck to the things we understand and are good at. We didn't go the GE Capital route when that was a hot notion. It didn't make a lot of sense for us. Our role is to help our customers buy CAT products."

Because Caterpillar Financial has a global footprint and completes thousands of financial deals weekly, it must deal quickly and efficiently with multiple foreign currencies. Caterpillar Financial borrows and lends in local currencies (this is a must if one wishes to serve local customers) but manages its currency positions throughout the world so that its exposure to currency fluctuations is minimized. It prudently hedges its currency positions with the objectives of eliminating all currency exposure on the company's balance sheet and reducing earnings volatility. Caterpillar Financial often makes money in its currency operations, but that is not its raison d'être. Assisting CAT customers with their financial needs is.

Caterpillar's public filings with the Securities and Exchange Commission provide ready evidence that Caterpillar Financial is successful in its lending efforts. In December 31, 2012, the company reported $28.58 billion in outstanding finance receivables ($19.89 billion with customers, $5.59 billion with dealers, and $3.1 billion in inventory receivables purchased from Caterpillar). Only $513 million of those receivables (1.8 percent) were classified as "nonperforming." This is an admirable performance that very few similarly situated corporations have been able to duplicate.

There is no pressure on Caterpillar Financial to make questionable loans or financial arrangements simply to sell product. Indeed, Caterpillar Financial's credit approval process is completely separate from Caterpillar, Inc. For example, it is Caterpillar Financial that determines the residual value of a machine owned by a customer who desires financing, not Caterpillar, Inc. The location of Caterpillar Financial's headquarters in Nashville, Tennessee, underlines its semiautonomous status.

INSIDER'S EDGE   *The story of Caterpillar Financial illustrates how CAT and other great companies approach the world: choose the battlefield carefully, determine what actions are critical to success, and then take the steps necessary to dominate the competitors in that space. Get so close to the customer that you enter his or her bloodstream. Don't expend resources on tasks or functions that are extraneous to those tasks.*

A Southern Strategy?

Caterpillar denies that it has a Southern Strategy of locating new facilities in right-to-work states, mostly in the U.S. South, and this term is not a part of its lexicon. Nevertheless, media large and small, unions, and academics routinely assert that the company is consciously locating new plants in southern states that have right-to-work laws to minimize labor problems. The diverse set of observers that has applied this label to Caterpillar's activities includes *Southern Business and Development,* the *Randle Report, Southern Auto Corridor, Triangle Business Journal, The Business Journal,* the *Wall Street Journal,* www.wikipedia.com, and the United Auto Workers.

What are right-to-work laws? There are three major union-management contractual models in the United States. An *open shop* arrangement means that workers do not have to join a union and do not have to pay dues to support any union that is present. Right-to-work laws guarantee an open shop; therefore, employees have the freedom to decide whether they wish to join a union and pay that union's dues. Caterpillar's relatively new plants in states such as North Carolina and Texas are open shops, and union activity in those locations is minimal.

An *agency shop* exists when a union has won the right to represent workers at a plant but the workers at that plant do not have to join the union. However, when an agency shop exists, employees must pay union dues and may not "free ride."

A *closed shop* contractual provision requires workers to join any union recognized for purposes of collective bargaining, and they must pay dues to that union. Caterpillar's collective bargaining agreements with its unions in location such as Aurora, Decatur, and East Peoria in Illinois include closed shop provisions.

Union dues are the mother's milk of trade unionism, and the steady flow of dues payments from members enables unions to wield power and carry out their programs. When the flow of dues is cut off, the union is in trouble. Evidence indicates that when workers have the option not to join a union and not pay dues to that union, many will decide not to do so. This directly threatens the viability of any union in that situation unless an agency shop exists and non-members must pay dues anyway.

The reduction in union power by right-to-work laws extends to the political arena. For at least a half century, a strong partnership has existed between most organized unions and the U.S. Democratic Party. Between 2005 and 2011, unions made $1.1 billion in direct political contributions and spent an additional $3.3

billion on political advocacy. Typically, more than 90 percent of those funds have supported the Democratic Party. The AFL-CIO national organization reported $282.40 million in political contributions and advocacy during that period, and the United Auto Workers national organization reported $63.05 million. Another big contributor, the National Education Association, reported $238.95 million in contributions and advocacy spending. Consequently, the AFL-CIO, the UAW, and the NEA have considerable political clout because of the political war chests they control and their ability to put union members to work electioneering during campaigns.

> **Use of union dues for political purposes**: *In a series of decisions, the U.S. Supreme Court has ruled that where agency shops exist, unions must give nonmember workers the opportunity to opt out from the use of any of their dues for political purposes. This has been a blow to union political power.*

Historically, political contributions by unions have had a positive payoff and typically have resulted in healthy support for union priorities by elected Democratic Party officials. This has been true especially in the case of public employees, whose wages, fringe benefits, and pensions are directly determined by the same elected officials who receive organized labor's financial support. In a few cases, those legislators also are members of public employee unions. The potential for conflict of interest is apparent.

> **After the state of Michigan** *adopted a contentious right-to-work law in December 2012, a* Wall Street Journal *article titled "Laws' Scant Effect on Wages" stated that the evidence on the wages issue was statistically inconclusive. This interpretation of the evidence tilts a bit in the direction of the Journal's editorial page but is somewhat defensible in light of the mixed evidence available.*

The end result has been the development of a symbiotic relationship between organized labor and the Democratic Party in heavily Democratic "blue" states such as New York, Illinois, and California. "We scratch each other's backs," a candid elected official who did not want to be identified told us. "They [the unions] provide us with contributions and election manpower, and we take care of their wages and pensions." It's not only about wages and fringe benefits, however. A multitude of other issues exist, such as whether there should be secret ballots on votes on union representation, how much public disclosure of union expenditures there should be, how unfair labor practice allegations are treated, and work conditions.

Right-to-work laws are an unambiguous threat to the symbiotic political-financial model just described, especially where public employees are concerned. If the flow of union political contributions to elected officials is cut off, those officials will be less likely to support union objectives and more likely to be defeated on Election Day. The result, union leaders argue, will be stagnating employee wages and fringe benefits.

Workers' wages typically are somewhat lower in right-to-work states. In 2012, private sector employees in right-to-work states were paid an average of a little more than $738 per week, whereas comparable workers in other states earned a bit more than $808 per week. Caterpillar has taken advantage of this situation. When the company moved some production from its Mossville, Illinois, plant to a new plant in Texas, the average wage of its production employees declined from about $17 per hour to about $10 per hour according to the *Peoria Journal-Star*. However, the Texas site was more cost-efficient in an additional way: CAT was able to reduce the costs it had been incurring from shipping large castings from Mexico to the United States.

However, unemployment rates typically are lower in right-to-work states. To some, this wage and employment information translates into an easy-to-understand rule: right-to-work laws result in lower wages but more jobs. We urge caution in this regard, however. Many other factors (e.g., tax rates) could have more influence on wages and employment in a state than that state's right-to-work status.

Several reputable economic studies have attempted to take account of the many factors (location, tax rates, infrastructure investments, and incentives offered) that could influence wage rates in a state in addition to right-to-work law status. After doing so, they typically conclude that wages are slightly lower in right-to-work states (holding many other things constant) but total employment is higher. What is undeniable, as we show below, is that the economies and employment levels in right-to-work states have been growing much more rapidly than have those in other states. Even so, it is not precisely clear why that is so or what the role of right-to-work laws in that growth is.

However, whatever the impact of right-to-work laws on wages and employment, there is little argument about the assertion that these laws have seriously eroded the power and political clout of unions. This erosion has occurred because right-to-work laws pulverize the union financial model. Given a choice, many workers decide not to join a union and not to pay union dues. Indeed, in 1992, Washington State adopted a "paycheck protection" system in which its public employees had to give annual written consent before unions could collect money from them for political purposes. This reduced the percentage of public school teachers opting to pay that portion of their dues from 82 percent to 11 percent. Caterpillar's apparent position and that of many employers in right-to-work states is that the existence of large numbers of non–dues payers provides ready evidence that the unions are not providing benefits equal to the dues they assess. Union supporters, in response, castigate free rider workers who don't join the union. In their view, the union exists and bargains for all employees and all employees receive the benefits, but the free riders don't pay the dues to support that bargaining.

It's no surprise that union officials "dread the spread of right-to-work laws" in the language of the *New York Times* and typically treat right-to-work laws as an existential threat An example is the statement by Randi Weingarten, president of the American Federation of Teachers: "They're throwing the kitchen sink at us. We're seeing people use the budget crisis to make every attempt to roll back workers' voices and any ability of workers to join collectively in any way whatsoever."

This view certainly is not new. In 1996, George Boze, a UAW-974 (East Peoria, Illinois) official, complained about Caterpillar: "They've had a Southern strategy for years . . . and they're still trying to move away from us as fast as they can." The *Wall Street Journal* seemingly agreed when it opined in 2012 that excessive labor contracts "helped to wreck the U.S. steel industry and drive General Motors and Chrysler into bankruptcy. . . . In order to avoid the same fate, Caterpillar expanded its non-union work forces in places like Arkansas and Texas."

Southern strategy or not, Caterpillar has been locating many new facilities in Southern right-to-work states. In November 2012, *Southern Auto Corridor News* almost casually noted that "Caterpillar's 'Southern Strategy' continued in February when the Illinois-based industrial giant picked Athens, GA, for its latest big plant. In recent years, CAT has sited plants in Winston-Salem, Little Rock, Victoria, TX, Seguin, TX and other locations in the south."

Figure 10.1 shows the distribution of Caterpillar production facilities in the United States in 1962, and Figure 10.2 shows the distribution in 2012. In 1962, CAT had no major production facility in the former Confederacy, but in 2012 it had more than a dozen. Consciously or not, Caterpillar has invaded the right-to-work states and the South in a big way.

There are economic reasons for this. First, Caterpillar plants and those of CAT suppliers are less likely to have to deal with work stoppages and strikes. Although the total number of work stoppages nationally has plummeted in recent years, they are virtually non-existent at large firms in right-to-work states. The Bureau of Labor Statistics reported that there were 19 work stoppages nationally

Figure 10.1   *Locations of Caterpillar's manufacturing facilities in the United States, 1962.*

Source: Caterpillar annual report, 1962

Figure 10.2 *Locations of Caterpillar's manufacturing facilities in the United States, 2012.*

Source: Caterpillar annual report, 2012

involving 1,000 or more employees in the United States in 2011. None of the firms involved was headquartered in a right-to-work state, and only one (the National Football League) had any locations in a right-to-work state.

Figure 10.3 shows the percentage of the workforce that is unionized in each state. It is apparent that Caterpillar has tended to locate

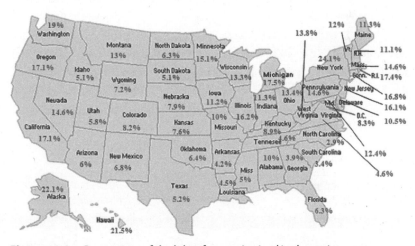

Figure 10.3 *Percentage of the labor force unionized in the various states.*

Source: Table 5 in "Union Affiliation of Employed Wage and Salary Workers by State," U.S. Bureau of Labor Statistics, www.bls.gov/news.release/union2.t05.htm

its new plants in states where organized unionism is not strong. Work stoppages and strikes threats are minimal in those locations.

Second, costs of production (including labor) typically are lower in right-to-work states. A rough and ready measure of these costs is the consumer price index for urban workers (CPI-U)· The CPI-U was 231.317 in October 2012 for the entire United States but was only 224.504 in the Bureau of Labor Statistics' South region. The comparable CPI-U for the Northeast region was 247.564, approximately 10 percent higher than that in the South. Although company location decisions ultimately reflect many different variables, production costs are an important consideration. Rational companies pay attention to such differentials.

Third, as Table 10.2 reveals, for whatever collection of reasons, right-to-work states have been growing more rapidly than have other states. Between 2000 and 2010, right-to-work states added 3.6 million jobs, whereas all other states together lost 900,000 jobs. In 2011 alone, there was a net in-migration of 364,000 people into right-to-work states from all other states. For the same reasons that Caterpillar has located in international growth markets such as Brazil and China, it has tended to locate its U.S. production facilities in the states with the most rapidly growing markets and populations. This makes long-term sense whether or not one is interested in right-to-work status.

Fourth, right-to-work states typically offer prospective employers more attractive financial incentives to locate in their states and accompany those incentives with lower long-term tax rates. One of the states where CAT really has rung the state financial incentive bell is North Carolina, where it received incentives valued at $87.9

Table 10.2 *Comparing Economic Growth and Incomes in Right-to-Work States Versus All Other States*

Percentage Change, 2000 to 2010	Right to Work States	All Other States
Private Employment	10.30%	1.90%
Private Sector Compensation	11.10%	0.70%
Real GDP Per Capita	9.70%	7.89%

Source: Carpe Diem Blog, http://mjperry.blogspot.com (February 1, 2012).

million between 2008 and 2012 for its new $426 million plant in Winston-Salem to build axle assemblies for mining equipment and its expanded manufacturing activities in Clayton. CAT also has done well negotiating incentives in Georgia, where its new plant near Athens will receive support valued at $78.2 million.

Although Texas is the undisputed leader in dispensing economic development incentives, Caterpillar has been only a modest recipient of that largesse. The *New York Times* reported in December 2012 that Texas spends $19.1 billion annually on incentives (an astonishing $759 per capita). The *Times* says CAT received $10.8 million to support its activities in Seguin and Victoria.

Caterpillar has been highly critical of the quality of the economic environment in its headquarters state, Illinois. On several occasions, CEO Doug Oberhelman has censured tax policies, workers' compensation laws, and public employee pension insolvency in the Land of Lincoln. The *New York Times* reported that Illinois spends $1.51 billion annually on economic development incentives, but Caterpillar's name has not appeared on the list of the top 100 recipients since 2007 despite the fact that CAT is the fifth largest private sector employer in Illinois (CAT had 26,000 employees in that state in December 2012) and despite the reality that the company has been progressively deciding to locate new facilities in other states.

> **The impact of right-to-work laws** *is disputed. The* Washington Post's *"fact checker" assigned two "Pinocchios" (out of four) to U.S. presidential candidate Mitt Romney, who pointed out that job growth in right-to-work states has exceeded that in other states over the last decade. The* Post *concluded that the statement was factually correct but deceptive and deserving of Pinocchios because many factors in addition to right-to-work status could have been responsible for the job growth. Romney's statement and the* Post's *reaction underscore the politicized nature of discussions about right-to-work laws.*

Some might question whether Caterpillar and the Democratic Party–dominated political power structure in Illinois have reached an unproductive loggerhead. In 2012, Governor Pat Quinn sent money to support workers who were on strike against CAT, and CAT CEO Doug Oberhelman pointedly informed the Economic Club of Chicago, "A lot of states, I go there and they tell me, 'Doug, why are you in Illinois?'" Some of Oberhelman's pique may reflect the fact that in recent years the state of Illinois has provided $161 million in financial incentives to Sears, $100 million to Google, and $87.5 million to Archer-Daniels-Midland but has given Caterpillar the back of its hand.

There is little doubt that Caterpillar has been attempting to nudge the state of Illinois to adopt policies that the company considers more business-friendly. The state is widely regarded as a financial basket case and apparently holds the national record for former governors sent to prison. The state's political system often is dysfunctional. In the short run, this situation may not be amenable to any financial solution that does not involve making Illinois even less attractive to prospective employers.

Caterpillar has responded to the Illinois economic-political world with both carrots and sticks. It has invested more than $500 million in modernizing its East Peoria production facility and in October 2012 opened a $37 million Caterpillar Visitors Center on the Peoria riverfront as a part of a larger city museum development project to which it contributed an additional $15 million. These are welcome economic pluses for the state of Illinois and for Peoria, though neither the state nor the city should doubt that these decisions represent carefully calculated choices by CAT in which it has meticulously weighed the alternatives.

As Caterpillar has made these decisions, it has continued to point out the shortcomings in the Illinois economic environment, almost as if to say, "We could do much more if you'd only change your policies." The company seldom shrinks from making its positions known to governmental units at any level.

A fifth reason Caterpillar's move into right-to-work states makes corporate sense is that like it or not, the willingness of companies such as Caterpillar to establish production sites in those states serves to discipline the labor unions the company deals with in other states. Our conversations with labor leaders indicate that they understand this dynamic rather well and that it has influenced their behavior. In the case of the United Auto Workers, national membership had fallen to 381,000 in December 2012, only about one-quarter of the number of members 35 years earlier. Whatever strategy the UAW has been following in recent decades, a huge stretch is required to conclude that it has been successful.

Sixth, Caterpillar's political support base has grown as Caterpillar has expanded its production and distribution network into more states. By no means is it any longer only an Illinois firm; it now can count upon political support across the United States. Figure 10.2 drills home the fact that CAT can anticipate a sympathetic ear from many governors and legislators because the company now is located in their states. This geographic dispersion of production and distribution has enhanced CAT's ability to stimulate states to compete with one another for Caterpillar's favor. Critical observers note that the whipsawing of one state against another by CAT to gain economic development incentives echoes the treatment the company once found objectionable in the pattern bargaining imposed by the United Auto Workers. Stimulating cities and states to compete against one another for its favor has become an important though unstated stratagem for CAT.

> **INSIDER'S EDGE** *Although some observers aren't pleased, right-to-work states have many attractions for firms such as Caterpillar. The reduced clout of organized labor is only part of the allure of these states, which have more rapidly growing markets and generally more favorable tax and regulatory climates. Astute firms take such factors into account.*

In sum, Caterpillar has many different reasons to diversify its geographic imprint in the United States. Caterpillar is not the only manufacturer to note these advantages and move to capitalize on them. The U.S. automobile industry has progressively established itself in the South over the last few decades, but so also have a host of other industries ranging from steelmaking to aircraft manufacturing.

Some people erroneously equate right-to-work states with the 11 states of the former Confederacy. True, all 11 former states of the Confederacy have right-to-work laws, but another 13 states, including Indiana (as of February 2012), Michigan (as of December 2012), Iowa, Kansas, and Arizona, also have these laws. Hence, rather than being a Southern Strategy, CAT's approach might be more accurately characterized as one in which the company exhibits a preference for right-to-work states wherever those states are. These states are growing more rapidly than the other states, and the company prefers not to deal with labor unions if that option is realistically available.

Reducing Plant Sizes

Southern Strategy or not, in recent years CAT has been opening small or moderate-size production assembly facilities primarily in right-to-work states such as Arkansas, Georgia, Mississippi, North Carolina, South Carolina, Tennessee, and Texas. CAT asserts that its optimal plant size is 500 to 1,500 employees, a dramatic reduction from employment levels at the huge plants that traditionally characterized its Illinois operations in cities such as Aurora, Decatur, and East Peoria. Table 10.3 gives employment informa-

Table 10.3 *Employment Levels at Four New Caterpillar Manufacturing Plants*

Location	Type of Production	Employment Level When Fully Utilized
Athens, GA	Small Tractors and Mini-Hydraulic Excavators	1,400
Winston-Salem, NC	Axles	500
Seguin, TX	Engines and Parts	1,400
Victoria, TX	Hydraulic Excavators	500

Source: The Athens employment number is found in Caterpillar's February 17, 2012, press release: www.caterpillar.com/cda/files/3325542/7/021712%20Caterpillar%Expands%20 Operations%20in%20United%States%20Athens%20Georgia.pdf. The Winston-Salem employment number is found in this November 30, 2011, press release: http://www .caterpillar.com/cda/files/3159306/7/111611%20Caterpillar%20Celebrates%20Grand%20 Opening%20of%20WinstonSalem.pdf. The Seguin employment number is found in this December 18, 2008, press release: http://governor.state.tx.us/news/press-release/11727/. The Victoria employment number is found in this June 17, 2011, press release: www .caterpillar.com/cda/files/2818387/7/061711%20Caterpillar%20Announces%20 Expansion%20Plans%20for%20Hydraulic%20Excavator%20Facility%20in%20Victoria.pdf.

tion on four manufacturing plants the company has opened in the South in recent years. The largest ones (Seguin, Texas, and Athens, Georgia) will have only 1,400 employees each when fully utilized.

Historically, heavy manufacturing firms such as Caterpillar have invested huge sums in plants; the presumption has been that they enjoy substantial economies of scale as output increases. CAT, however, argues that the smaller plants are easier to manage because managers are able to have daily face-to-face contact with employees and because smaller plants allow the company to focus on a smaller number of products and processes. The company's leaders assert that this more intimate atmosphere increases both productivity and employee morale. Of course, this also means that such plants ordinarily cannot produce CAT's largest pieces of equipment (such as the D9, D10, and D11 tractors) because of the capital-intensive nature of such production. CAT has produced these large tractors only in East Peoria, Illinois.

A side benefit that accrues to Caterpillar is that small plant sizes reduce the impact on the company if work stoppages occur. Whatever the cause of a work stoppage—labor problems, weather, or input supply disruptions—CAT has less to worry about if it operates multiple small plants, some of which perform the same tasks. This again underscores Caterpillar's pursuit of flexibility. It does not wish to be held captive by local labor conditions, bad weather, or difficulties in obtaining inputs. Also, if CAT decides it is necessary to limit or halt the production of a specific product or even leave a market permanently, these decisions can be more easily carried out if smaller plants exist that produce a narrower range of products and services. When this is the case, the disruption to all parties concerned is likely to be reduced. This is a lesson that many global firms have learned.

Organized labor leaders tend to cast jaundiced eyes on Caterpillar's small plant phenomenon because they realize it effectively reduces union and worker leverage while increasing that of the company (and not just in a single location). In addition, the same political and economic development officials who compete strenuously to attract Caterpillar plants soon come to understand that it is much easier for the company to dial down production levels in a small plant or even close down a small plant than would be true for a large plant that produces many different products and perhaps is an essential, irreplaceable link in Caterpillar's overall production arrangements. Thus, smaller plants diffuse the local and regional economic impact—positive or negative—of Caterpillar.

INSIDER'S EDGE   *Great firms such as Caterpillar cherish flexibility. They do their best to avoid being held hostage by single-source input suppliers, labor union problems, unusual weather, difficult local politicians, or any other developments that reduce their range of choices.*

CHAPTER 11

PLANNING FOR THE TROUGH: CATERPILLAR TRANSFORMS CHALLENGE INTO OPPORTUNITY

Caterpillar is a firm whose sales and profits always have been highly attuned to the ups and downs of the business cycle. Figure 11.1 illustrates this vividly. After a 14.2 percent increase in sales and revenues in 2008, the company's sales and revenues fell a momentous 36.9 percent in 2009 but then grew 31.5 percent in 2010, 41.2 percent in 2011, and 9.5 percent in 2012.

These sales and revenue changes translated to changes in operating profit. After declining 9.6 percent in 2008, operating profit fell 87.0 percent in 2009. However, like sales, operating profit recovered sharply in 2010 with an astounding 586 percent gain, followed by an 80.5 percent increase in 2011. Operating profit in 2012 increased to $8.6 billion, lower than it might have been because of a worldwide economic slowdown in construction spending

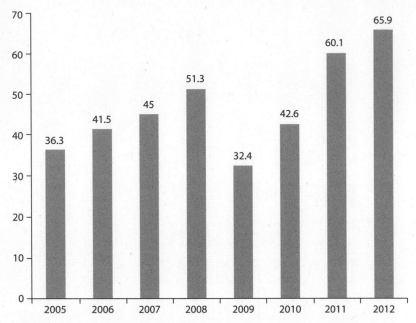

Figure 11.1 *Caterpillar's consolidated sales and revenues, 2005–2012 (in billions of $).*
Source: Caterpillar annual reports

and Caterpillar's $580 million write-off associated with the ERA accounting fraud (Figure 11.2).

Fortune magazine's Geoff Colvin put it this way in a laudatory 2011 article about Caterpillar: "When the economy is strong, customers always find money for new, cutting-edge earthmovers. But when corporate budgets tighten, the multi-decade longevity of Caterpillar's machines works against the company. It's easy for a customer to put off buying a new locomotive or excavator in a downturn. And cash-strapped owners flood the market with used machines that have lots of life left in them."

The production of the predominantly durable goods that are the centerpiece of Caterpillar's existence always has been more volatile than is true for most other products. Figure 11.3 contrasts the growth rates of durable goods production with those of nondurable goods for the United States between 1985 and 2009. Although the value of durable goods production accounts for only a bit

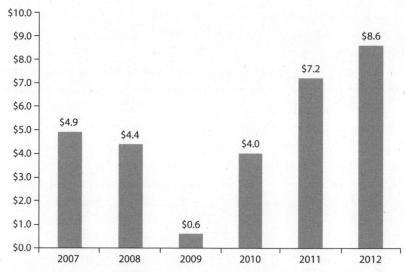

Figure 11.2   *Caterpillar's operating profits, 2007–2012 (in billions of $).*
Source: Caterpillar annual reports

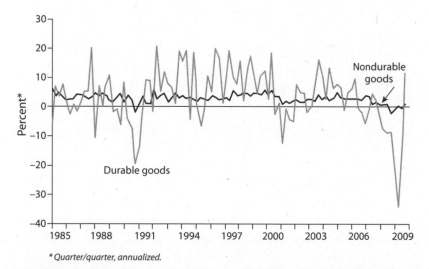

* Quarter/quarter, annualized.

Figure 11.3   *Durable goods production is more volatile than nondurable goods production.*

Source: Jian Wang, "Durable Goods and the Collapse of Global Trade," *Economic Letter,* Federal Reserve Bank of Dallas, 5 (February 2010), www.dallasfed.org/assets/documents/research /eclett/2010/el1002.pdf

more than 20 percent of U.S. gross domestic product, that value increases to almost 60 percent when we focus only on the value of U.S. exports.

Not surprisingly, the share price of Caterpillar stock tends to reflect the hills and valleys of industrial production: the stock's beta coefficient was 1.98 in mid-July 2013. This means that a 10 percent change in the collective prices of all stocks in the S&P's 500 Index typically is accompanied by an almost 20 percent change in CAT's share price. Hence, there's general agreement that the company's performance is highly dependent on national and global economic conditions. However, it is useful to know that Caterpillar's sales and revenues often are a leading economic indicator and usually fulfill the same role as the proverbial canary in the coal mine. When CAT's sales and revenues begin to decline, nearly always this means that overall economic conditions are likely to decline soon afterward. CAT's prosperity, in turn, usually signals that macroeconomic expansion is on the horizon.

> **McDonald's,** *another of the "Big Ten" firms identified in Chapter 1, is similar to Caterpillar in that it benefits from very strong brand identification, is global in its reach, and has sales that are sensitive to the business cycle. Although McDonald's is a well-managed firm, it has had less success than Caterpillar in adjusting its scale to economic trough conditions.*

Thus very few would argue with the proposition that Caterpillar's sales, revenues, and profits are sensitive to the business cycle. However, this sensitivity also exists for many other well-known firms, including financial giants such as Citigroup and Bank of America; industrial firms such as John Deere, Ingersoll Rand, Nucor, and U.S. Steel; and technology firms such as Advanced Micro Devices, Hewlett-Packard, and 3M.

What's very different about Caterpillar is the way the company handles the vicissitudes of the business cycle that all these firms confront. Caterpillar has emerged as an exemplar in terms of how it "plans for the trough" and subsequently deals with economic recession. We have not discovered a large publicly traded firm or small privately owned company that does it as well. In fact, relatively few companies formally do this type of planning at all.

Planning for the Trough

More so than any other individual, CEO Jim Owens (2004–2010) pushed CAT to plan for the trough, that is, to prepare annual detailed contingency plans for cutting expenditures and downsizing operations quickly and efficiently when required by business conditions Owens viewed economic contraction as inevitable and, in light of CAT's undeniable responsiveness to macroeconomic conditions, believed Caterpillar should be neither surprised nor timid when economic troughs appeared.

Owens became Caterpillar's chairman/CEO in 2004; in 2005 he pushed the company to move ahead of the curve and come to grips with the economic troughs of the future. Doug Oberhelman, who was to succeed Owens as chairman/CEO in 2010, observed, "No one wanted to talk about it," and so the organization had to be goaded by its CEO to go through contingency planning exercises that detailed how each part of CAT would deal with sales declines of varying magnitudes, including some as large as 80 percent. The individual plans then were critiqued, modified, and eventually incorporated into a corporation-wide contingency plan.

The contingency plan would be useful, however, only if it preserved and increased Caterpillar's organizational flexibility:

- CAT needed to ensure that significant portions of its costs would become variable rather than fixed so that necessary changes (reductions being the most difficult) could be implemented promptly and efficiently. Although this clearly meant adjusting the number of company employees, it also entailed finding ways to increase Caterpillar's flexibility and options in purchasing, energy consumption, and a host of other areas.

- However, the contingency plan also had to reflect institutional coordination; it wouldn't work if one business unit's reductions effectively destroyed another business unit's operational ability. Thus, it was critical that it be an integrated company plan rather than a series of business unit plans pasted together.

- Further, any reductions had to take into account the needs of CAT's dealers, customers, and suppliers. Antagonizing them clearly would come back to bite the company when economic conditions improved. Working with dealers, customers, and suppliers to maintain their viability and ability to scale became a priority consideration.

- CAT also was insistent that it maintain faith with its investors by continuing to generate operational profits, retaining its strong credit rating, and paying a respectable dividend.

- Finally, even if times became difficult, CAT hoped to increase employee engagement and maintain morale by communicating openly with its employees about the company's situation and, whenever possible, offering them assistance designed to help them deal with their own challenges.

Proof of the concept came in fall 2008 when a worldwide Great Recession hit with the force of one of Caterpillar's D11 tractors. Group President Ed Rapp told us that the company's sales did not fall off the table until around Thanksgiving 2008, and that is accurate. This was also more than two months after the Federal Housing Finance Agency (FHFA) had placed Fannie Mae and Freddie Mac under government conservatorship, Bank of America was persuaded to purchase Merrill-Lynch, and Lehman Brothers filed for bankruptcy. The financial crisis did not immediately lead to a crisis in industrial production and sales.

However, despite the lag, when the recession hit durable goods sales, it hit hard. As Figure 10.4 shows, the real value of U.S. exports declined almost 20 percent in the fourth quarter of 2008 and almost 30 percent in the first quarter of 2010. If there was anything positive in the situation, it was that the export activity of Germany and Japan declined even more. We now know that real gross domestic product in the United States would decline for the first three quarters of 2009 and that Caterpillar's consolidated sales

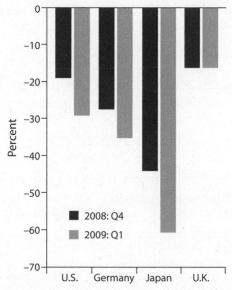

Figure 11.4   *The decline in the real value of U.S. exports, 2008Q4–2009Q1.*

Source: Jian Wang, "Durable Goods and the Collapse of Global Trade," *Economic Letter,* Federal Reserve Bank of Dallas, 5 (February 2010), www.dallasfed.org/assets/documents/research/eclett/2010/el1002.pdf

and revenues would decline 36.8 percent from $51.32 billion to $32.40 billion in that year. It was a grueling time period for virtually every industrial firm.

> **When economic recession hits***, many companies react in an unproductive way. "We can't control the economy," managers complain, and begin to point fingers, accentuate company politics, criticize leadership, and point out alleged flaws in structure and operations. All these behaviors create scars that make it more difficult to recover and scale upward when economic conditions improve. Caterpillar minimizes such inefficient conduct by making trough planning a regular and accepted part of its operating methodology.*

Although most companies were confused and stunned at the collapse, Caterpillar reacted swiftly. As Rapp put it, "We didn't have to scurry around" because the trough plans already existed. It was a matter of implementing those plans, and CAT did just that over the next few months.

Chairman/CEO Jim Owens said it all in *How We Win: 2009 Year in Review* when he remarked, "In my 37 years at Caterpillar, this was the most difficult economic environment I've seen. The industries we serve were among the hardest hit. And our sales and revenues plummeted."

A series of work teams met daily and weekly to carry out the overall trough plan, chart progress in specific areas, and deal with hiccups. Jim Owens delegated overall responsibility to Doug Oberhelman to oversee the process.

Measurables

The implementation of the trough plan touched every part of Caterpillar and changed the way the company did business. Among the more noticeable adjustments made by the company were the following:

- Overall company end-of-year employment declined by 19,074 between 2008 and 2009 (though *Fortune*'s Geoff Colvin reported that at one juncture Caterpillar's employment numbers fell by 35,000).

- Overtime hours were reduced, and in some cases weekly employee hours were reduced as well. Caterpillar's motor grader production facility in Decatur, Illinois, was shut down for the entire month of July 2009.

- The total value of inventories declined by more than $3 billion. This transformed Caterpillar even more into a just-in-time manager of its inventories.

- Executive compensation was reduced by as much as 30 to 50 percent. This set a tone within the organization and sent a message to all employees about the need for joint effort and sacrifice.

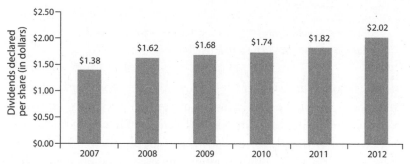

Figure 11.5   *Caterpillar dividends paid per share, 2007–2012.*
Source: Caterpillar annual reports

- Caterpillar not only continued to pay a dividend to its share-holders, but it also actually increased that dividend on a per share basis in 2009 (Figure 11.5). This impressed investors and financial analysts. Here was a company that knew how to manage through tough times.

Bouncing Back

Caterpillar emerged from the worst recession since the Depression financially sound and well positioned for expansion. To achieve that, however, it had to do more than simply cut costs. Simultaneously, it had to position itself for economic recovery. Its goal was to leapfrog most of its competitors by being financially healthy and ready to go when economic conditions improved. Doug Oberhelman felt that the company had emerged from the business cycles of the 1980s and 1990s "weak" and therefore wasn't as well positioned for subsequent expansion as it might have been. This time things would be different.

Moderating the Bullwhip Effect

When Caterpillar's output declines, its orders from its own input suppliers usually also contract. However, when Caterpillar bounces back, its input suppliers also bounce back. Sometimes this occurs so dramatically that CAT's suppliers have difficulty scaling up to the new levels of demand.

INSIDER'S EDGE   *Caterpillar's thinking, even in the middle of the worst economic trough since the Great Depression, is exemplary and should be emulated by other firms.*

A portion of Caterpillar's trough planning is done with its input suppliers to minimize the bullwhip effect. This refers to situations in which "small increases in demand cause a big snap in the need for parts and materials further down the supply chain." During the Great Recession, Caterpillar monitored its critical suppliers to ensure that they would not be wiped out. In 2010, the company actually informed several of its steel suppliers that it would more than double its purchases of steel from them even if CAT's sales did not rise significantly. Caterpillar had at least two motivations. First, during 2009, it had drawn down on its inventories and now needed to replenish them even if sales did not increase. Second, when economic conditions eventually improved, Caterpillar wanted to make sure that its suppliers would be capable of meeting its increased demand for inputs.

By some reports, Caterpillar visited approximately 500 of its suppliers in 2009–2010 in an attempt to ascertain if they had the ability to scale up their outputs rapidly if Caterpillar increased its orders.[17] Further, the company assisted some of its suppliers by making firm commitments so that it would be easier for them to obtain financing on the basis of their receivables (some of which would be from Caterpillar).

Planning for the Trough Now Is Company Wisdom

Jim Owen's planning for the trough innovation has become an article of faith at Caterpillar and now is seen by outsiders as a differentiating strength of the company. CAT has developed the ability to contract its operations and reduce its costs more quickly than is the case at most large corporations. This has occurred primarily because determined managers have succeeded in turning many previously fixed costs into variable costs.

Victory has many fathers, and Caterpillar's success with trough planning and execution is no exception. Jim Owens was the primary proponent, and Doug Oberhelman the primary implementer. As chairman/CEO, Oberhelman continues to regard planning for the trough and subsequent execution as vitally important activities. However, the proverbial rubber met the road in planning for the trough in the form of thousands of critical assessments made by production floor employees and managers. They were among the very best judges of how the company could increase its operational flexibility. One example: today's CAT production line employees and managers are cross-trained so that large numbers of them are capable of filling the shoes of others when necessary. The number of employee job classifications has been cut by 90 percent in some cases; the net effect has been to increase Caterpillar's flexibility and options.

Caterpillar did not neglect its customers and dealers in its drive for increased flexibility. The company's representatives talked with input suppliers at their factories, interacted with customers on job sites, and sought the advice of its dealers, all with the goal of arriving at mutually satisfactory conclusions about what costs and activities legitimately could be made more scalable up and down without breaking faith with those suppliers, customers, and dealers. A primary motivation behind Caterpillar's decision making was its desire to establish the basis for the next expansion. It would be foolish to scale down in ways that would destroy the very suppliers, customers, and dealers that would be crucial to scaling up.

Some of Caterpillar's increased operational flexibility has been derived from labor contracts that it gradually renegotiated. In contrast to the 1970s and 1980s, CAT's labor contracts today grant the company great discretion in allocating its capital, locating production, and sourcing inputs. Caterpillar CEOs memorably asserted in the 1980s and 1990s that their struggles with organized labor ultimately would determine who was going to run the company. It's now clear that it is Caterpillar's management that runs the company and makes the critical operational decisions. If this had not occurred, Caterpillar's trough planning today would largely be a symbolic exercise because the company's ability to scale its activities up and down would be seriously diminished.

Caterpillar's current executives, nearly all of whom were with the company during those critical periods, stand on the shoulders of the giants who triumphed in those skirmishes. Even so, today's employees and managers operate with what can only be termed a flexibility mindset. They are encouraged and rewarded for developing options, whether it is alternative sources of supply, cross-trained employees, or multiple locations for production. This is a mindset that differentiates Caterpillar from many other large corporations, some of which reward employees and managers for "doing the same old thing" repetitively and for avoiding considerations and alternatives that might challenge someone within their firms (an observation by a Caterpillar supplier).

It would be a mistake, however, to place too much emphasis on increased labor flexibility. Caterpillar also has devoted considerable time to developing productive and cooperative relationships with suppliers. The company now typically has multiple sources of supply for important inputs and gradually has acquired the ability to observe the activities of its suppliers (some CAT suppliers believe *monitor* is a more accurate term) to ensure both uninterrupted production and Six Sigma quality. Further, as already noted, even though deteriorating economic conditions severely tested Caterpillar in 2009 and 2010, the company extended favorable financial terms to some dealers and customers and kept them in the game. This maintained the company's options.

Internally, most managers now have enhanced ability to "turn the spigot" (a description by one manager) to adjust production levels, input purchases, and support activities. At the corporate level, the gradual move of Caterpillar toward a larger number of smaller plants has provided executives with a greater ability to adjust production levels without focusing on a single large facility. It's much easier to dial back production or even shutter several small plants than it is to achieve the same reduction of production in a single large plant. Simply put, the economic and social grief is parceled out and dissipated in different locations rather than being concentrated in a single location.

Reducing production and employment involves employees' lives and livelihoods and never can be taken as a given. If it were easy to do and carry out, many more companies would plan for the trough. Nevertheless, planning for the trough is close to becoming institutionalized at Caterpillar. Jim Owens's vision has become reality, and the worldwide economic slowdown in spring 2013 once again put that vision to the test.

CHAPTER 12

SETTING THE STAGE: THE BOUCHARD-KOCH FORECAST MODEL FOR CATERPILLAR

In this chapter and the next two chapters, we present our proprietary analysis of Caterpillar's financial performance and its stock.

We've said many good things about Caterpillar in previous chapters, primarily because the company's stock has been an amazing investment over the last 30 years. Figure 12.1 provides the details. Between January 1, 1981, and December 31, 2011, Caterpillar's stock price rose from $3.58 per share to $89.61 per share, a 25-fold increase. The compound annual rate of return on the stock was 10.9 percent. By contrast, two of the most visible major stock market indexes—the Dow Jones Industrial Average and the S&P 500—had compound annual growth rates of 8.26 percent and 7.87 percent, respectively. Over almost the same period, the U.S. economy had a real compound annual growth rate of only 2.69 percent.

Quite simply, Caterpillar's stock has been one of the very best-performing long-term investments. This is the major reason why it is important not only to explain why Caterpillar has been so successful but also to chart its future.

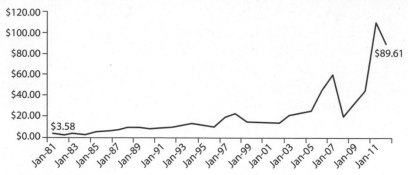

Figure 12.1 *Caterpillar's share price (adjusted for dividends): January 1, 1981–January 3, 2012.*
Source: Capital IQ

The owners of Caterpillar stock were rewarded with more than just a stock that moved fairly steadily upward. Caterpillar also paid its shareholders $18.12 per split-adjusted share in dividends between 1996 and 2012 and has averaged a 2.5 percent dividend over the last five years. By contrast, the average dividend paid by S&P 500 firms over the last five years was 2.1 percent, and it was only 1.3 percent for Dow Jones Industrial Average firms. Stockholders who invested in CAT in 1996 and held their shares through 2012 realized an 8.2 percent average annual rate of return (10.7 percent if they reinvested their dividends)

We hope that board members, managers, and employees in corporations of all sizes will learn from the decisions of Caterpillar's board and managers over the last 30 years. Our readers should admire what CAT accomplished; more important, they should learn how to identify winning management teams such as those at CAT and be able to pinpoint the companies that are most likely to succeed. It is essential that investors learn to avoid management teams that are not up to the challenges of scaling to higher levels of size and performance. Our task here and in the next two chapters is to capitalize on lessons drawn from Caterpillar's success to identify companies that will outperform the stock market over the next few decades.

All investors face thousands of potential investment choices. In the United States alone, there are over 15,000 publicly traded companies. With this surfeit of choices, it's not easy to figure out how to invest one's funds. Focusing on companies such as Caterpillar is a helpful way to separate the financial wheat from the chaff. Very few of these 15,000 publicly traded companies have done so well for such an extended period. Hence, it is well worth our time to examine the principles Caterpillar has relied on to scale to its current size and scope.

In this chapter, we are going to discuss why out of those 15,000 choices it would have made great sense to put money into Caterpillar stock throughout the last 30 years. We will put our investor's hat on, discussing things we like as well as things we don't like about Caterpillar as a stock investment. Along the way, we'll give you a better sense of how we evaluate companies. You'll see that our approaches don't have much in common with the colorful advertisements that boast that investors who follow their advice will be able to double their money in six months. We focus on methods that will make it much less likely that you will make a mistake. Our first-order task is to cut off the left-hand (below-average) segment of the probability distribution to eliminate investment losses.

We will provide you with our predictions of what we think Caterpillar shares will be worth in the future—another Insider's Edge. However, the principles that we apply to the evaluation of Caterpillar also can be applied to assessing the future worth of any company for which public performance data are available.

Good Management Ultimately Produces Good Returns for Investors

Setting aside rumors, short-term dislocations, and illegal activity, there are only two circumstances that will support an enduring increase in the market value of a company:

- **Higher company earnings.** Higher profits can pay for increased growth or can be used to pay dividends to investors; both make a company more valuable.

- **Higher multiples applied to company earnings.** Investors decide to place a higher value on each dollar of the company's earnings, probably because they believe the company's future is brighter or perceive that the risk attached to the company has declined.

Our model focuses like a laser on earnings because this is where the rubber meets the road for successful investors. Some companies generate very small profits or even record losses. Perhaps we are carrying coals to Newcastle when we observe that when a company cannot generate profits, it must raise money from investors or borrow money to continue to operate.

When a company's earnings grow, the value of that company increases. Thus, we concentrate on companies and investment opportunities in which earnings have the potential to rise significantly. We're always on the outlook for reasons why a company's earnings can grow.

The pathways to higher earnings growth are so obvious that some investors miss them. They are as follows:

- **Grow revenue.** Are the conditions in place that will cause a business to increase its revenue faster (or slower) in the future?

- **Increase margins.** For every dollar the company takes in as revenue, how many cents in profit are created for the company's owners? Are there ways management can turn a larger proportion of each dollar of revenue into earnings? (Reducing costs is one avenue for doing this.)

- **Manage capital astutely.** On occasion, companies buy back their own shares, sometimes by borrowing the funds required to do so. When carried out at a propitious time, this can increase the price of the firm's stock and generate higher earnings per share as well.

Let's focus for the moment on companies that increase their margins because this is one of the areas where Caterpillar has excelled. Over the years, we've seen management teams effectively increase their margins of revenues over costs by means of a number of different strategies:

- **Making acquisitions.** Some choose to acquire companies that provide new products, new markets, and sales channels that enable them to push up revenues and/or reduce costs.

- **Increasing company scale.** Increased profitability can occur for mundane reasons, for example, spreading fixed costs over more units of output.

- **Expanding company scope.** Profitability may increase because the company expands its scope (the breadth of its activities) if the marginal cost of doing that is low.

  We've seen this occur when firms do not need to add new salespeople or administrative people or build or acquire new space to generate additional sales or expand their product lines. (Consider the simplest kind of example: a Mary Kay salesperson adding one additional cosmetic to her sales line without incurring much additional cost.) If this is the case, the next sale (the marginal sale) probably will be very profitable. It makes sense to look at marginal profitability on additional sales to assess whether a company can benefit from scaling to a larger size. Arguably, the advent of the Internet has enabled companies such as Amazon to expand their scope at minimal expense because most of the "work" is accomplished digitally.

- **Engaging in turnarounds, reorganizations, or restructurings:** Firms big and small often announce downsizings, "rightsizings," and reductions in the workforce. Sometimes they trumpet the adoption of new processes such as lean manufacturing. Or, like Caterpillar, they introduce business units and incentives designed to track and stimulate productive behavior.

> **INSIDER'S EDGE** *The advent of the Internet has enabled companies such as Amazon to increase their scope without incurring comparable increases in their costs. Many Internet firms are said to take advantage of a "long tail" because digitization enables them to sell items whose unit sales are very low. Digitization also enables firms, including Caterpillar, to create new personalized bundles of goods and services with the click of a computer mouse.*

Caterpillar has used each of these four strategies at various times during the 30-year period that is our primary focus. For example, in 2011 the company acquired Bucyrus, giving it a dominant position in the global mining industry. Although most financial analysts believe CAT paid a high price for Bucyrus (we agree), the acquisition did provide the company with significant potential to increase its scale. It situated CAT in a gigantic global industry in which it had been a marginal player; simultaneously, it established the company as one of the worldwide leaders in mining equipment and machinery. Yet that's not all. The acquisition enabled CAT to amortize its SG&A (selling, general, and administrative) expenses and corporate overhead over a larger output base. This was a textbook example of spreading fixed costs over more units of output while making other costs joint so that they could be shared.

As we have seen, Caterpillar has done lots of other things as well. It has undergone a number of reorganizations, fundamentally altered the way in which it records and evaluates the performance of its units and managers, changed its operating segments, adopted new manufacturing systems, shuttered plants, developed alternative sources of supply, increased product quality and reliability, improved its inventory controls, enhanced its already good relationships with its dealers, negotiated more favorable labor agreements, developed superb information technology capabilities, planned for the trough, and vastly increased its corporate flexibility. Each of these initiatives either reduced costs or increased potential revenues; their net effect was to increase Caterpillar's profitability.

INSIDER'S EDGE *Caterpillar's acquisition of Bucyrus received flak from some analysts and investors because of its timing and the price CAT paid. However, we predict that 10 years from now it will be seen as a wise strategic move that simultaneously increased CAT's scale and increased its profitability.*

Of course, Caterpillar hasn't been the only company that has taken such initiatives. What is distinctive about Caterpillar is the extended duration of its thrust toward larger scale and global leadership. For Caterpillar, it has been a continuous, never-ending 30-year drive that seldom has been replicated. Although many corporations enjoy what might best be labeled hot streaks when they surge forward and capture the imagination of analysts and investors, this usually dissipates over time. Such leaps forward usually are driven by dynamic, decisive, charismatic CEOs (Steve Jobs at Apple and David Packard at Hewlett-Packard) whose visions propel their corporations to levels of performance never seen previously. Legendary CEOs such as Jobs and Packard were able to scale their companies to much larger sizes, generate enviable profit streams, and generously reward stockholders. However, their conspicuous successes could not be maintained by the managers who followed.

Caterpillar's three-decade surge forward is a rara avis that sets Caterpillar apart. Why has CAT been able to achieve leadership in circumstances that frustrated or destroyed similarly situated companies? In our view, this occurred because the company's management has been willing to make tough decisions, both strategic and operational, when necessary, though always with the requirement that it reward its stockholders. A recent example: when the Great Recession hit Caterpillar in late fall 2008, the company found a way to maintain its dividend payment to its stockholders despite what was to be an 86.3 percent decline in its operating profit the next year. It implemented its trough plans by contracting employment, slashing managerial salaries, and reducing inventories, but it did not decrease its dividend payment.

Caterpillar's management consistently has made decisions that maximize the earnings the company delivers to its shareholders. This may seem to be a pedestrian explanation, but it is an important part of the secret sauce we look for as investors. Expressed another way, we look for management teams that care about us and are prepared to sacrifice their personal welfare to honor that commitment. Witness CAT's executives giving themselves major compensation cuts during the Great Recession in 2008–2009. This impressed us; it also has impressed other investors and is one reason why the stock has performed so well.

As Figure 12.2 shows, Caterpillar has grown its earnings per share significantly from 1990 to 2012.

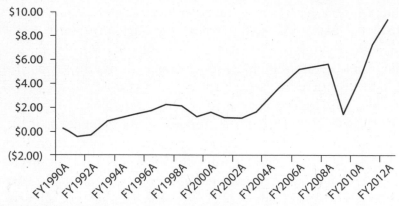

Figure 12.2   *Growth in Caterpillar's earnings per share.*
Source: Capital IQ

A basic principle of the Bouchard-Koch model and efficient market models in general is that markets are discounting mechanisms. This means that markets have a "view" of what the future will hold for a company. These expectations are reflected in each company's stock price. Stock prices move when the market's expectations about future sales and profits change.

On occasion, equity markets can be frenetic because investors' expectations change dramatically. Figure 12.3, which depicts Caterpillar's forward price/earnings ratio between 1999 and 2012, provides striking evidence of this. The graph shows Caterpillar's stock price divided by its forward earnings (what analysts forecast Caterpillar would earn in profits over the succeeding 12 months). CAT's price/earnings multiple bounced from a low of around 7× to a high of around 43×. But this graph also calls into question the research and opinions of investors since over the long term, CAT's forward P/E multiple typically has varied between 10× and 20×. If investors had known about Caterpillar's planning for the trough, their investment behavior might have been different.

This brings us to a key to examining Caterpillar on a "go-forward" basis. Can the company consistently generate the higher earnings needed to drive returns for shareholders in the next generation?

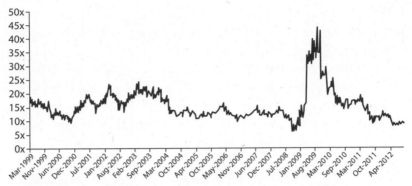

Figure 12.3 *Caterpillar's forward price/earnings ratio, 1999–2012.*
Source: Capital IQ

Company Research That Counts

In many ways, Caterpillar is a very simple company: it produces machinery (engines, turbines, bulldozers, mining trucks, excavators, and the like) that it sells through a network of dealers to customers around the globe. If all goes right, the company will sell the machinery for more than it costs to make and will earn an attractive profit. This will cause CAT's stock price to rise, and nearly everyone will be happy.

Of course, nothing is quite so simple in the world of Wall Street or, for that matter, in most industries. Caterpillar actually is a complex company to analyze. To understand CAT, one must make an accurate reading of the global economy, have a handle on global mining capital expenditures, figure out international manufacturing cost dynamics, and understand commercial construction growth in the developed and developing nations as well as master the exotic topic of foreign exchange risks and, as a necessity, not a luxury, figure out China.

While writing this book, we got to know many key individuals at Caterpillar and were able to talk with numerous individuals outside the company who interact with CAT. However, we are not Caterpillar employees. We do not have access to its financial results or economic outlook beyond what a normal investor or outsider might have. Put simply, we will never know as much about

Caterpillar as do the people who work there, though on occasion our status as outsiders will provide us with a valuable perspective that Caterpillar employees may not have.

In many Fortune 500 companies, there are so many divisions, offices, and product lines that even insiders don't have the whole picture of what's going on. On occasion, the insiders who may think they have the whole picture—the CEO, the CFO, the board, and so on—are remarkably parochial and cannot see the forest for the trees.

> **As we analyze Caterpillar**, *our situation is roughly analogous to that of Americans in the U.S. Department of State who attempt to explain and predict the behavior of the government of the People's Republic of China. American diplomats can talk a good game about China but are unlikely ever to understand fully the intricate cultural, political, and economic puzzle that is the real China. What they do, however, is conduct thorough research and then make educated inductions based on that research. We do the same with respect to Caterpillar.*

Even the most knowledgeable manager cannot know what company earnings or revenues will look like years into the future. He or she can only make educated judgments that are subject to change. Caterpillar exemplified this in 2011, when it projected 2015 sales and revenues of $100 billion with earnings per share (EPS) of $15 to $20. A year later, CAT revised those figures down to $80 to $100 billion in revenue and EPS of $12 to $18. This revision, approved by Doug Oberhelman and the board, was supported by more than 20 inside economists, thousands of salespeople in the field, constant customer contact, and an intelligently well-assembled worldview.

Caterpillar's changing views about its outlook for 2015 reflect the reality that CAT operates in a cyclical business and that a wide range of complex issues drive its ultimate results. Both they and we must form opinions by piecing together information from a broad and deep variety of sources. We must accept that we will never know with certainty what the future will bring. Managers and investors must also force themselves to recognize the certainty of uncertainty.

Investing in and managing companies thus becomes an exercise in evaluating the likelihood of different outcomes. Since we cannot know the future with certainty, the Bouchard-Koch model evaluates investments the old-fashioned way: with scenario analysis. Upside scenarios, expected scenarios, and trough scenarios must all be fairly represented to estimate with any accuracy what the potential range of outcomes will be.

Wise individuals use these scenarios either to help them manage their companies or to make their own investments. We constantly update our scenarios so that we have an informed view of the range of potential outcomes. It is complicated, difficult, and time-consuming work, but if we do it right, the payoffs can be extraordinary because most managers and investors take shortcuts.

Taking Inventory: What We Like to See and What Bothers Us

As we gather information, we create lists of what we like and don't like about a particular company. These lists help us understand where the upside to a particular investment may reside. The lists also help uncover risks that could cost us money. What we aim for is a realistic view of a company and its prospects; this means we need to get to know the company well. However, it is essential that investors resist identifying emotionally with an investment because this often leads to inferior decision making.

Things We Like About Caterpillar When We Put On Our Investor Hats

When we look at Caterpillar, we see many things to like. Not only does the company's basic story about what it is attempting to do make sense, but also CAT has an established record of success. The company has several core strengths. We are especially impressed by the following:

- Caterpillar has been an outstanding performer for decades and is operating in market segments that are destined to grow faster than both the U.S. and world economies.

- The company's dealer network is superb and perhaps unmatched.

- The company has dominant market shares in nearly all of its businesses.

- The company's parts and service model reminds one of Gillette's legendary pairing of razors and razor blades.

- Caterpillar's management has demonstrated a remarkable ability to adjust to changes in its markets.

Let's examine the strengths in greater detail.

Caterpillar's End Markets Will Exhibit Long-Term Growth

Gerard Vittecoq, Caterpillar's influential and recently retired group president, told us that "Caterpillar is in the right business at right time, and this has been true for a long time." Caterpillar's theory of the future is that a burgeoning, increasingly urbanized, and prosperous world population will require roads, schools, and infrastructure and construction of all types. CAT will supply the equipment and tools that will bring these developments to fruition and extract the natural resources and minerals (copper, iron ore, coal, oil, natural gas, etc.) that underpin economic growth.

Vittecoq constructed a list of the 10 most attractive worldwide industries in terms of long-term return on invested capital. They included mining, oil and gas, food and agriculture, and electrical generation. He pointed out that Caterpillar has a major position in 8 of these 10 industries. In the words of a competitor, "Those guys are well positioned for the long term." We agree.

The Caterpillar Dealer Network

One of the things we look for when we invest is a strong competitive position because such a position makes it easier to continue to make money for an extended period. We think the dealer network is Caterpillar's core competitive strength. None of CAT's competitors have anything like it.

The dealer network keeps Caterpillar in close contact with its customers and places those customers in a position of depending on CAT. For example, the cost of downtime for mining equipment can be critical and, when it occurs, can far exceed the initial purchase price. A mining truck, for instance, might cost as much as $5 million to buy. During a single year, depending on the type of mine, a single truck might carry $250,000 to $750,000 per day in mining product. If the truck breaks down for a single day, the mining company may lose the same amount in revenue. If the truck needs to be sent out for repairs and is out of commission for two weeks, the loss to the mining company could easily reach millions of dollars. Thus, mining companies are much more concerned with uptime and downtime and their ability to get equipment repaired quickly and easily. They want to go—indeed, they need to go—to a high-quality repair shop nearby. Caterpillar dealers provide that essential service for CAT's customers.

This reliability generates enormous customer loyalty. Reflect on this: If you've ever owned a car or a computer, haven't you wanted to own the most hassle-free car or computer? Caterpillar customers are the same way, only on a much larger scale. That's why so many of those customers turn out to be repeat customers. They know they can trust the company and its dealer network to be there when they need them. CAT and the dealer occupy a place in the bloodstream of the customer.

INSIDER'S EDGE   *"After-market" parts and service revenues are extremely important to firms that operate in cyclical industries. They bind customers to the firm, prep them for the eventual sale of a new machine, and provide badly needed revenue when sales of new machines decline. Firms that only give lip service to these realities do themselves great harm.*

Since Caterpillar and its dealers are in constant contact with customers throughout the life of a product, they learn very quickly what those customers need and want. Both CAT and the dealers then can develop products that respond to those needs and wants. It's a very close relationship that generates benefits for the customer, for the dealer, and for CAT. The knowledge that comes out of this process is much deeper than anything CAT could acquire through focus groups or the other marketing research tools on which many of its competitors rely.

Beyond customer knowledge and loyalty, the dealer network has financial advantages for Caterpillar. A key fact about that network is that CAT doesn't own the dealers; they are independent businesses that have invested billions of dollars to support the distribution of CAT products. In 2012, Caterpillar's dealers had a collective net worth of $21.30 billion; CAT did not have to provide those funds, and that freed up those dollars for other company purposes.

Caterpillar has established conditions that make it possible for its dealers to prosper. Four of its dealers are publicly traded; hence, their revenues and profitability are known. Their 2011 EBIT margins ranged from the 6.5 percent of Finning International to the 11.4 percent of Toromont, with Barloworld and Sime Darby recording intermediate EBIT margins of 7.2 percent and 10.4 percent, respectively.

These profits inspire an obvious question: Why hasn't Caterpillar decided to own the entire dealer network itself and retain that profit stream within the company? We believe that the primary reason is that the network of independent dealers enables CAT to avoid many of the financial requirements associated with developing and maintaining that kind of network. Though the company may have sacrificed profit by having an independent dealer network, there are major benefits to that strategy:

- Caterpillar is able to generate higher margins and higher returns on the capital its invests because that capital is not drawn off to support a dealer network.

- Caterpillar's dealers are regarded as locals rather than corporate interlopers from afar.

- Caterpillar avoids many of the regulatory hassles that could be involved in operating in many different states and countries, thus reducing the overall risk of operating its business.

Let us issue a caveat, however. In our view, it has yet to be established that the Caterpillar dealer and service model applies equally well to customers in all segments of emerging markets such as China and India. CAT's dealer network may offer advantages in large mining equipment. There, equipment uptime is a core issue, and the company's extensive dealer network clearly differentiates CAT from its customers. In other industries, however, the uptime issue may be less important (construction is an example).

Our experience suggests that local customers in emerging markets often devise their own jerry-rigged solutions to equipment problems and necessary repairs as they emerge. In that type of environment, CAT dealers, though still valuable, are less important than they are elsewhere in the world. This is an issue Caterpillar must continue to monitor as it increases its presence in emerging markets.

We also wonder what other opportunities may exist for Caterpillar with respect to its dealer network. Could CAT choose to outsource some of its manufacturing and evolve in some locations into being an enterprise—perhaps more akin to a tech company—that designs products, creates marketing plans, and then distributes those products through its dealer network? Or should CAT choose to lease (share) its dealer network to companies that want to make or distribute complementary products? The company's dealer network could provide additional significant sources of profitability in the future.

Dominant Market Share in a Number of Businesses

Companies with dominant market shares often derive significant advantages from that status. Dominant firms with highly identifiable, trustworthy brands are able to charge higher prices. Their margins are higher. In our view, Caterpillar has this ability in a number of its product lines.

Consider the market for mining trucks. We estimate (we can only make estimates because Caterpillar does not disclose market share information) that CAT's share grew from approximately 45 percent of the global installed base of mining trucks in 1992 to over 60 percent in 2011.

A similar dynamic plays out across many parts of the Caterpillar product portfolio. CAT may have a greater than 50 percent market share in mining equipment and also in oil and gas equipment. In construction markets outside of China, the company's global market share ranges between 30 and 40 percent.

Success breeds success. Caterpillar sells high-quality products that generate customer loyalty and retention. When customers require new equipment, they know precisely where to go for superb products, excellent service, and honest treatment. It is precisely because its customers are so loyal that CAT has the ability to charge premium prices; in China, for example, CAT's competitors assert that the company's prices may be up to 30 percent higher than their own for visually comparable pieces of equipment.

The Razor/Razor Blade Character of CAT's Business

Parts and service are key considerations for Caterpillar's equipment customers. Customers buy the initial equipment and return over the years for parts and service. In many cases, they spend significantly more on parts and service than they spent buying the original equipment. This is why former chairman/CEO Don Fites described CAT's parts and service operations as having the character of an annuity that continually pays benefits over time.

Among investors, this phenomenon often is referred to as the razor/razor blade model in reference to the model Gillette pioneered many years ago. Gillette earned more from the sale of its blades than it did from the sale of the original razor. One could point to similarities with Caterpillar's business model, which provides stability and predictability in its sometimes volatile revenue and earnings even when original sales turn down. The razor/razor blade model creates a "bank" of future sales for CAT and its dealers. This is a characteristic of companies with the ability to make money for a *long* time.

In Caterpillar's case, customers may often spend two to three times more on service and parts compared to what they spent on the original equipment. Although CAT provides only limited disclosure on this issue, its competitor Komatsu and one if its dealers, Finning, have been more forthcoming. In various presentations to investors, they revealed that for many products, customers will buy parts at least equal to the price of the original piece of equipment. For major products like mining trucks, the total spent can be even higher.

As we project Caterpillar's financial performance into the coming years, we are impressed with the bank of future parts sales that the company has already created. As Figures 12.4 and 12.5 show,

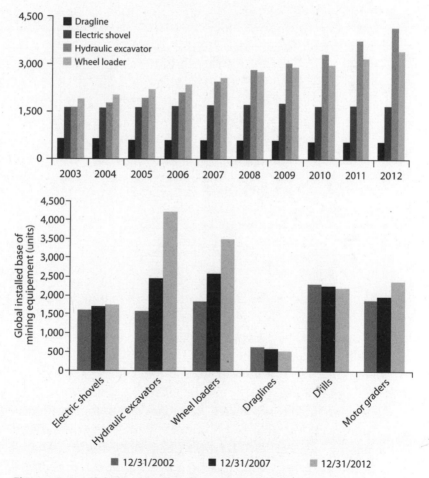

Figure 12.4 *Global installed base for various types of mining equipment.*
Source: Parker Bay Company Global Mining Database

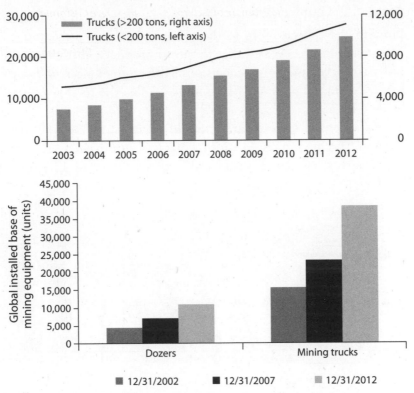

Figure 12.5   *Global mining truck installed base.*
Source: Parker Bay Company Global Mining Database

over the last decade the installed base of many mining equipment products has doubled. In many types of equipment, the growth of CAT's installed base has outpaced the growth of the market. This is especially significant in the market for mining trucks, where the overall installed base has almost tripled and CAT's market share has increased significantly.

Indeed, as Table 12.1 shows, Caterpillar's largest four customers (Rio Tinto, Vale, Yamana, and Shenhua) all are primarily situated in the mining business. This represents both opportunity and peril for CAT. Nevertheless, when such companies are expanding, CAT is a major beneficiary.

Table 12.1 *Bloomberg's Estimate of Caterpillar's Largest Five Customers Worldwide, 2013*

Name of Company	Percentage of Caterpillar's Sales Derived from This Company
Rio Tinto (mining)	2.50
Vale (mining)	2.28
Yamana Gold (mining)	1.76
Shenhua (mining)	1.72
Arcelor Mittal (steel)	1.65

Source: Bloomberg (accessed May 6, 2013)

Caterpillar's Adaptability to Changing Business Environments

One of the things about Caterpillar that consistently impresses external observers is the company's demonstrated ability to adapt to changing business environments. Caterpillar has developed a culture of constant experimentation and an ability to undertake change that is unusual for a large organization. Perhaps this culture always was present at CAT; however, it has particularly been in evidence over the last 30 years.

Large organizations are notoriously resistant to change, but our conversations with Caterpillar employees at all levels reveal that as one production line employee told us, "We can't use the same game plan two seasons in a row." Thus Caterpillar employees expect things to change, and when the unexpected appears, they tend to thrive.

Here is a simple example. In 2006, according to Trefis, construction might have produced up to 60 percent of Caterpillar's operating profits (Caterpillar says the percentage was considerably smaller). However, the construction equipment market is highly competitive, with a large number of strong global players. It's also a business in which a local manufacturer can beat a global player because construction companies often like to buy local. Construction markets in many parts of the world, including the United States and China, were white hot in 2006, so much so that CAT understood that existing activity levels were unsustainable. Retrenchment was inevitable. Understanding this, the company consciously chose to focus on construction markets in which it already had a more dominant market share, faced fewer competitors, and earned more profits. It limited its attempts to penetrate and expand in other markets.

At the same time, Caterpillar moved aggressively into mining and natural resources, where there were opportunities to achieve higher growth rates. By 2012, construction accounted for about 22 percent of CAT's business, whereas natural resources had expanded to approximately 53 percent.

Some might regard this as a simple reactive change in product mix. It was not. It reflected careful forward-looking analysis that resulted in Caterpillar fundamentally repositioning itself.

The Things That We Don't Like When We Put On Our Investor Hats

Nobody's Perfect has been the title of at least 20 popular films, books, albums, and songs. The ubiquity of the title conveys the reality that both individuals and organizations sometimes fall short of their own lofty visions and standards. So it is with Caterpillar. Despite its dazzling successes, there have been bumps in the road, and the company's positioning and decision making haven't always been spotless.

These are the major drawbacks in our opinion:

- Caterpillar's financial reporting is kept at highly aggregated levels (probably for competitive reasons) and therefore is not always informative.

- The company's end markets in many cases are heavily reliant on government regulation or spending.

- As already noted, Caterpillar's businesses are highly cyclical, and the world economy may be stagnating yet again.

- Caterpillar has been losing market share in some Chinese markets.

- The company has a high fixed cost base.

- Caterpillar's management's timing has not always been flawless.

Caterpillar's Financial Reporting Can Be Obscure

Joel Tiss, an analyst with BMO Capital Markets, put it to us succinctly: "Caterpillar's reporting is more opaque than their competitors. CAT tells nothing." This is a harsh evaluation, but the truth is that CAT sometimes is parsimonious as it parcels out nuggets of information. For example, the company refuses to disclose the names of its largest dealers even though several, such as Finning International, are public firms.

Caterpillar's financial reporting sometimes does not contain information that many investors and analysts would like to have. On occasion, one must guess about variables, such as market share, that many believe are important to an understanding of the company's performance. For example, until 2009, the company didn't disclose enough information for investors to understand the profitability of specific product lines. Today, even though CAT sells a tremendous number of engines to oil and gas drillers, it does not always report its activities in that end market.

As a recent example, we saw only a limited amount of disclosure about Bucyrus after its acquisition by Caterpillar in 2011. When Bucyrus was an independent company, investors received information about its original equipment sales and its follow-on service. CAT has eliminated that disclosure. In fact, even though follow-on parts are an essential component of future revenue, CAT does not disclose parts sales for any of its businesses.

We firmly believe that Caterpillar's parts and service business model is compelling. Nevertheless, it is not easy to predict how that business will grow in the coming years. We were forced to piece together information by talking to both CAT's dealers and its competitors.

What's especially interesting about Caterpillar's reticence is that its competitors often do not behave that way. As just noted, Bucyrus formerly disclosed its original equipment sales and parts revenue.

CAT's competitor Joy Global continues to disclose this information. Thus, it does not appear to us that there are any essential trade secrets hidden in these data.

> **We'd like Caterpillar** *to disclose more information than it does. However, the company is entirely transparent on the most important financial variables of interest to investors, such as sales, sales by major product category, and earnings.*

Caterpillar is especially reluctant to provide market share data even though reputable outlets such as the *Financial Times* are not reluctant to do so for CAT and its major competitors. This aversion may be understandable since market share data could have competitive implications. CAT executives told us that market share data provided by various companies seldom are comparable because of the wide variety of definitions and time periods used to define market shares. Thus, in the company's view, it is better not to contribute to additional misunderstanding by dispensing market share data that may not be either accurate or comparable.

Nevertheless, investors dislike uncertainty. Caterpillar's reporting reticence may create a small drag on the company's stock price.

Caterpillar's End Markets Often Are Dependent on Government Regulation and Spending

Many of Caterpillar's end markets depend extensively on government decision making. In mining as well as oil and gas, governments around the world are heavily involved in leasing land, issuing permits, creating regulations around mining and extraction operations, and levying taxes. Environmental concerns abound, and those who wield governmental power instinctively are attracted by such matters.

Governmental units often also get heavily involved in providing tax incentives that stimulate private construction projects and sometimes supplement those incentives with infrastructure support such as highways and bridges. Caterpillar's Mossville, Illinois, plant exemplifies the latter with four-lane highway access in several directions.

Further, governments nearly always conduct a host of regulatory activities that impinge on projects in which Caterpillar equipment is used. These interventions range from requiring permits to inspecting ongoing construction sites for health and safety.

In construction, a significant proportion of projects involving Caterpillar equipment depends on government funding. Witness the tremendous spur to Caterpillar's growth that the funding of the federal interstate highway system provided. Thus, the impact of government on Caterpillar can be highly positive.

Even so, what the Lord giveth, the Lord can take away. The sometimes unpredictable nature of governmental funding and the sometimes arbitrary and capricious nature of governmental regulation can have distinctly negative effects on Caterpillar. Further, these events sometimes occur for reasons that have very little to do with CAT. For instance, the government may refuse to issue mining permits for environmental reasons unconnected to the company's machines or cut infrastructure spending because of a decline in tax receipts.

Caterpillar's exposure to government decision making is a reality of its business. In some cases, this works out very well. The Chinese government, for instance, has been a very strong financial supporter of infrastructure projects, driving demand for the company's construction equipment. At the same time, however, that government operates state-run enterprises that compete with CAT, and those enterprises benefit from subsidies and preferences not available to Caterpillar. Not so subtly, the Chinese government sometimes favors privately owned Chinese firms over foreign firms such as CAT.

Enforcement of property rights and contracts and the availability of evenhanded judicial remedies do not exist in some governmental jurisdictions. Caterpillar's worldwide footprint renders it more vulnerable to such vagaries than most large corporations are.

There's No Doubt Caterpillar's Business Is Highly Cyclical

We need not beat this topic into the ground. We've shown in earlier chapters that Caterpillar's sales are highly sensitive to the business cycle. The company knows this and engages in a variety of practices designed to mitigate the effects of the cyclicality, including nurturing its steady parts and service operation, its diverse multicontinent production and sales base, and its celebrated planning for the trough. CAT's economists also have become skilled at predicting business cycle turning points, and that information is quite useful even though it cannot immediately generate more sales.

> **Caterpillar's head economist, Don Johnson,** *focuses on the yield curve—the gap between the 10-year U.S. government bond rate and the federal funds rate—to predict macroeconomic turning points in the United States. That gap has predicted the last seven U.S. recessions. When the gap declines or even becomes negative, economic problems soon follow.*

Caterpillar Is Losing Market Share in China

According to the *Financial Times,* Caterpillar has been struggling to maintain market share in China. In one important market (crawler excavator sales), it trails both Komatsu and China's Sany. Sany's sales were virtually zero at the turn of the century, but it now has an approximately 12 percent market share in crawler excavators. CAT's share approximates 7 percent according to the *Financial Times.* CAT's 2012 excavator sales appear to have fallen about 30 percent.

Caterpillar Operates in a High Fixed Cost Business

The central premise of Caterpillar's planning for the trough activities has been a desire to gain organizational flexibility. More than anything else, this implies attaining cost flexibility, that is, turning previously fixed costs into variable costs.

That's not easy to do at a company like Caterpillar, which operates in markets where plants and operations are characterized by large initial capital requirements and high ratios of fixed to variable costs. Thus, between 2008 and 2009, CAT's revenues fell by 37 percent but its earnings per share declined by 74 percent. This reflected the company's inability to cut certain costs promptly despite planning for the trough. Virtually every business confronts this phenomenon to some extent; there are overhead costs related to the core organization and tasks that cannot easily be eliminated or powered down: accounting, legal, and the like.

Our interviews with financial analysts suggest that Caterpillar still has a distance to travel in terms of making its processes more flexible and thus more responsive to changes in the business cycle. Chairman/CEO Doug Oberhelman has placed emphasis on this objective, but as one analyst commented to us, "Oberhelman's projects took CAT's systems from the 1950s into the 1990s. He's still got 20 years to go." This view is overly severe but underlines the need for progress in this arena at CAT.

The Timing of Caterpillar's Decision Making Has Not Always Been Optimal

Although we admire Caterpillar for its ability to adapt to changing business environments, there have been a few times in its history when its enthusiasm arguably caused it to acquire other firms for premium prices at less than optimal points in time. CAT purchased the Bucyrus mining business in 2011 for $8.8 billion, but that was just as the price of global commodities was beginning to decline. Many mining companies canceled or delayed their expansion plans, causing them to defer purchases from Bucyrus, and that precipitated a decline in the value of the acquisition.

Caterpillar's hard-charging approach to China resulted in the company acquiring ERA/Siwei in November 2011 for a price that could go as high as $677 million; it did this even though *Forbes* magazine opines that there were "warning signs . . . flashing" concerning the ERA/Siwei's performance and health.

When a company decides to increase its market share over time and expand aggressively to conquer new global markets, situations such as this are likely to occur. Charitably, one might pass off such instances as the cost of acquiring a ticket to a much more profitable long-term big show. Nonetheless, with the advantage of hindsight, we can say that these acquisitions have not been well timed in terms of subsequent events in the mining industry.

In our view, these stumbles have been momentary in nature and have not altered the company's long-term prospects, which continue to be quite favorable. Characteristically, Caterpillar was quick to learn its lessons and has taken swift action to remediate any associated problems. Although CAT as a company visibly values its past, it seldom ruminates excessively over irretrievable sunk costs and situations that cannot be reversed. This forward-looking attitude is an important ingredient in its success.

CHAPTER 13

VALUING CATERPILLAR: THE GLOBAL QUESTIONS

In recent years, Caterpillar has derived between 60 and 70 percent of its total consolidated sales and revenues (a term that includes Caterpillar Financial's activities) from outside the United States. Hence, any financial analyses and forecasts for the company must analyze its global position and reach clear conclusions about its international position.

The two most important factors that will influence Caterpillar's global success over the next few years are (1) global mining capital expenditures and (2) global construction spending. Analyses of CAT can be clothed in fancy terminology, but the essential reality is that these two factors ultimately will tell the company's tale. We will discuss each of these influences in depth because periodically the role and interpretation of each have not been well understood in the investment community.

Global Mining, Capital Expenditures, and the Mining Supercycle

The year 2002 was a momentous one in global commodities markets. China joined the World Trade Organization, and spectacular growth followed. The World Bank reported that between 2002 and 2011 Chinese GDP grew at a 19.7 percent compound rate annually. Its GDP increased from $1.64 trillion (U.S.) in 2002 to $7.30 trillion in 2011. In 2010, the PRC overtook Japan to become the second largest economy in the world.

Growth of this magnitude had a huge impact on global commodity markets. To support its growth, China consumed vast quantities of cement, iron ore, coal, steel, lead, aluminum, and copper. Rather quickly, the PRC became the world's largest consumer of all of those commodities. Figure 13.1 presents data on Chinese consumption of basic resources and commodities, which we previewed in Chapter 4. By 2011, China dominated the world consumption of iron ore (47.7 percent), coal (46.9 percent), steel (45.4 percent), and copper (38.9 percent).

> **Nominal commodity prices** *have risen for many commodities, such as oil and copper, in recent years. However, "real" (price-deflated) commodity prices, as represented by the Dow Jones–AIG commodity index, have trended downward since the 1930s. This is an often ignored phenomenon. It also suggests that demands for many commodities are price-elastic in real terms.*

Global miners could not keep up with this explosion in demand, and the prices of their commodities increased. For many mining firms, this produced record high profits. Between 2002 and 2009, the Brazilian miner Vale was able to grow its earnings from BRL 2.0 billion to BRL 10.3 billion, an annual compound growth rate of 26 percent. Table 13.1 shows profit data for three major mining companies: Vale, Rio Tinto, and BHP Billiton Plc. It was *laissez les bons temps rouler*—let the good times roll—for most mining companies in the first decade of this century.

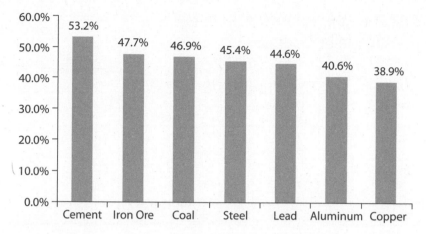

Figure 13.1 *China's share of world consumption of basic resources and commodities.*

Source: Data are taken from "High Exposure to China Could Be Trouble for These Companies," *Seeking Alpha Blog* (June 17, 2011), http://seekingalpha.com/article/275396-high-exposure-to -china-could-be-trouble-for-these-companies

Higher prices and profits stimulated miners to increase production fairly significantly over this period. Table 13.2 illustrates the growth in production during the last decade for three basic commodities: iron ore, copper, and thermal coal.

Increased profits and production drive additional capital expenditures. As Figure 13.2 shows, mining capital expenditures have grown significantly since the turn of the century. Between 2002 and 2009, for example, from our representative sampling of major

Table 13.1 *Profits of the Top Mining Companies, 2002 and 2009*

Company	Profit FY 2002	Profit FY 2009	Compound Annual Growth Rate
Vale	BRL 2.0 billion	BRL 10.3 billion	26.4%
Rio Tinto	GBP 404.5 million	GBP 3.0 billion	33.2%
BHP Billiton Plc	GBP 1.1 billion	GBP 3.6 billionn	18.5%

Source: Capital IQ

Table 13.2   *Growth in World Production of Iron Ore, Copper, Thermal Coal, and Met Coal, 2002 and 2009*

	Production 2002	Production 2009	Compound Annual Growth Rate
Iron ore	1.16 billion metric tons	2.30 billion metric tons	10.3%
Copper	13.4 billion metric tons	15.8 billion metric tons	2.4%
Coal–thermal	5.1 billion short tons	7.1 billion short tons	5.2%
Coal–met	390 million short tons	573 million s hort tons	5.7%

Sources: U.S. Geological Service, Energy Administration Agency

mining companies, total global mining capital spending grew at a 37 percent annual compound rate.

Each of these developments—rising commodity prices, rising mining profits, expanded mining production, and increased capital expenditures—was enormously beneficial to Caterpillar and its competitors. Caterpillar, of course, is a major supplier of the excavators, bulldozers, engines, and mining equipment that do the work

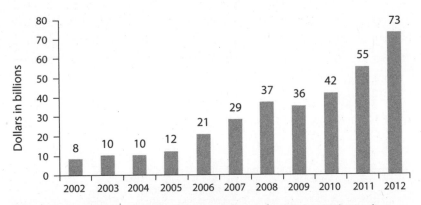

Figure 13.2   *Global mining capital expenditures for representative major mining companies, 2002–2009*.*

Includes BHP Billiton PLC, Vale, Rio Tinto, Ango-American, BarrickGold, Freeport McMoRan, Goldcorp, and Peabody Energy.
Source: Capital IQ

of digging mines, removing ore, and transporting mining commodities to market. As Figures 13.3 and 13.4 reveal, global sales of mining equipment grew dramatically from 2003 to 2012; the dollar value of shipments sextupled.

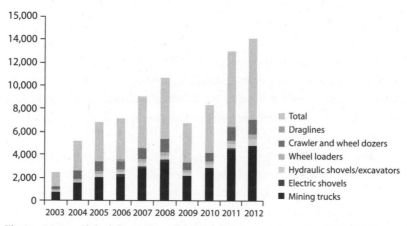

Figure 13.3   *Global shipments of mining equipment (in units), 2003–2012.*
Source: Parker Bay Company Mining Database

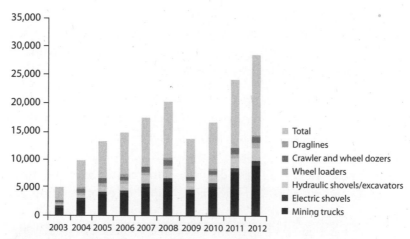

Figure 13.4   *Global shipments of mining equipment (in millions of $), 2003–2012.*
Source: Parker Bay Company Mining Database

The Evolving Nature of Natural Resource Extraction

China was not the only reason spending on mining capital equipment increased during the last decade. The gradually evolving character of many natural resource commodity markets also played a role.

Whenever possible, mining firms are cost minimizers. Given a choice and holding other things constant, they usually do their mining in the least expensive locations. Metaphorically speaking, however, most of the low-hanging, low-cost resource fruit already has been picked worldwide. Hence, to augment their mining output, companies now must focus on locations that tend to be more remote and on methods that often are more expensive. Three major trends are at work here:

1. **Overburden has been growing.** Most shale oil and gas projects today require much deeper (and longer) penetrations into the earth than was true for older mines. In some shale deposits, vertical drilling into the ground may go as deep as two miles; horizontal drilling into productive strata may extend another three miles. Miners refer to the rock and soil above a deposit of minerals, oil, or gas as *overburden*. The greater the overburden is, the more expensive and time-consuming it is to extract the ore, oil, or gas. This may not be good for mining firms but is quite good for CAT as it frequently translates into increased demand for Caterpillar's machines and engines.

2. **Unconventional plays are becoming more important.** Many shale oil and gas wells involve significant overburden. Therefore, these wells require drilling down through significant amounts of rock before the fracking process can proceed. Pressurized water and chemicals then are injected, often horizontally, into the sandstone and siltstone strata to loosen up the "tight" oil and gas there. The larger the overburden and the tougher the rock, the greater the engine horsepower required to penetrate the strata, inject the well, and capture the oil and gas. Rob Wertheimer of Vertical Research Partners notes that shale gas wells use up

to 250 times more horsepower than do traditional wells. This stimulates the demand for Caterpillar engines or at least for a greater number of larger, more powerful engines.

3. **Mineral yields have been declining.** In some varieties of mining, companies must dig a load of dirt or ore that they subsequently process or filter to obtain the minerals they are seeking. Unfortunately, for several decades, mineral mining yields have tended to decline. Companies must dig more dirt to obtain the same amount of mineral and ore as previously. Figure 13.5 illustrates that copper yields have slowly been deteriorating for more than a century. This has benefited Caterpillar because the additional digging and extraction required stimulates the demand for its trucks and equipment.

Even though recovery rates for oil and gas have not declined as much as those for copper, they can be quite low. The Bakken shale formation in North Dakota and Montana illustrates this situation. Less than 10 percent of all the barrels of oil believed to be there are likely to be recovered. This translates directly to the demand for Caterpillar machines and equipment. In

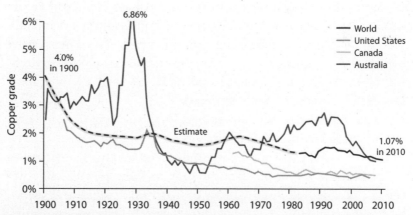

Figure 13.5   *Declining quality of copper ore yields as a percentage of ore mined, 1900–2008.*

Source: Richard Schodde, managing director, Minex Consulting, "The Key Drivers behind Resource Growth: An Analysis of the Copper Industry over the Last 100 Years," MEMS Conference Presentation, Phoenix, Arizona, March 2010

general, the lower the recovery rates, the greater the need for Caterpillar's products.

Thus, Caterpillar has benefited from both a large upswing in mining capital expenditures and the evolving nature of resource extraction processes. The salient consideration is how these dynamics will play out in the coming years. Will capital spending for mining-related equipment continue to trend upward? Will Caterpillar maintain or increase its share of the pie? We conclude that the answer is yes to both questions even though there probably will be bumps in the road and variations around the long-term trend.

Growing populations and increasing urbanization will stimulate world demand for many different types of minerals as well as for oil and gas. Caterpillar is ideally positioned to help the world meet this increasing demand. CAT's 2011 acquisition of Bucyrus vastly increased the company's presence in mining both above and below ground. Further, Caterpillar did not acquire just any company. Bucyrus was an acknowledged leader in the area of mining equipment, and now Bucyrus/Caterpillar's products are generally considered to be superior to those offered by the major competitor, Joy Global.

It's appropriate, however, to issue a caveat here. Because the history of mining is replete with boom and bust cycles, the future demand for Caterpillar's mining products probably will vary substantially around a long-term upward trend. Nevertheless, we believe that Caterpillar will perform tolerably well in this environment even if mining companies cut back on their overall capital spending (this occurs every few years).

This will be true for two reasons. First, the long-term resource consumption trendline is positively sloped, and there is unanimity in the view that the world's consumption of resources such as iron ore and copper will be much larger 10 years from now. Second, over the last decade, the installed base of Caterpillar equipment owned by mining companies has more than doubled. Thus, unless mining companies choose to idle equipment or shut down completely, they will have to patronize CAT dealers for parts and service. As already noted, such expenditures can average two to four times the purchase price of the original piece of equipment.

The Global Construction Cycle

In a variety of ways, the global mining dynamics we have just described also apply to global construction expenditures. China has been a huge marginal consumer of construction machinery, similar to what has been true in mining. Figure 13.6 illustrates the tremendous growth in fixed asset investments that has occurred in China since 1970. Much of this investment requires machines and equipment that Caterpillar manufactures and services.

Road building continues to be a very important source of construction equipment expenditures. Since 2004, China has added 5,000 to 10,000 kilometers to its expressway system every year and has added 130,000 kilometers annually to its paved roads. By way of comparison, the United States added 20,000 to 30,000 kilometers per year.

This spurt in road building has spurred demand for the equipment that is used in construction: bulldozers, excavators, engines, trucks, and the like. During the early 2000s, approximately 30,000 excavators were sold in China annually by all sellers. By 2010, that number had risen to 100,000. Once again, Caterpillar is optimally positioned to be a prime supplier of such equipment.

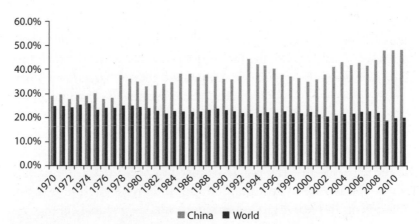

Figure 13.6 Gross capital formation as a percentage of GDP: China and the world, 1970–2012.

Source: www.data.worldbank.org

The sometimes explosive nature of investments in construction machines and equipment is undeniable. Mike DeWalt, Caterpillar's corporate controller, told us that a 5 percent increase in the value of global economic output could lead to as much as a 25 percent increase in global construction spending. One reason for this is that Caterpillar customers often defer replacement of worn-out machines during slack economic times. Hence, when economic conditions improve, these customers find themselves "undermachined" and need to spike their orders upward. This can translate into major increases in orders received by CAT.

> **INSIDER'S EDGE**   *Caterpillar is one of many firms whose sales are closely tied to gross domestic product. What differentiates CAT from many other companies in the same situation is the large amount of income CAT consistently receives from its parts and service business and its planning for the economic troughs that sooner or later always appear. These are important reasons why CAT was not forced to decrease its dividend during the Great Recession. Though CAT cannot conquer the business cycle, its pursuit of these strategies dramatically reduces the negative effects of economic recession on the company.*

DeWalt also noted that the demand for Caterpillar construction machines in the United States is closely tied to increases in U.S. gross domestic product (GDP). Annual growth rates of U.S. GDP above 2.5 percent have multiplier-like impacts on construction spending and therefore on Caterpillar. He estimated, for example, that a 3 percent increase in U.S. GDP in 2013 could translate into as much as a 20 percent increase in sales of CAT construction machinery.

A salient question for Caterpillar is how long the current expansion of expenditures on construction equipment will last. Much of the expansion of the last few years has been driven by China; however, it is wise to bear in mind that the PRC's enormous recent investments in fixed assets are rather unusual in a global context. As Table 13.3 shows, China is already an outlier compared with other industrialized nations. China has been investing a far greater percentage of its GDP than have nearly all other countries.

Table 13.3 *Critical Investment Ratios by Country, 1973–2011*

	China	Japan	U.S.	Korea	Taiwan	Thailand	Indonesia	India
Investment/ GDP ratio 2010	46.2	20.5	15.5	28.6	21.7	24.7	32.2	31.8
Historical peak	46.2	36.4	23.2	38.0	30.9	41.6	32.2	35.8
Year of historical peak	2010	1973	1943	1991	1975	1991	2010	2007

Sources: Adapted from Ichiro Muto and Tomoyuki Fukumoto, "Rebalancing China's Economic Growth; Some Insights from Japan's Experience," *Bank of Japan Working Paper Series*, No. 11-E-5, July 2011, p. 4

A 2012 International Monetary Fund (IMF) report alleged that because the Chinese economy is so heavily dependent on investment, it is out of balance, and this needs to be changed. More emphasis should be placed on increasing the less volatile Chinese consumption, according to the IMF. The Chinese government claims to be taking steps to achieve this, but it has made such statements in the past without observable effect.

Nevertheless, to the extent that the Chinese government is able to make the Chinese economy more consumption-oriented, this will affect Caterpillar, probably in terms of diminishing the rate of growth of CAT's Chinese sales. Nevertheless, the Chinese government is quite unlikely to pitch its economy into recession by making meat-ax reductions in investment; the reality is that it still has a tremendous backlog of ambitious infrastructure projects it says it intends to pursue. More modest and contemplative investment expenditures in China will benefit Caterpillar in the longer term because such a posture by the Chinese will reduce the volatility of CAT's Chinese equipment sales and diminish the probability that an overheated Chinese construction equipment market will crash and burn.

INSIDER'S EDGE   *The International Monetary Fund is not the only authority that argues that the Chinese economy is dangerously out of balance because of its exceptionally high dependence on investment. If and when the Chinese rebalance and increase consumption expenditures, this will moderate the demand for some*

of Caterpillar's products, but only in the short term. Consumption
expenditures also drive investment expenditures, though less
directly than do activities such as mining and construction. It is the
overall rate of growth of the Chinese economy that is the ultimate
key for Caterpillar and similarly situated firms. As long as it remains
high, firms such as CAT will do well.

If history provides a valid precedent, over this decade China's fixed investment will fall as a percentage of its GDP. Even as this occurs, Caterpillar still should have the opportunity to expand its construction business in China for the remainder of this decade because the Chinese market remains underserved with respect to construction equipment. Rob Wertheimer of Vertical Research Partners points out that China consumes about 60 percent of the world's cement yet has only one-third of the world's excavators. Just to reach the world average for excavator utilization, China needs to double its current fleet of excavators.

Wertheimer also observes that data on Chinese equipment suggest that the Chinese utilize their equipment more hours each day than does most of the rest of the world. They do this because it reduces their immediate need to purchase additional equipment. However, this practice also will lead to increased replacement demand in the longer term because their machines will wear out more quickly.

Putting all these factors together, Wertheimer believes that Chinese demand for construction equipment is likely to remain healthy even though it will be cyclical. We agree.

From Doug Oberhelman on down at Caterpillar, there is absolutely no doubt that the company has placed a high priority on increasing its market share in China. Even so, CAT is unlikely to become number one in the area of construction equipment in China by 2015. Indeed, in several product lines, it has been "bleeding market share" to China's Sany, according to the *Financial Times*. Still, CAT's willingness to take a long view of what is needed to succeed in China bodes well for its future there. CAT Group President Ed Rapp, who has responsibility for China, speaks of "a systematic build out" of the company's "complete business model" in that country. Rapp also speaks of methodically developing a "pipeline of local leaders."

The maturation of Caterpillar's complete business model in China will take time, but the company repeatedly asserts that it is in China for the long run. If CAT is patient and does roll out its complete business model in China, we believe its dealer network and high-quality products will enable it to succeed. The company may not become number one in China in the area of construction equipment, but it will do well.

In the judgment of the *Financial Times*, however, Caterpillar has on several occasions "misjudged" the Chinese market for heavy machinery. As a consequence, the company's earlier optimism about being able to vault rather quickly to market leadership in China has given way to realism. If CAT does move to leadership status in China during this decade, it will have been the result of a long, hard slog.

INSIDER'S EDGE *Western companies hoping for quick success in China are likely to be disappointed. Even firms with Asian backgrounds such as Komatsu and Samsung have found the economic terrain to be uncertain and success to require long-term investment and attention. Culture, politics, and history all come into play. Only some of the rules that apply to the rest of the world pertain to China.*

The measuring sticks are a bit different in China. A slowdown in the Chinese economy still translates to an annual rate of growth of 7 to 8 percent per year in real terms. Even at this "leisurely" pace, the Chinese economy will double in size in less than a decade. Thus, even if fixed asset investments decline as a percentage of GDP (and this is probable), as time passes, the absolute size of such expenditures is going to grow. Thus, despite some hiccups, there is reason for Caterpillar to have long-term optimism about its Chinese prospects.

CHAPTER 14

THE BOUCHARD-KOCH MODEL FORECASTS CATERPILLAR'S FUTURE

How much is Caterpillar worth? How much will it be worth in the future? It's time to answer these critical questions. To do that, we model Caterpillar in terms of its operating segments. Caterpillar reports its sales and revenues in two major subdivisions:

- Machinery and Power Systems

- Financial Products

Within Machinery and Power Systems, the company provides a further breakdown into

- Construction Industries

- Resource Industries

- Power Systems

- All Other

Our forecast scenarios depend on our assumptions about the growth of sales and revenue and costs in each segment.

The scenarios depend on our accumulated knowledge of Caterpillar, the many different markets in which the company competes, global economic conditions, our interpretations of events, and common sense. Arguably, we now know more about Caterpillar than all but a very few individuals outside the company, but at the same time we have acquired the ability to take a more detached view of CAT than most individuals inside the company. This is an enviable position, and we readily acknowledge that we would not occupy it without the cooperation of Caterpillar. However, all the forecasts and other forward-looking statements in this book are solely those of Craig Bouchard and Jim Koch. The forecasts have not been approved or endorsed by Caterpillar and do not necessarily reflect the company's views.

We make explicit assumptions about factors that may drive profit margins higher or lower in each of Caterpillar's activity segments. Further, we consider the investments in fixed assets and working capital that the company will need to make to execute its plans and grow its business:

- We examine working capital by turns (the number of times each year that inventory turns over) rather than simply by the percentage of assets, although we recognize that ultimately the two methods are roughly equivalent. An advantage of this approach is that this is how Caterpillar forecasts and manages its working capital internally.

- With respect to capital expenditures, we assume that capital expenditures will be a percentage of sales. Caterpillar is a growth company. This implies that except in unusual situations, CAT's capital expenditures will exceed its depreciation and amortization expense allocations.

We also make a number of assumptions about Caterpillar's approach to capital management and investment. Our model shows the company generating healthy cash flows in the future. We assume the following priorities for CAT's use of that cash:

- Scheduled debt service is the first priority use of Caterpillar's cash.

- Caterpillar will pay gradually increasing dividends per share that will be consistent with the growth in its earnings. Further, it will not decrease its dividend even in years when the company faces a temporary cyclical hit to its earnings.

- Caterpillar will continue to pursue acquisitions requiring an average of $1 billion to $2 billion in cash every several years. We stipulate that we do not have inside information about CAT's acquisition plans, but in light of the company's history and our conversations with its senior executives, it makes sense to assume periodic acquisitions. After all, in the recent past, CAT acquired MWM (for $810 million in 2011), Bucyrus (for $8.8 billion in 2011), and ERA Mining Machinery/Siwei (for $677 million in 2012). We do not assume Bucyrus-sized acquisitions during the next decade, but such initiatives can't be ruled out.

- Caterpillar's $580 million write-off relating to ERA/Siwei in January 2013 was a setback for the company but represented less than 1 percent of what we believe CAT currently is worth. Further, it will have very little effect on CAT's future activities in mining and zero impact on the company's activities in areas such as construction.

This is what we assume about the next decade:

- Global population will continue to grow, and that growth will occur at a faster pace in emerging countries than in developed countries, where falling birthrates will produce population stagnancy in any mature country that does not accept large numbers of immigrants.

- Global GDP will grow at an average of over 3.0 percent per year and a minimum of over 5.0 percent annually in China. However, average economic growth rates in developing countries will be higher than this, although the variance of those economic growth rates also will be higher because of countries' irregular patterns of growth. Developed countries' growth will average closer to 2.0 percent annually.

- Developing countries will continue to invest in infrastructure such as roads and buildings, often simply because their existing infrastructure is wearing out. However, in most developing countries, we assume infrastructure investment will grow faster than annual average GDP growth rates.

- The continued growth of developing countries will create increasing worldwide demand for commodities. China will be the dominant player here, and its activities will have a profound influence on total world consumption and prices.

Relying on these general assumptions; our analysis of world construction, mining, and resource markets that was presented in Chapters 12 and 13; and our knowledge of Caterpillar, we have created three scenarios. We believe the range of these scenarios provides excellent insight into the array of potential outcomes for CAT over the coming decade. We have included our full models in the Appendix.

The Base Case

Our base case is the one we believe is the most probable; we think it has a 70 percent probability of occurring. If the forecasts generated by the base case are on target, Caterpillar will be a very compelling and profitable investment over the next eight years.

Key assumptions particular to the base case include the following:

- Natural resources

  - Mining capital spending will continue to grow, but at a slower rate than we have seen during the last decade.

  - A higher installed base of Caterpillar mining and construction equipment will drive higher demand for its maintenance, parts, and repair services.

- Construction

  - Construction spending will grow in the United States and China, but at more subdued rates than those in the last decade.

- Power generation

  - Power generation, both fixed and mobile, will grow slightly faster than our expectation of 3.0+ percent average annual global GDP growth.

- China

  - Caterpillar will continue to invest in China, emerge from its momentary funk there, and gradually increase its market share.

In our base case scenario, Caterpillar's sales and revenues grow from $65.88 billion in 2012 to $117.96 billion by 2020, a compound annual growth rate of 7.55 percent. This is a healthy increase but less than the 9.6 percent annual growth rate in sales and revenue the company has averaged since its founding. CAT's net income will rise from $5.68 billion to $14.06 billion, a compound annual growth rate of 12 percent.

Caterpillar will be able to increase its operating profit much faster than its revenues because it will be able to expand its margins. We are impressed by the company's ability to control its costs as it scales upward. For example, its business unit managers are graded and compensated at least partly on their demonstrated ability to retard the growth of fixed costs as output and activities increase.

Caterpillar has developed what we term *expectation curves* that generate cost containment targets for managers as their business units and the company grow larger. Consistent with the CAT tradition of "everyone owns their own numbers," managers understand that controlling costs and overhead is a critical consideration both for the company and for their own progress as a manager. CAT's unusual commitment to planning for the trough makes all of this easier because it places a premium on managers creating flexibility in their business units by making costs variable rather than fixed. Hence, managers already have at their fingertips some of the critical tools required to control costs and increase margins.

It is instructive to contrast Caterpillar's cost containment strategies with those of many other corporations and organizations where the accumulation of "managerial slack"—substantial overhead, numerous assistants, plentiful reportages, and so on—is regarded as a sign of managerial stature and success. This is not the case at CAT, and that is one of the reasons that we forecast gradually improving margins for the company during the remainder of this decade.

We acknowledge that in today's world of slow global growth, the base case numbers presented in Table 14.1 are higher than those usually bandied about on the street. Nevertheless, it's our belief that the base case makes common sense. Why?

Here's a quick summary:

- Caterpillar has diversified its business both by product and by geography.

- The company is "well located"; it produces products and provides services that respond directly to the resource extraction and infrastructure needs of a world whose population is growing and becoming more urbanized.

- CAT has high market shares in most markets.

- Caterpillar's branding is quite powerful, even a weapon, and the company has been astute in the way it has developed off-brand products in developing countries.

- Few competitors can match the quality of CAT's products.

Table 14.1 Projected Caterpillar Consolidated Sales and Revenues, Net Income, Margins, and Growth Rates: Base Case for 2012 and 2020

	2012	2020	Compound Annual Rate of Growth
Consolidated sales and revenues (billions of dollars)	$65.88	$117.96	7.55%
Net income (billions of dollars)	$5.68	$14.06	12.00%
Percent margin	8.62%	11.92%	4.13%

Source: 2012 data from Caterpillar's Year in Review 2012; 2020 data are projections from the Bouchard-Koch model's base case.

- The company's dealer network–customer connection is unmatched and is one of the best in any industry.

- The Caterpillar management team is cohesive, and its leadership is tough.

- The company steadily has invested the resources to have the capacity to grow with its end markets.

- Caterpillar has consistently invested in the research and development necessary to provide a very strong, up-to-date product line and equipment that satisfies Tier 4 emissions standards. CAT stands to benefit as developing countries gradually adopt those standards.

- The company's cost containment and planning for the trough activities are first rate and put some distance between it and several of its competitors.

- Our base case assumes a slower rate of growth in Caterpillar's sales and revenues than the 9.6 percent average annual increase that has been the case throughout its history.

The Optimistic Case

Our optimistic case may seem impossible to some observers, yet it is not pie in the sky. We believe there is a 15 percent chance that some or all of the critical features of this case will hold sway in the remainder of this decade. In essence, in this scenario we assume that the world economy soon will return to the levels of growth it had in its best years since the turn of the century. We assume the following:

- Mining capital spending continues to grow at the pace of the last decade. The trends of resource scarcity and increased global demand continue. Caterpillar continues to sell additional equipment into the field.

- Construction spending recovers in the United States and China.

- Caterpillar is able to install its complete business model in China and therefore is able to increase market share there.

- A higher installed base of Caterpillar equipment drives higher demand for CAT's maintenance, parts, service, and repair businesses.

- The United States deals effectively with its deficit and spending challenges by adopting something close to Simpson-Bowles. As a result, GDP growth in the United States surges and averages 3.0 percent annually. This stimulates the demand for Caterpillar equipment of all types, including power systems, which grow by multiples of GDP growth rates.

In this upside scenario, CAT's revenues grow from $65.88 billion in 2012 to $160.53 billion by 2020, a compound growth rate of 11.78 percent per year (Table 14.2). The company's net income rises from $5.68 billion to $25.68 billion, an increase of 20.76 percent per year. As the fast pace of earnings growth indicates, this case holds that Caterpillar will be able to grow profits faster than revenues by expanding its margins fairly consistently from 2012 to 2020.

The Downside Case

A very smart way to invest is to find opportunities that will protect your principal even when things don't go well for the company in

Table 14.2 *Projected Caterpillar Consolidated Sales and Revenues, Net Income, Margins, and Growth Rates: Optimistic Case for 2012 and 2020*

	2012	2020	Compound Annual Rate of Growth
Consolidated sales and revenues (billions of dollars)	$65.88	$160.53	11.78%
Net income (billions of dollars)	$5.68	$25.68	20.76%
Percent margin	8.62%	16.00%	8.04%

Source: 2012 data from Caterpillar's *Year in Review for 2012*; 2020 data are projections from the Bouchard-Koch model's optimistic case.

which you invest. Let's examine how Caterpillar would perform in this kind of world. As we do so, we harken back mentally 30 years ago to a time when CAT's business was much more troubled. Our downside case assumptions include the following:

- Mining spending plateaus or even declines as a consequence of slower global demand. In essence, we project a repeat of the 1970s and 1980s for mining expenditures. To be sure, this is not what we see today, but we already have predicted that mining spending is likely to diminish in coming years and that the decline will affect Caterpillar.

- Construction spending also declines. The major premise here is that the Chinese economy has expanded too rapidly and that this has resulted in that country overinvesting in many areas, including infrastructure. Hence, a correction will be required.

- Customers delay maintenance on Caterpillar equipment. We assume that mining capital expenditures and construction spending fall and customers begin to use their machines less intensively. Thus, the machines experience less wear and tear and customers defer spending on parts and maintenance.

In this scenario, Caterpillar's revenues grow only modestly from $65.88 billion in 2012 to $74.91 billion in 2020, a compound growth rate of only 1.62 percent per year. At the same time, CAT's net income declines from $5.68 billion to $4.21 billion because its costs rise faster than its consolidated sales and revenues. Simultaneously, CAT's profit margins deteriorate from 8.62 percent to 5.61 percent between 2012 and 2020 (Table 14.3).

We believe that the probability of this occurring is only about 15 percent. Population growth, urbanization, and economic growth in the developing world will stimulate sales of Caterpillar's products. Once again, CAT is well positioned to take advantage of any growth that does occur.

What is remarkable about our downside case is that despite very sluggish demand, Caterpillar's profits are not destroyed and the company maintains its dividend payments to its stockhold-

Table 14.3   *Projected Caterpillar Consolidated Sales and Revenues, Net Income, Margins, and Growth Rates: Downside Case for 2012 and 2020*

	2012	2020	Compound Annual Rate of Change
Consolidated sales and revenues (billions of dollars)	$65.88	$74.91	1.62%
Net income (billions of dollars)	$5.68	$4.21	−3.81%
Percent margin	8.62%	5.61%	−5.52%

Source: 2012 data from Caterpillar's *Year in Review 2012*; the 2020 data are projections from the Bouchard-Koch model's downside case.

ers. In this downside world, an investment in Caterpillar stock in the period 2013–2020 would constitute "dead money" if one were interested in a capital gain; however, such an investment would not be a disaster because we have assumed the company would continue to pay an attractive dividend. CAT demonstrated it had both the ability and the will to do so in the Great Recession of 2009–2010.

Figures 14.1, 14.2, and 14.3 illustrate our forecasts for Caterpillar's financial performance for each of the three scenarios.

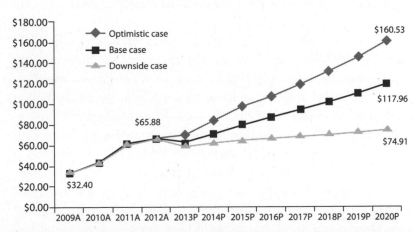

Figure 14.1   *Actual and projected values for Caterpillar's consolidated sales and revenues: optimistic, base, and downside scenarios, 2009–2020 (in billions of $).*

A = actual, P = projected
Source: Bouchard-Koch model

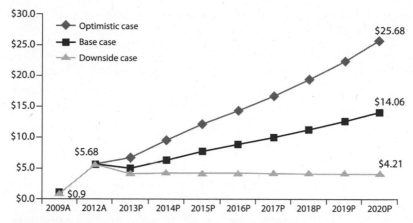

Figure 14.2 *Actual and projected values for Caterpillar's net income: optimistic, base, and downside scenarios, 2009–2020 (in billions of $).*
A = actual, P = projected
Source: Bouchard-Koch model

Figure 14.1 details Caterpillar's consolidated sales and revenues, Figure 14.2 supplies analogous estimates for CAT's net income, and Figure 14.3 presents similar estimates for CAT's net margin.

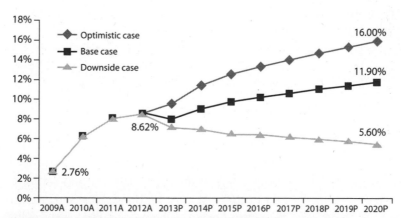

Figure 14.3 *Actual and projected values for Caterpillar's net margin: optimistic, base, and downside scenarios, 2009–2020.*
A = actual, P = projected
Source: Bouchard-Koch model

Valuing Caterpillar

Valuation of companies and their stocks remains both an art and a science. Just as very few individuals ever become highly accomplished violin players, very few active stock pickers ever achieve great success in the stock market. Therefore, it should not be a surprise that a frequently cited study by Fama and French found that active fund managers underperformed the market by an average of 0.8 percent per year between 1984 and 2006. Even smart people find it difficult to value firms and their stocks accurately.

Numerous studies reveal that many investors shoot themselves in the foot by ill-timed trades, costly churning of their portfolios, inappropriate diversification, and bad individual stock selections. For a large majority of investors, bad stock selection simply means that they attempt to pick their own stocks rather than indexing their investments.

We value businesses on the basis of how much cash they are able to create. In the long run, stock prices reflect the market's expectations of the flow of cash a business will generate today and in the future. Because the cash is spread out over time, it's necessary to find the present value of that future stream of cash. This is straightforward. However, to make this approach operational, an additional important step must be taken: it's necessary to figure out the amount of capital investment required to generate the future stream of cash. Most investors miss this subtle but critical ingredient.

Faint Praise for EBITDA

Investors often value companies on the basis of their EBITDA (earnings before interest, taxes, depreciation, and amortization), but we view EBITDA as a very limited measure of company performance. It excludes a number of very real costs that every company we have ever owned, bought, or managed has encountered. For instance, taxes are excluded from EBITDA, but we have yet to participate in a tax-free company.

The EBITDA metric also excludes depreciation and amortization. How many machines that never wear out are used in any business? How many roofs live forever? In the case of a traditional manufacturing companies like Caterpillar, it is preposterous to exclude the real cost of the aging of the plants and machinery that are required to run the business.

Some may respond to our critique by noting that EBITDA does provide a view of the operating cash flow of a business that enables analysts to compare different businesses in an industry. After all, companies have different capital structures, different tax situations, and different levels of capital investment, and EBITDA irons out those differences by not considering them.

We understand this point of view, yet it is a point of view that also assumes that investors have an almost mysterious level of control over the business that investors ordinarily do not have. For example, as investors, we can neither change Caterpillar's tax domicile nor alter its tax rates. We can't force CAT to raise debt or pay down debt. We certainly can't change the speed with which the company's assets age. The bottom line is this: investors can demand, suggest, or hope for all the changes they wish. Nevertheless, if management does not agree, absent a revolution, those changes will not occur.

Hence, although we have no objection to computing EBITDA (Caterpillar's trailing 12-month EBITDA was $11.97 billion on February 15, 2013), we do not value companies and their stocks on the basis of traditional EBITDA multiples. If forced to hobnob with bankers who dote on EBITDA, we'll talk the EBITDA talk, but then we'll go home and make allowances and adjustments to EBITDA to account for tax expenses. That is, we will calculate cash flow.

We define *cash flow* in a very simple way:

Cash flow = net income + D&A – capex – investment in working capital

where
D&A = depreciation and amortization
capex = capital expenditures
working capital = operating liquidity of the business

> **Don't forget the cash flow formula.** *This could be the most important tip we give you. Measure cash flow properly, and the world of successful management and investing will open up before your eyes.*

Note that capital expenditures and working capital represent real investments in any business. Of the two, we pay particular attention to working capital. As we have learned over and over, working capital management often can make or break a business.

Enterprise Value, Not Market Cap

The discussion of working capital and capital expenditures brings us to another area where our approach distinguishes us from many other investors. We firmly believe it is important to focus on the entire value of the enterprise, not just its market capitalization. This brings us to total enterprise value, which is calculated as follows:

Total enterprise value = market capitalization +
debt + minority interest + preferred shares –
total cash and cash equivalents

Total enterprise value (TEV) represents what it would cost to acquire all the outstanding shares of a company's common stock, plus its preferred stock, plus outstanding debt that must be assumed, minus its cash holdings. The cash is subtracted because once a firm has been acquired, any cash on hand reverts to the new owner. The relevant point, however, is that total enterprise value adjusts market capitalization to take debt and cash into account.

Why are such adjustments important? Over the years, we have taken on debt to build our businesses. That debt represented a real obligation of our companies. We have never discussed the purchase or sale of any of our companies in terms of their market caps alone. One must know many other things, such as a firm's debt structure and its liquidity position. It is palpably unwise to ignore significant financial obligations that a company has created, especially if they are debt obligations that have priority over the earnings available to common shareholders. Focusing only on a company's equity market cap can be highly misleading.

The place to look to get an initial handle on a company's debt circumstance is the interest expense line in that company's earnings statement. It will tell you what the company is expending to service its debt. However, one needs to look further to ascertain the nature and term structure of the debt, determine whether it is adjustable or callable, and pin down other debt changes that may exist just over the horizon. In any case, very large debt service requirements should constitute a red flag for investors; this is largely independent of the size of a firm's market cap. There always is an opportunity cost attached to debt service dollars—dividends not granted, investments not made, stock repurchases not carried out, and so forth— and so large debt service requirements should inspire caution. Huge debt service requirements hobble what a firm can do.

The most commonly cited investment metric may well be the price/earnings (P/E) ratio, but it provides only a limited picture of what a company might be worth. We confess that we sometimes use the traditional P/E metric even in this book (see Figure 14.4),

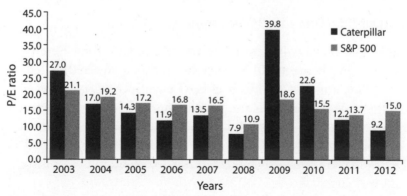

Figure 14.4 *Average annual P/E ratios for Caterpillar and the S&P Index firms, 2003–2012.*

primarily because it is so well entrenched in the thinking of the investment community. Nevertheless, we take a more comprehensive view of valuation in our daily investing lives and will do so for the remainder of this book.

So how have Caterpillar's valuations changed over time? Figure 14.4 reports CAT's P/E ratios between 2003 and 2012 and compares them with the average P/E ratios in the same years for the companies in the S&P 500 index. During this period, CAT's P/E ratio varied between 7.9 and 39.8, whereas the less variable S&P Index P/E ratio ranged between 10.9 and 21.1. Caterpillar's 2012 P/E was 9.2, and the comparable average P/E for the firms in the S&P 500 was 15.0. Prima facie, the market has not been valuing Caterpillar's earnings as highly as it has the earnings of the typical firm in the S&P 500 Index.

Although we do not regard P/E ratios as decisive evidence of the value of a company, P/E data do provide collateral evidence for the proposition that investors often have undervalued Caterpillar. The S&P 500 P/E multiple of 15.0 reflects a 63 percent premium over Caterpillar's 9.2 multiple, a very steep penalty even after taking into account the greater variability of CAT's sales, profit, and stock price. In light of CAT's enviable market position, persistent long-term profitability, and demonstrated ability to maintain its dividend payments to its stockholders even in bad times, the market's substantial P/E adjustment is based on inadequate analysis.

Our Total Enterprise Value Estimates

Table 14.4 presents our estimates of Caterpillar's Total Enterprise Value (TEV) between 2012 (actual) and 2020 (projected) based on 17×, 20×, and 23× multiples of CAT's net income. Lest one conclude that these multiples are too generous, we hasten to point out that between 1994 and 2013, Caterpillar's median TEV/net income multiple on a daily basis was 23.9. Thus, the TEVs presented in Figure 14.5 are not overly bullish; they correspond to CAT's historical experience.

Nonetheless, it is immediately apparent that in any scenario other than our downside case, Caterpillar's TEVs soon become very

Table 14.4 Total Enterprise Value (TEV) Under the Downside, Base, and Optimistic Cases and 17×, 20×, and 23× Earnings Multiples (Billions of $)

Cases	FY2012A*	FY2013P*	FY2014P	FY2015P	FY2016P	FY2017P	FY2018P	FY2019P	FY2020P
Downside	$95.1A								
17×		$72.9	$74.3	$72.6	$72.9	$72.9	$72.7	$72.3	$71.5
20×		$85.7	$87.4	$85.5	$85.7	$85.8	$85.6	$85.1	$84.1
23×		$98.6	$100.5	$98.3	$98.6	$98.7	$98.5	$97.8	$96.7
Base	$95.1A								
17×		$84.0	$108.5	$132.2	$150.6	$169.9	$19102	$214.0	$239.0
20×		$98.9	$127.6	$155.6	$177.1	$199.9	$224.7	$251.7	$281.2
23×		$113.7	$146.8	$178.9	$203.7	$2,229.9	$258.5	$289.5	$323.4
Optimistic	$95.1A								
17×		$113.7	$162.4	$205.5	$243.0	$284.0	$329.6	$380.3	$436.6
20×		$133.7	$191.0	$241.8	$285.8	$334.0	$387.7	$447.4	$513.6
23×		$153.8	$219.7	$278.1	$328.7	$384.2	$445.9	$514.5	$590.6

*A = actual, P = projected
Source: Bouchard-Koch model.

259

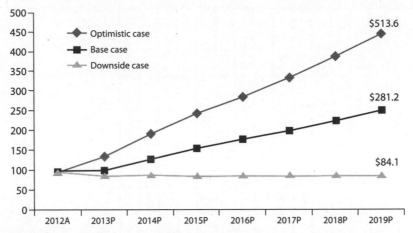

Figure 14.5 *Changes in Caterpillar's total enterprise value (TEV) between 2013 and 2020: pessimistic, base, and optimistic cases, assuming a 20× multiple of net income (in billions of $).*
A = actual, P = predicted
Source: Bouchard-Koch model

large. In 2020, at a 23× multiple (slightly below CAT's historical experience), we predict CAT's TEV will be $323.4 billion in the base case and $590.6 billion in the optimistic case. These valuations contrast to the company's actual 2012 TEV of $95.1 billion. If we discard the optimistic case as being, well, too optimistic, it's still true that even the base case TEV of $323.4 billion represents a 2020 valuation of Caterpillar well beyond that of most analysts and institutional investors.

Figure 14.5 provides a visual representation of the data found in Table 14.4 and assumes a 20× multiple (conservative in terms of Caterpillar's history) and then projects forward CAT's TEV through 2020 under the assumptions of the pessimistic, base, and optimistic cases. The upward trajectory of CAT's TEV is both impressive and, we believe, realistic, especially if one focuses on our base case scenario.

In fact, Caterpillar is very favorably positioned to be a cash-generating machine for the remainder of this decade. This will produce significant annual increases in the company's total enterprise value. Table 14.5 notes that the compound annual increases in CAT's TEV between 2012 and 2020 range from 14.51 percent in the base

Table 14.5 *Compound Annual Rates of Growth in Caterpillar's Total Enterprise Value (TEV) Between 2012 and 2020 Under Varying Assumptions*

	20× Multiple Net Income	23× Multiple Net Income
Base Case	14.51%	16.53%
Optimistic Case	23.47%	25.64%

Source: Bouchard-Koch model

case with a very reasonable 20× multiple on net income to a high of 25.64 percent for the optimistic case with a 23× multiple (which is still below the company's historical average).

Projecting Caterpillar's Future Share Price

To place a value on Caterpillar in 2020, the Bouchard-Koch forecast model for the company applies enterprise value multiples of 17×, 20×, and 23× to our earnings forecasts of the company's 2020 earnings (Table 14.6). We derive price targets from these multiples. Caterpillar's stock hovered around $86 per share in mid-July 2013 but had (and has) a tremendous upside. CAT's superb upside potential will come as a surprise to most investors because our estimates of the company's future revenues and profits exceed those that the market currently appears to be expecting. Even our downside scenario for Caterpillar, which involves stagnant sales and profits, produces a situation in which investors experience only a very modest capital loss at a 23× valuation (the historical average) even while they receive a 2.0+ percent dividend annually. If this represents disaster, many investors would be happy to have it befall them in light of their misfortunes in recent years.

Table 14.6 *Forecasting Caterpillar's 2020 Share Price Under Alternative Sets of Assumptions, Viewed from 2013 and Assuming an $86 per Share Starting Price*

Earnings Multiple	Downside Scenario	Base Scenario	Optimistic Scenario
17×	$55.04 (–42.5%)	$357.55 (272%)	$949.49 (889%)
20×	$75.27 (–21.6%)	$439.29 (358%)	$1,150.17 (1,097%)
23×	$95.49 (–0.5%)	$521.03 (443%)	$1,350.84 (1,307%)

Source: Bouchard-Koch earnings model

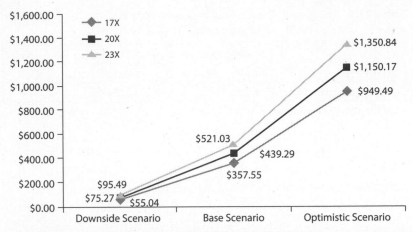

Figure 14.6 *Forecasting Caterpillar's 2020 share price under alternative sets of assumptions, presuming an $86 per share starting price in 2013.*
Source: The Bouchard-Koch model

Our starting point in each of the share price scenarios outlined in Table 14.6 and illustrated in Figure 14.6 is a share price of $86 for Caterpillar. One can see that what we regard as the highly reasonable base scenario forecasts a $357 price for CAT stock in 2020 with a 17✕ multiple, $439 with a 20✕ multiple, and $521 with a 23✕ multiple. The optimistic scenario share price forecasts are comparably higher, and the downside forecasts comparably lower.

Why Do We Forecast Higher Revenues and Share Prices Than Many Other Analysts?

You might ask why we have forecast revenues and share prices that are higher than those being churned out by major financial analysts. For example, in December 2012, 17 analysts who covered Caterpillar projected average 2014 consolidated sales and revenues of $68.94 billion; this was before the worldwide economic slowdown that became apparent in spring 2013. If they had predicted the slowdown, their 2014 consolidated sales and revenues estimates for CAT probably would have been even lower.

By contrast, in our base case scenario, we now forecast $70.17 billion in consolidated sales and revenues for 2014. Why do these analysts undervalue Caterpillar? There are seven reasons:

1. Most observers are only dimly aware of Caterpillar's planning for the trough and penchant for gaining organizational flexibility by turning fixed costs into variable costs.

2. Many analysts have not yet assimilated Caterpillar's ability to control costs and the success it has experienced in retarding the growth of its overhead costs.

3. Caterpillar's network of dealers is widely acknowledged to be beneficial, but many of those who follow Caterpillar for their employers have not gotten close enough to the company to fully comprehend how distinctive that network actually is and how much value it adds to the company.

4. Caterpillar is not the only large company to tell its managers, "You own your own numbers," or to place strong emphasis on individual business units. It is one of the few, however, where reality matches rhetoric on this score, and this is one factor that pushes its performance above that of the crowd.

5. Most analysts understand that Caterpillar is very well positioned to capitalize on global economic and population growth and accelerating urbanization, but only a few have delved into the company to understand its ability to defend or increase its margins in all but the worst times.

6. Caterpillar's leaders sometimes make mistakes, but they are quick to acknowledge their missteps and driven to convert failures into successes. Failing that, they cut their losses and move on to other opportunities.

7. Caterpillar's distinguishing company culture and history are insufficiently understood by some who regard Peoria, Illinois, as flyover territory.

We make no claim that Caterpillar is the only large company that exhibits these characteristics. Very few companies, however, have excelled so clearly or for so long. Despite its status as a component of the Dow Jones Industrial Average, Caterpillar is in the end an underappreciated company whose actual position is understood by only a few.

CHAPTER 15

LESSONS LEARNED

The world certainly does not lack for books, Internet sites, management gurus, and financial advisors promoting their distinctive (and of course always profitable) approaches to managing and investing. How many times has your life been interrupted by someone attempting to convince you that his or her distinctive investment rules are the best thing since sliced bread?

You, the reader, may decide to hurl us into the same "I can afford to ignore this" file on the floor of your office along with ubiquitous mass mailings and political ads. Knowing this is so (we've done the same thing numerous times), we'd like to tell you why our analyses of Caterpillar and the Bouchard-Koch financial model deserve your attention. It is not our argument that managers always will prosper or that investors always will get rich by following our approach, though we do contend that our methods maximize the probability of managing and investing wisely in large, publicly traded enterprises.

Let's begin with our analysis of Caterpillar.

Why Do We Forecast Higher Share Prices for Caterpillar Than Most Other Analysts Do?

It now is legitimate for you to ask, Why do Bouchard and Koch forecast share prices that are higher than those being issued by major financial analysts? Why do we conclude that many institutional investors undervalue Caterpillar? Let's reiterate the 12 most important reasons:

1. Most observers are only dimly aware of Caterpillar's planning for the trough techniques and penchant for increasing organizational flexibility by turning fixed costs into variable costs. The company's ability to adjust output levels quickly and reduce costs without damaging its recovery prospects is one of the most important differentiating features of Caterpillar.

2. Many analysts have not yet assimilated Caterpillar's ability to control its costs and the success it has experienced in retarding the growth of its overhead costs. How many companies actually tie a portion of a manager's performance evaluation and salary to his or her ability to avoid cost inflation and empire building?

3. Related to this, only a few investors have delved deeply enough into Caterpillar to understand its ability to edge its margins upward in all but the worst times. Independent of the growth in demand for its products that Caterpillar reasonably can anticipate, CAT has an unusual ability to extract more profit from each dollar of sales. It is skilled at spreading its fixed costs as it scales upward.

4. Caterpillar's network of dealers is widely acknowledged to be beneficial, but many observers have not gotten close enough to that network to comprehend fully how distinctive it is and how much value it adds to the company. The dealer network is CAT's crown jewel and would be nearly impossible for any competitor to duplicate. The cost of doing that today would be prohibitively high. The decades of close customer interaction at the dealer level can't be duplicated. A surprising number of ana-

lysts covering the company, plus individuals who speak about its prospects, have never visited a dealership or talked with CAT dealers. We'll observe simply that this is a mistake.

5. Caterpillar is neither the only large company to tell its managers, "You own your own numbers," nor the only one to place strong emphasis on accountable individual business units inside the company. It is one of the few, however, in which reality matches rhetoric in this area. More than most large companies, CAT closely tracks both the performance of units in the company and the profitability of individual products. Each unit of this global company has a full understanding of the concept of the cost of capital. The company's devotion to this regimen pushes its performance above that of the crowd.

6. Virtually all analysts understand that Caterpillar is very well positioned to capitalize on global economic and population growth and accelerating urbanization, yet only some have taken the time to do the mathematics on how this reliably translates to an increased demand for Caterpillar products. Higher than average global economic growth generates explosive expansion at CAT.

7. Caterpillar's culture and history are imperfectly understood by some who regard Peoria, Illinois, as flyover territory. It is sexier to spend time deconstructing the likes of Apple and Citibank. Such analyses perhaps are easier to do as well because the home bases of a majority of analysts and major institutional investors are on the two coasts. Of course, these parties have access to the usual financial reporting numbers; this is not the problem. Instead, it is the use they make of these numbers because they are less likely to put their boots on the ground at key Caterpillar sites, including Peoria. Our experience suggests that analysts and institutional investors are more public information–driven with respect to CAT than they are for many other large company stocks. They've seen CAT's familiar yellow machine outside their windows on construction projects, but for many, Big Yellow remains a semiexotic entity they don't completely under-

stand because the company does not produce familiar items such as automobiles, computers, and media that they utilize on a daily basis.

8. Caterpillar may have something to do with the lack of understanding that surrounds it because the company sometimes makes it difficult to for analysts to follow it in detail by declining to divulge a variety of data sets, including market share information. Unscientifically, we estimate that this reluctance, along with Caterpillar's headquarters location, may cut 1 or 2 percent from the company's share price. True, sources such as Bloomberg can diminish some of the data mystery, but many analysts and investors either do not have access to the likes of Bloomberg or fail to use it.

9. Caterpillar's leaders sometimes make mistakes, but they are quick to acknowledge their missteps and absolutely driven to convert failures into successes or to cut their losses and move on to other opportunities.

10. In any case, too many analysts and institutional investors pay attention to the wrong numbers. The easy way out is to focus on price/earnings (P/E) ratios, position in the business cycle, and EBITDA metrics. It takes more effort and skill to understand cash creation spurred by business geography, the process of squeezing out working capital efficiencies, the accretive or diluting nature of acquisitions, and dividend policy and tax management. It's even more difficult to dig into the value created by scaling successfully to output levels larger than those of competitors. We refer to that illusive celestial place where scale economies create global purchasing and operating efficiencies. Caterpillar is a cash generator, and it is this that should occupy the attention of analysts and investors.

11. Large manufacturing firms nearly always struggle with labor costs and labor unions. The potentially adverse effects that collective bargaining can have on work rules, work stoppages, seniority, outsourcing restrictions, and legacy pension costs are real, though not always easy to measure. The authors have con-

siderable experience in the collective bargaining arena; we are comfortable in stating that Caterpillar is the best in its class in managing the collective bargaining process for the benefit of the company and its stockholders. External observers too often give short shrift to this organizational comparative advantage.

12. Financial data sites such as Bloomberg, Morningstar, and Yahoo Finance don't automatically pump out metrics that accurately reflect the strengths noted above. Thus, although Caterpillar's critical organizational assets may be acknowledged, they are not incorporated in the data sets or predictive models utilized by analysts and institutional investors unless those parties have taken the time to get to know CAT. Smaller investors nearly always follow the larger institutional pack in this regard.

Of the 12 reasons, the 4 most important in terms of differentiating Caterpillar from its contemporaries are its discipline in planning for the trough, its ability to control its costs, its lean/human resource/union optimization, and its network of dealers. Appreciate these and you will grasp the essence of Caterpillar's imposing prospects for growth. Understand their centrality and you will be a more productive manager and a more successful investor.

We do not assert that Caterpillar is the only large company that exhibits these characteristics. Very few companies, however, have excelled so clearly or for so long as has Caterpillar. Despite its status as a component of the Dow Jones Industrial Average, CAT is in the end an underappreciated company whose actual position is understood by only a few. Only a scattering of analysts and large institutional investors have come to our conclusion, primarily because most haven't taken the time to bore into Caterpillar and find out what makes it tick. Instead, many analysts trot out tired evaluations of CAT and other companies that are based on old staples such as P/E ratios and EBITDA metrics. Unfortunately, these metrics can be uninformative about some of the critical aspects of a company's real financial position, management ability, and future promise.

In Chapter 14, we presented a concise summary of our financial projections for Caterpillar in the form of the Bouchard-Koch model. In the Appendix, we provide additional detail. Those who want our full analysis (it is highly detailed) and perhaps wish to emulate this analysis for other companies should go to our book website, www.bouchardkochmodel.com.

Paying Attention to the Most Critical Things

A well-known Buddhist proverb warns, "To every man is given the key to the gates of heaven; the same key opens the gates of hell." Similar words may be found in the *Summa Theologica* of Saint Thomas Aquinas and in a number of other philosophical approaches to life. Alas, more than a few managers and investors ultimately have endured the sting presaged by the second half of this proverb. They pay attention to evaluation metrics they believe will improve their management and investment performance, but their choices lead to mediocre results and even to their financial destruction.

It is not enough to learn the lingo of managing and investing. One also must have the ability to remove largely irrelevant noise from investment markets. Revenue and earnings measures are not without value, but they don't reveal some of the most important things we need to know about a company. Measures such as EBITDA omit too much and provide some investors with a false sense of having at their fingertips unbiased metrics that enable them to compare companies on what often is labeled a level playing field. Only indirectly do such measures provide us with information about topics as diverse as a firm's financial liquidity, its skill in collective bargaining negotiations, the manner in which it obtains its inputs and manages its inventory, how it deals with unexpected change, its long-term positioning in world markets, and its management succession. Hence, on occasion, these metrics do constitute the proverbial keys to financial mediocrity or ruin.

We've also noted that the typical actively managed hedge fund does not perform as well as overall market indexes. This occurs because hedge fund managers too often make bad investment choices and tend to make too many choices overall, saddling themselves with higher transaction costs. In essence, these active traders believe they are smarter than the overall market and consequently press ahead with investment choices that too often are misguided and generate excessive switching costs. Piles of empirical evidence have accumulated that reveal retrospectively that such funds and investors would have been better off if they had simply indexed their investments to the entire market. John Bogle and other advocates of investment indexing have been right much more often than they have been wrong. Unless you have inside information and exercise it illegally or have some other advantage over other investors such as a millisecond faster ability to exercise trades, over the long term you are better off indexing your investments to the market. (The best ways to do this are well known, and Bogle's analyses are a very good place to start.)

Our model focuses on what is really important to managers and investors: cash generation and measures such as TEV/net income that tell us how productive management has been over time and how much companies actually are worth. Though these metrics help narrow down our set of choices, they do not eliminate the need for intimate knowledge of the workings of a company. They cannot foretell future events or, for example, tell us how a firm's management will react in times of crisis.

Intelligent managing and investing, then, require narrowing the set of possible choices by focusing on the appropriate metrics (cash creation, TEV, and TEV/net income) and then acquiring extensive knowledge of the inner workings of a company. But here's the reality: if you don't have that on-site knowledge, you must depend on the judgments of a trustworthy person who does. Since comparatively few financial organizations and funds have individuals who have acquired such knowledge about Caterpillar and very few individual investors are that well informed, it follows that their evaluations of Caterpillar's value as a company and share price often have been off target.

Because Caterpillar as a company has performed so well and its share price has surged so significantly in recent decades, the extent to which analysts and institutional investors have been off target (and ultimately have been too modest in their judgments) has been disguised. In fact, analysts, institutional investors, and other managers consistently have undervalued Caterpillar.

INSIDER'S EDGE   *Intelligent managing and investing require a focus on cash creation and TEV/net income. This necessarily involves acquiring intimate knowledge of a firm: its actual and potential positioning in the world, the quality and continuity of its managers and board, how it makes choices (especially when times are tough), its risk management, and the things the company culture values. If you don't know such things personally (and most of us don't), whether you are a manager or an investor, you must rely on someone who does. Some managers and financial analysts understand these realities and rely on that knowledge to make intelligent decisions and provide valuable advice. However, the lackadaisical performance of many managerial decision makers over the last two decades and the mediocre performance of mutual funds in general (and hedge funds in particular) strongly suggest that many managers and many large institutional investors ultimately do not have a command of the critical cash creation/TEV essentials. Their failure to grasp the significance of Caterpillar's achievements and their consistent undervaluing of Caterpillar's shares provide specific evidence of these inadequacies.*

Appendix

Table A.1   *Caterpillar—Bouchard-Koch Model: Total Enterprise Value Caterpillar (CAT)*

CAT Share Price over Time—Base Case
(Based on Various Total Enterprise Value to Net Income Multiples)

Multiple	FY2013P	FY2014P	FY2015P	FY2016P	FY2017P	FY2018P	FY2019P	FY2020P
23.0x	$113,713	$146,753	$178,949	$203,700	$229,919	$258,455	$289,512	$323,411
20.0x	$98,881	$127,611	$155,608	$177,131	$199,930	$224,743	$251,749	$281,227
17.0x	$84,049	$108,469	$132,266	$150,561	$169,940	$191,032	$213,987	$239,043

CAT Share Price over Time—Optimistic Case
(Based on Various Total Enterprise Value to Net Income Multiples)

Multiple	FY2013P	FY2014P	FY2015P	FY2016P	FY2017P	FY2018P	FY2019P	FY2020P
23.0x	$153,763	$219,657	$278,093	$328,705	$384,173	$445,897	$514,478	$590,630
20.0x	$133,707	$191,006	$241,820	$285,831	$334,064	$387,736	$447,372	$513,591
17.0x	$113,651	$162,355	$205,547	$242,956	$283,954	$329,576	$380,266	$436,553

CAT Share Price over Time—Downside Case
(Based on Various Total Enterprise Value to Net Income Multiples)

Multiple	FY2013P	FY2014P	FY2015P	FY2016P	FY2017P	FY2018P	FY2019P	FY2020P
23.0x	$98,607	$100,506	$98,281	$98,607	$98,659	$98,445	$97,832	$96,722
20.0x	$85,745	$87,396	$85,462	$85,745	$85,791	$85,604	$85,071	$84,106
17.0x	$72,883	$74,287	$72,642	$72,883	$72,922	$72,764	$72,311	$71,490

Table A.2 *Caterpillar—Bouchard-Koch Model: Stock Price*

CAT Share Price over Time—Base Case
(Based on Various Total Enterprise Value to Net Income Multiples)

Multiple	FY2013P	FY2014P	FY2015P	FY2016P	FY2017P	FY2018P	FY2019P	FY2020P
23.0x	$132.58	$182.25	$233.09	$277.76	$327.12	$383.42	$447.61	$521.03
20.0x	$109.22	$151.39	$194.53	$232.47	$274.39	$322.22	$376.76	$439.29
17.0x	$85.86	$120.53	$155.96	$187.18	$221.66	$261.01	$305.91	$357.55

CAT Share Price over Time—Optimistic Case
(Based on Various Total Enterprise Value to Net Income Multiples)

Multiple	FY2013P	FY2014P	FY2015P	FY2016P	FY2017P	FY2018P	FY2019P	FY2020P
23.0x	$190.37	$297.85	$406.68	$521.42	$662.01	$839.28	$1,062.83	$1,350.84
20.0x	$158.51	$250.31	$343.14	$441.05	$561.15	$712.69	$903.85	$1,150.17
17.0x	$126.66	$202.77	$279.60	$360.67	$460.29	$586.10	$744.86	$949.49

CAT Share Price over Time—Downside Case
(Based on Various Total Enterprise Value to Net Income Multiples)

Multiple	FY2013P	FY2014P	FY2015P	FY2016P	FY2017P	FY2018P	FY2019P	FY2020P
23.0x	$109.24	$111.50	$107.26	$106.90	$105.67	$103.62	$100.26	$95.49
20.0x	$89.20	$90.78	$86.83	$86.31	$85.05	$83.04	$79.80	$75.27
17.0x	$69.16	$70.06	$66.40	$65.72	$64.42	$62.46	$59.35	$55.04

Table A.3 *Caterpillar-Bouchard-Koch Model: Base Case*

CAT Share Price over Time—Base Case
(Based on Various Total Enterprise Value to Net Income Multiples)

Multiple	FY2013P	FY2014P	FY2015P	FY2016P	FY2017P	FY2018P	FY2019P	FY2020P
23.0x	$132.58	$182.25	$233.09	$277.76	$327.12	$383.42	$447.61	$521.03
20.0x	$109.22	$151.39	$194.53	$232.47	$274.39	$322.22	$376.76	$439.29
17.0x	$85.86	$120.53	$155.96	$187.18	$221.66	$261.01	$305.91	$357.55

Income Statement

FYE Dec ($ millions)	FY2009A	FY2010A	FY2011A	FY2012A	FY2013P	FY2014P
Revenues						
Machinery and Power Systems	29,544	39,932	57,431	63,115	58,258	67,086
Financial Products	3,139	2,946	3,003	3,090	3,268	3,436
less: Corporate	(287)	(290)	(296)	(330)	(308)	(353)
Total Revenue	32,396	42,588	60,138	65,875	61,218	70,169
% y/y growth	(36.9%)	31.5%	41.2%	9.5%	(7.1%)	14.6%
Gross Profit	7,465	11,307	15,734	18,023	15,304	17,542
% margin	23.0%	26.5%	26.2%	27.4%	25.0%	25.0%
EBITDA	3,866	6,342	9,691	11,517	10,178	12,389

% margin	11.9%	14.9%	16.1%	17.5%	16.6%	17.7%
less: D&A	2,336	2,296	2,527	2,813	3,310	3,434.7
EBIT	1,530	4,046	7,164	8,704	6,868	8,954
% margin	4.7%	9.5%	11.9%	13.2%	11.2%	12.8%
% incremental margin				26.8%	39.4%	23.3%
EBT	1,524	3,803	6,700	8,379	7,128	9,129
% margin	24.7%	8.9%	11.1%	12.7%	11.6%	13.0%
Taxes	(270)	968	1,720	2,528	2,174	2,739
% tax rate	(17.7%)	25.5%	25.7%	30.2%	30.5%	30.0%
Net Income	895	2,700	4,928	5,681	4,944	6,381
% margin	2.8%	6.3%	8.2%	8.62%	8.1%	9.1%
EPS	1.43	4.15	7.4	8.48	7.79	10.29
% y/y growth	(74.7%)	190.2%	78.3%	14.6%	(8.2%)	32.1%
Weighted Diluted Shares Outstanding	626.0	650.4	666.1	669.5	635.0	620.3

Table A.3 *Caterpillar-Bouchard-Koch Model: Base Case (continued)*

Income Statement						
FYE Dec ($ millions)	FY2015P	FY2016P	FY2017P	FY2018P	FY2019P	FY2020P
Revenues						
Machinery and Power Systems	75,885	81,993	88,607	95,772	103,535	111,947
Financial Products	3,996	4,498	4,952	5,451	5,999	6,602
less: Corporate	(399)	(432)	(468)	(506)	(548)	(593)
Total Revenue	79,482	86,058	93,091	100,717	108,987	117,957
% y/y growth	13.3%	8.3%	8.2%	8.2%	8.2%	8.2%
Gross Profit	19,870	21,514	23,273	25,179	27,247	29,489
% margin	25.0%	25.0%	25.0%	25.0%	25.0%	25.0%
EBITDA	14,639	16,120	17,766	19,618	21,678	23,955
% margin	18.4%	18.7%	19.1%	19.5%	19.9%	20.3%
less: D&A	3,432	3,374	3,390	3,467	3,596	3,772
EBIT	11,206	12,746	14,376	16,151	18,082	20,184
% margin	14.1%	14.8%	15.4%	16.0%	16.6%	17.1%
% incremental margin	24.2%	23.4%	23.2%	23.3%	23.4%	23.4%
EBT	11,387	12,931	14,567	16,346	18,282	20,375
% margin	14.3%	15.0%	15.6%	16.2%	16.8%	17.3%

Taxes	3,416	3,879	4,370	4,904	5,485	6,112
% tax rate	30.0%	30.0%	30.0%	30.0%	30.0%	30.0%
Net Income	7,780	8,857	9,996	11,237	12,587	14,061
% margin	9.8%	10.3%	10.7%	11.2%	11.5%	11.92%
EPS	12.85	15.10	17.58	20.40	23.62	27.25
% y/y growth	25.0%	17.4%	16.4%	16.1%	15.8%	15.4%
Weighted Diluted Shares Outstanding	605.3	586.6	568.7	550.8	533.0	516.1

Table A.3 Caterpillar-Bouchard-Koch Model: Base Case (continued)

Working Capital (ex-finance operation)						
FYE Dec ($ millions)	**FY2009A**	**FY2010A**	**FY2011A**	**FY2012A**	**FY2013P**	**FY2014P**
Net Working Capital	8,901	12,002	16,563	18,886	14,981	17,003
Investment in (Benefit from) Working Capital	(4,450)	3,101	4,561	2,323	(3,905)	2,022
Working Capital Analysis (ex-finance operation)						
Receivables Days	62 days	71 days	62 days	56 days	56 days	55 days
Inventory Days	93 days	112 days	120 days	119 days	95 days	95 days
Payables Days	44 days	68 days	67 days	52 days	50 days	50 days
Fixed Assets						
FYE Dec ($ millions)	**FY2009A**	**FY2010A**	**FY2011A**	**FY2012A**	**FY2013P**	**FY2014P**
Net PP&E	9,285	9,628	11,516	16,461	15,736	14,923
Free Cash Flow						
FYE Dec ($ millions)	**FY2009A**	**FY2010A**	**FY2011A**	**FY2012A**	**FY2013P**	**FY2014P**
Net Income	895	2,700	4,928	5,681	4,944	6,381
plus: D&A	2,275	2,220	2,294	2,813	3,786	3,619
less: Capex	(2,472)	(2,586)	(3,924)	(3,350)	(3,061)	(2,807)
less: Investment in (Benefit from) Working Capital	(4,450)	3,101	4,561	2,323	(3,905)	2,022
Free Cash Flow	5,148	(767)	(1,263)	2,821	9,574	5,171

Uses of Free Cash Flow

FYE Dec ($ millions)	FY2009A	FY2010A	FY2011A	FY2012A	FY2013P	FY2014P
Dividends					1,351	1,446
Pension Contribution					500	500
Acquisitions					1,000	1,000
Debt (Paydown)/Increase					(2,955)	0
Share Buyback					3,768	2,225

Cash and Debt

FYE Dec ($ millions)	FY2009A	FY2010A	FY2011A	FY2012A	FY2013P	FY2014P
Cash and Short-Term Investments	2,648	1,840	1,844	5,490	5,490	5,490
Total Debt (ex-Finance Operation)	6,395	5,210	9,066	10,415	7,460	7,460
Net Debt	3,747	3,370	7,222	4,925	1,970	1,970
Dividends per Share	$1.68	$1.74	$1.82	$1.99	$2.19	$2.40

Table A.3 Caterpillar-Bouchard-Koch Model: Base Case (continued)

Working Capital (ex-finance operation)

FYE Dec ($ millions)	FY2015P	FY2016P	FY2017P	FY2018P	FY2019P	FY2020P
Net Working Capital	19,069	20,385	21,888	23,440	25,103	26,813
Investment in (Benefit from) Working Capital	2,066	1,316	1,503	1,552	1,663	1,710

Working Capital Analysis (ex-finance operation)

	FY2015P	FY2016P	FY2017P	FY2018P	FY2019P	FY2020P
Receivables Days	55 days	54 days	54 days	53 days	53 days	52 days
Inventory Days	94 days	94 days	93 days	93 days	92 days	92 days
Payables Days	50 days	50 days	50 days	50 days	50 days	50 days

Fixed Assets

FYE Dec ($ millions)	FY2015P	FY2016P	FY2017P	FY2018P	FY2019P	FY2020P
Net PP&E	14,670	14,738	15,072	15,634	16,398	17,345

Free Cash Flow

FYE Dec ($ millions)	FY2015P	FY2016P	FY2017P	FY2018P	FY2019P	FY2020P
Net Income	7,780	8,857	9,996	11,237	12,587	14,061
plus: D&A	3,432	3,374	3,390	3,467	3,596	3,772
less: Capex	(3,179)	(3,442)	(3,724)	(4,029)	(4,359)	(4,718)
less: Investment in (Benefit from) Working Capital	2,066	1,316	1,503	1,552	1,663	1,710
Free Cash Flow	5,967	7,473	8,159	9,124	10,161	11,405

Uses of Free Cash Flow

FYE Dec ($ millions)	FY2015P	FY2016P	FY2017P	FY2018P	FY2019P	FY2020P
Dividends	1,545	1,640	1,741	1,846	1,956	2,073
Pension Contribution	500	500	500	500	500	500
Acquisitions	1,000	1,000	1,000	1,000	1,000	1,000
Debt (Paydown)/Increase	0	0	0	0	0	0
Share Buyback	2,922	4,333	4,919	5,778	6,705	7,424

Cash and Debt

FYE Dec ($ millions)	FY2015P	FY2016P	FY2017P	FY2018P	FY2019P	FY2020P
Cash and Short-Term Investments	5,490	5,490	5,490	5,490	5,490	5,898
Total Debt (ex-Finance Operation)	7,460	7,460	7,460	7,460	7,460	7,460
Net Debt	1,970	1,970	1,970	1,970	1,970	1,562
Dividends per Share	$2.63	$2.88	$3.15	$3.46	$3.79	$4.15

Table A.3 *Caterpillar-Bouchard-Koch Model: Base Case (continued)*

Segment Revenue						
FYE Dec ($ millions)	FY2009A	FY2010A	FY2011A	FY2012A	FY2013P	FY2014P
Machinery and Power Systems—External Sales						
Construction Industries	8,507	13,572	19,667	19,334	18,947	22,358
Resource Industries	5,857	8,667	15,629	21,158	16,926	19,465
Power Systems	13,389	15,537	20,114	21,122	21,333	24,107
All Other	1,791	2,156	2,021	1,501	1,051	1,156
Total—Machinery and Power Systems	29,544	39,932	57,431	63,115	58,258	67,086
Financial Products	3,139	2,946	3,003	3,090	3,268	3,436
Eliminations	(287)	(290)	(296)	(330)	(308)	(353)
Total Revenue	32,396	42,588	60,138	65,875	61,218	70,169
Operating Profit Before Tax						
FYE Dec ($ millions)	FY2009A	FY2010A	FY2011A	FY2012A	FY2013P	FY2014P
Machinery and Power Systems						
Construction Industries	(768)	783	2,056	1,789	1,692	2,545
Resource Industries	288	1,789	3,334	4,318	3,260	3,895
Power Systems	1,660	2,288	3,053	3,434	3,487	4,180
All Other	625	720	837	1,014	525	552
Total—Machinery and Power Systems	1,805	5,580	9,280	10,555	8,965	11,172

	FY2009A	FY2010A	FY2011A	FY2012A	FY2013P	FY2014P
Financial Products	399	429	583	741	763	785
Corporate & Consolidating Adjustments	(1,627)	(2,046)	(2,710)	(2,723)	(2,859)	(3,002)
Total Operating Profit Before Tax	577	3,963	7,153	8,573	6,868	8,954
% Margin						
Machinery and Power Systems						
Construction Industries	(9.0%)	5.8%	10.5%	9.3%	8.9%	11.4%
Resource Industries	4.9%	20.6%	21.3%	20.4%	19.3%	20.0%
Power Systems	12.4%	14.7%	15.2%	16.3%	16.3%	17.3%
All Other	34.9%	33.4%	41.4%	67.6%	50.0%	47.7%
Total—Machinery and Power Systems	6.1%	14.0%	16.2%	16.7%	15.4%	16.7%
Financial Products	12.7%	14.6%	19.4%	24.0%	23.3%	22.8%
Corporate & Consolidating Adjustments	566.9%	705.5%	915.5%	825.2%	929.4%	851.4%
Total	1.8%	9.3%	11.9%	13.0%	11.2%	12.8%

Financial Products Segment

FYE Dec	FY2009A	FY2010A	FY2011A	FY2012A	FY2013P	FY2014P
Total Receivables		22,743	24,758	27,234	25,051	28,847
Total Revenue		2,986	3,057	3,160	3,268	3,436
Operating Income		386	583	741	763	785
% margin		13%	19%	23%	23%	23%
Profit to CAT		349	453	555	574	590

Table A.3 *Caterpillar-Bouchard-Koch Model: Base Case (continued)*

Segment Revenue

FYE Dec ($ millions)	FY2015P	FY2016P	FY2017P	FY2018P	FY2019P	FY2020P
Machinery and Power Systems—External Sales						
Construction Industries	25,712	27,511	29,437	31,498	33,703	36,062
Resource Industries	22,385	23,952	25,629	27,423	29,342	31,396
Power Systems	26,517	29,169	32,086	35,294	38,824	42,706
All Other	1,271	1,360	1,456	1,557	1,666	1,783
Total—Machinery and Power Systems	75,885	81,993	88,607	95,772	103,535	111,947
Financial Products	3,996	4,498	4,952	5,451	5,999	6,602
Eliminations	(399)	(432)	(468)	(506)	(548)	(593)
Total Revenue	79,482	86,058	93,091	100,717	108,987	117,957

Operating Profit Before Tax

FYE Dec ($ millions)	FY2015P	FY2016P	FY2017P	FY2018P	FY2019P	FY2020P
Machinery and Power Systems						
Construction Industries	3,383	3,833	4,315	4,830	5,381	5,971
Resource Industries	4,625	5,017	5,436	5,884	6,364	6,878
Power Systems	4,783	5,446	6,175	6,977	7,859	8,830
All Other	581	603	627	652	679	708
Total—Machinery and Power Systems	13,371	14,898	16,552	18,343	20,284	22,387

	FY2015P	FY2016P	FY2017P	FY2018P	FY2019P	FY2020P
Financial Products	987	1,157	1,300	1,457	1,630	1,820
Corporate & Consolidating Adjustments	(3,152)	(3,310)	(3,475)	(3,649)	(3,832)	(4,023)
Total Operating Profit Before Tax	11,206	12,746	14,376	16,151	18,082	20,184
% Margin						
Machinery and Power Systems						
Construction Industries	13.2%	13.9%	14.7%	15.3%	16.0%	16.6%
Resource Industries	20.7%	20.9%	21.2%	21.5%	21.7%	21.9%
Power Systems	18.0%	18.7%	19.2%	19.8%	20.2%	20.7%
All Other	45.7%	44.3%	43.0%	41.9%	40.8%	39.7%
Total—Machinery and Power Systems	17.6%	18.2%	18.7%	19.2%	19.6%	20.0%
Financial Products	24.7%	25.7%	26.2%	26.7%	27.2%	27.6%
Corporate & Consolidating Adjustments	789.2%	765.4%	742.9%	721.0%	699.6%	678.7%
Total	14.1%	14.8%	15.4%	16.0%	16.6%	17.1%

Financial Products Segment

FYE Dec	FY2015P	FY2016P	FY2017P	FY2018P	FY2019P	FY2020P
Total Receivables	32,631	35,257	38,101	41,182	44,520	48,137
Total Revenue	3,996	4,498	4,952	5,451	5,999	6,602
Operating Income	987	1,157	1,300	1,457	1,630	1,820
% margin	25%	26%	26%	27%	27%	28%
Profit to CAT	735	857	958	1,071	1,194	1,331

Table A.4   *Caterpillar-Bouchard-Koch Model: Optimistic Case*

CAT Share Price over Time—Optimistic Case
(Based on Various Total Enterprise Value to Net Income Multiples)

Multiple	FY2013P	FY2014P	FY2015P	FY2016P	FY2017P	FY2018P	FY2019P	FY2020P
23.0x	$190.37	$297.85	$406.68	$521.42	$662.01	$839.28	$1,062.83	$1,350.84
20.0x	$158.51	$250.31	$343.14	$441.05	$561.15	$712.69	$903.85	$1,150.17
17.0x	$126.66	$202.77	$279.60	$360.67	$460.29	$586.10	$744.86	$949.49

Income Statement

FYE Dec ($ millions)	FY2009A	FY2010A	FY2011A	FY2012A	FY2013P	FY2014P
Revenues						
Machinery and Power Systems	29,544	39,932	57,431	63,115	66,468	79,675
Financial Products	3,139	2,946	3,003	3,090	3,488	4,006
less: Corporate	(287)	(290)	(296)	(330)	(350)	(418)
Total Revenue	32,396	42,588	60,138	65,875	69,607	83,263
% y/y growth	(36.9%)	31.5%	41.2%	9.5%	5.7%	19.6%
Gross Profit	7,465	11,307	15,734	18,023	17,402	20,816
% margin	23.0%	26.5%	26.2%	27.4%	25.0%	25.0%
EBITDA	3,866	6,342	9,691	11,517	12,669	16,886

% margin	11.9%	14.9%	16.1%	17.5%	18.2%	20.3%
less: D&A	2,336	2,296	2,527	2,813	3,310	3,434.7
EBIT	1,530	4,046	7,164	8,704	9,359	13,451
% margin	4.7%	9.5%	11.9%	13.2%	13.4%	16.2%
% incremental margin				26.8%	17.5%	30.0%
EBT	1,524	3,803	6,700	8,379	9,634	13,658
% margin	24.7%	8.9%	11.1%	12.7%	13.8%	16.4%
Taxes	(270)	968	1,720	2,528	2,938	4,097
% tax rate	(17.7%)	25.5%	25.7%	30.2%	30.5%	30.0%
Net Income	895	2,700	4,928	5,681	6,685	9,550
% margin	2.8%	6.3%	8.2%	8.62%	9.6%	11.5%
EPS	1.43	4.15	7.4	8.48	10.62	15.85
% y/y growth	(74.7%)	190.2%	78.3%	14.6%	25.2%	49.2%
Weighted Diluted Shares Outstanding	626.0	650.4	666.1	669.5	629.6	602.7

Table A.4 *Caterpillar-Bouchard-Koch Model: Optimistic Case (continued)*

Income Statement							
FYE Dec ($ millions)	FY2015P	FY2016P	FY2017P	FY2018P	FY2019P	FY2020P
Revenues							
Machinery and Power Systems	91,914	101,687	112,508	124,489	137,756	152,448
Financial Products	4,796	5,515	6,217	7,006	7,894	8,891
less: Corporate	(484)	(536)	(594)	(657)	(728)	(807)
Total Revenue	96,226	106,666	118,131	130,838	144,921	160,532
% y/y growth	15.6%	10.8%	10.7%	10.8%	10.8%	10.8%
Gross Profit	24,056	26,667	29,533	32,709	36,230	40,133
% margin	25.0%	25.0%	25.0%	25.0%	25.0%	25.0%
EBITDA	21,005	24,203	27,781	31,812	36,333	41,386
% margin	21.8%	22.7%	23.5%	24.3%	25.1%	25.8%
less: D&A	3,627	3,678	3,814	4,023	4,302	4,645
EBIT	17,378	20,525	23,967	27,789	32,031	36,741
% margin	18.3%	19.4%	20.5%	21.4%	22.2%	22.9%
% incremental margin	30.3%	30.1%	30.0%	30.1%	30.1%	30.2%
EBT	17,591	20,744	24,180	27,974	32,176	36,837
% margin	18.3%	19.4%	20.5%	21.4%	22.2%	22.9%

Taxes	5,277	6,223	7,254	8,392	9,653	11,051
% tax rate	30.0%	30.0%	30.0%	30.0%	30.0%	30.0%
Net Income	12,091	14,292	16,703	19,387	22,369	25,680
% margin	12.6%	13.4%	14.1%	14.8%	15.4%	16.00%
EPS	2L18	26.79	33.62	42.20	53.00	66.89
% y/y growth	33.7%	26.5%	25.5%	25.5%	25.6%	26.2%
Weighted Diluted Shares Outstanding	570.8	533.4	496.8	459.4	422.1	383.9

Table A.4 *Caterpillar-Bouchard-Koch Model: Optimistic Case (continued)*

Working Capital (ex-finance operation)							
FYE Dec ($ millions)	FY2009A	FY2010A	FY2011A	FY2012A	FY2013P	FY2014P	
Net Working Capital	8,901	12,002	16,563	18,886	16,223	19,178	
Investment in (Benefit from) Working Capital	(4,450)	3,101	4,561	2,323	(2,663)	2,955	
Working Capital Analysis (ex-finance operation)							
Receivables Days	62 days	71 days	62 days	56 days	55 days	54 days	
Inventory Days	93 days	112 days	120 days	119 days	90 days	90 days	
Payables Days	44 days	68 days	67 days	52 days	50 days	50 days	
Fixed Assets							
FYE Dec ($ millions)	FY2009A	FY2010A	FY2011A	FY2012A	FY2013P	FY2014P	
Net PP&E	9,285	9,628	11,516	16,461	16,155	15,77	
Free Cash Flow							
FYE Dec ($ millions)	FY2009A	FY2010A	FY2011A	FY2012A	FY2013P	FY2014P	
Net Income	895	2,700	4,928	5,681	6,685	9,550	
plus: D&A	2,275	2,220	2,294	2,813	3,786	3,716	
less: Capex	(2,472)	(2,586)	(3,924)	(3,350)	(3,480)	(3,331)	
less: Investment in (Benefit from) Working Capital	(4,450)	3,101	4,561	2,323	(2,663)	2,955	
Free Cash Flow	5,148	(767)	(1,263)	2,821	9,654	6,981	

Uses of Free Cash Flow

FYE Dec ($ millions)	FY2009A	FY2010A	FY2011A	FY2012A	FY2013P	FY2014P
Dividends					1,339	1,404
Pension Contribution					500	500
Acquisitions					1,000	1,000
Debt (Paydown)/Increase					(2,456)	0
Share Buyback					4,358	4,077

Cash and Debt

FYE Dec ($ millions)	FY2009A	FY2010A	FY2011A	FY2012A	FY2013P	FY2014P
Cash and Short-Term Investments	2,648	1,840	1,844	5,490	5,490	5,490
Total Debt (ex-Finance Operation)	6,395	5,210	9,066	10,415	7,959	7,959
Net Debt	3,747	3,370	7,222	4,925	2,469	2,469
Dividends per Share	$1.68	$1.74	$1.82	$1.99	$2.19	$2.40

Table A.4 *Caterpillar-Bouchard-Koch Model: Optimistic Case (continued)*

Working Capital (ex-finance operation)						
FYE Dec ($ millions)	FY2015P	FY2016P	FY2017P	FY2018P	FY2019P	FY2020P
Net Working Capital	21,900	23,919	26,238	28,702	31,764	35,089
Investment in (Benefit from) Working Capital	2,722	2,018	2,320	2,464	3,061	3,325
Working Capital Analysis (ex-finance operation)						
Receivables Days	53 days	52 days	51 days	50 days	50 days	50 days
Inventory Days	90 days	90 days	90 days	90 days	90 days	90 days
Payables Days	50 days	50 days	50 days	50 days	50 days	50 days
Fixed Assets						
FYE Dec ($ millions)	FY2015P	FY2016P	FY2017P	FY2018P	FY2019P	FY2020P
Net PP&E	15,992	16,580	17,492	18,703	20,198	21,974
Free Cash Flow						
FYE Dec ($ millions)	FY2015P	FY2016P	FY2017P	FY2018P	FY2019P	FY2020P
Net Income	12,091	14,292	16,703	19,387	22,369	25,680
plus: D&A	3,627	3,678	3,814	4,023	4,302	4,645
less: Capex	(3,849)	(4,267)	(4,725)	(5,234)	(5,797)	(6,421)
less: Investment in (Benefit from) Working Capital	2,722	2,018	2,320	2,464	3,061	3,325
Free Cash Flow	9,147	11,685	13,472	15,713	17,812	20,578

Uses of Free Cash Flow

FYE Dec ($ millions)	FY2015P	FY2016P	FY2017P	FY2018P	FY2019P	FY2020P
Dividends	1,455	1,487	1,514	1,530	1,535	1,524
Pension Contribution	500	500	500	500	500	500
Acquisitions	1,000	1,000	1,000	1,000	1,000	1,000
Debt (Paydown)/Increase	0	0	0	0	0	0
Share Buyback	6,192	8,698	10,041	12,047	14,072	16,774

Cash and Debt

FYE Dec ($ millions)	FY2015P	FY2016P	FY2017P	FY2018P	FY2019P	FY2020P
Cash and Short-Term Investments	5,490	5,490	5,907	6,542	7,246	8,027
Total Debt (ex-Finance Operation)	7,959	7,959	7,959	7,959	7,959	7,959
Net Debt	2,469	2,469	2,052	1,417	713	(68)
Dividends per Share	$263	$2.88	$3.15	$3.46	$3.79	$4.15

Table A.4 *Caterpillar-Bouchard-Koch Model: Optimistic Case (continued)*

Segment Revenue

FYE Dec ($ millions)	FY2009A	FY2010A	FY2011A	FY2012A	FY2013P	FY2014P
Machinery and Power Systems—External Sales						
Construction Industries	8,507	13,572	19,667	19,334	20,301	24,361
Resource Industries	5,857	8,667	15,629	21,158	22,216	27,770
Power Systems	13,389	15,537	20,114	21,122	22,601	25,991
All Other	1,791	2,156	2,021	1,501	1,351	1,554
Total—Machinery and Power Systems	29,544	39,932	57,431	63,115	66,468	79,675
Financial Products	3,139	2,946	3,003	3,090	3,488	4,006
Eliminations	(287)	(290)	(296)	(330)	(350)	(418)
Total Revenue	32,396	42,588	60,138	65,875	69,607	83,263

Operating Profit Before Tax

FYE Dec ($ millions)	FY2009A	FY2010A	FY2011A	FY2012A	FY2013P	FY2014P
Machinery and Power Systems						
Construction Industries	(768)	783	2,056	1,789	2,079	3,297
Resource Industries	288	1,789	3,334	4,318	4,635	6,302
Power Systems	1,660	2,288	3,053	3,434	3,878	4,895
All Other	625	720	837	1,014	675	736
Total—Machinery and Power Systems	1,805	5,580	9,280	10,555	11,267	15,229

	FY2009A	FY2010A	FY2011A	FY2012A	FY2013P	FY2014P
Financial Products	399	429	583	741	869	1,054
Corporate & Consolidating Adjustments	(1,627)	(2,046)	(2,710)	(2,723)	(2,777)	(2,833)
Total Operating Profit Before Tax	577	3,963	7,153	8,573	9,359	13,451
% Margin						
Machinery and Power Systems						
Construction Industries	(9.0%)	5.8%	10.5%	9.3%	102%	13.5%
Resource Industries	4.9%	20.6%	21.3%	20.4%	20.9%	227%
Power Systems	12.4%	14.7%	15.2%	16.3%	17.2°/o	18.8%
All Other	34.9%	33.4%	41.4%	67.6%	50.0%	47.4%
Total—Machinery and Power Systems	6.1%	14.0%	16.2%	16.7%	17.0%	19.1%
Financial Products	12.7%	14.6%	19.4%	24.0%.	24.9%	26.3%
Corporate & Consolidating Adjustments	566.9%	705.5%	915.5%	825.2%	794.1%	677.1%
Total	1.8%	9.3%	11.9%	13.0%	13.4%	16.2%

Financial Products Segment

FYE Dec	FY2009A	FY2010A	FY2011A	FY2012A	FY2013P	FY2014P
Total Receivables		22,743	24,758	27,234	28,581	34,260
Total Revenue		2,986	3,057	3,160	3,488	4,006
Operating Income		386	583	741	869	1,054
% margin		13%	19%	23%	2 5%	26%
Profit to CAT		349	453	555	650	783

Table A.4 *Caterpillar-Bouchard-Koch Model: Optimistic Case (continued)*

Segment Revenue

FYE Dec ($ millions)	FY2015P	FY2016P	FY2017P	FY2018P	FY2019P	FY2020P
Machinery and Power Systems—External Sales						
Construction Industries	27,771	30,548	33,603	36,964	40,660	44,726
Resource Industries	33,324	36,656	40,322	44,354	48,789	53,668
Power Systems	29,109	32,603	36,515	40,897	45,804	51,301
All Other	1,709	1,880	2,068	2,275	2,502	2,752
Total—Machinery and Power Systems	91,914	101,687	112,508	124,489	137,756	152,448
Financial Products	4,796	5,515	6,217	7,006	7,894	8,891
Eliminations	(484)	(536)	(594)	(657)	(728)	(807)
Total Revenue	96,226	106,666	118,131	130,838	144,921	160,532

Operating Profit Before Tax

FYE Dec ($ millions)	FY2015P	FY2016P	FY2017P	FY2018P	FY2019P	FY2020P
Machinery and Power Systems						
Construction Industries	4,320	5,153	6,070	7,078	8,187	9,407
Resource Industries	7,968	8,967	10,067	11,277	12,607	14,071
Power Systems	5,830	6,878	8,052	9,366	10,839	12,488
All Other	783	834	891	953	1,021	1,096
Total—Machinery and Power Systems	18,901	21,833	25,079	28,674	32,654	37,061

	FY2015P	FY2016P	FY2017P	FY2018P	FY2019P	FY2020P
Financial Products	1,367	1,639	1,894	2,182	2,506	2,870
Corporate & Consolidating Adjustments	2,890	(2,947)	(3,006)	(3,067)	(3,128)	(3,190)
Total Operating Profit Before Tax	17,378	20,525	23,967	27,789	32,031	36,741
% Margin						
Machinery and Power Systems						
Construction Industries	15.6%	16.9%	18.1%	19.1%	20.1%	21.0%
Resource Industries	23.9%	24.5%	25.0%	25.4%	25.8%	262%
Power Systems	20.0%	21.1%	22.1%	22.9%	23.7%	24.3%
All Other	45.8%	44.4%	43.1%	41.9%	40.8%	39.8%
Total—Machinery and Power Systems	20.6%	21.5%	22.3%	23.0%	23.7%	24.3%
Financial Products	28.5%	29.7%	30.5%	31.1%	31.7%	323%
Corporate & Consolidating Adjustments	597.6%	549.9%	506.5%	466.4%	429.5%	395.5%
Total	18.1%	19.2%	20.3%	21.2%	22.1%	22.9%

Financial Products Segment

FYE Dec	FY2015P	FY2016P	FY2017P	FY2018P	FY2019P	FY2020P
Total Receivables	39,523	43,725	48,378	53,530	59,235	65,552
Total Revenue	4,796	5,515	6,217	7,006	7,894	8,891
Operating Income	1,367	1,639	1,894	2,182	2,506	2,870
% margin	29%	30%	30%	31%	32%	32%
Profit to CAT	1,007	1,201	1,384	1,589	1,821	2,082

Table A.5 *Caterpillar-Bouchard-Koch Model: Downside Case*

CAT Share Price over Time—Downside Case
(Based on Various Total Enterprise Value to Net Income Multiples)

Multiple	FY2013P	FY2014P	FY2015P	FY2016P	FY2017P	FY2018P	FY2019P	FY2020P
23.0x	$109.24	$111.50	$107.26	$106.90	$105.67	$103.62	$100.26	$95.49
20.0x	$89.20	$90.78	$86.83	$86.31	$85.05	$83.04	$79.80	$75.27
17.0x	$69.16	$70.06	$66.40	$65.72	$64.42	$62.46	$59.35	$55.04

Income Statement

FYE Dec ($ millions)	FY2009A	FY2010A	FY2011A	FY2012A	FY2013P	FY2014P
Revenues						
Machinery and Power Systems	29,544	39,932	57,431	63,115	56,029	59,130
Financial Products	3,139	2,946	3,003	3,090	3,208	3,157
less: Corporate	(287)	(290)	(296)	(330)	(296)	(311)
Total Revenue	32,396	42,588	60,138	65,875	58,941	61,975
% y/y growth	(36.9%)	31.5%	41.2%	9.5%	(10.5%)	5.1%
Gross Profit	7,465	11,307	15,734	18,023	14,735	15,494
% margin	23.0%	26.5%	26.2%	27.4%	25.0%	25.0%
EBITDA	3,866	6,342	9,691	11,517	9,232	9,514

% margin	11.9%	14.9%	16.1%	17.5%	15.7%	15.4%
less: D&A	2,336	2,296	2,527	2,813	3,310	3,434.7
EBIT	1,530	4,046	7,164	8,704	5,922	6,080
% margin	4.7%	9.5%	11.9%	13.2%	10.0%	9.8%
% incremental margin				26.8%	40.1%	5.2%
EBT	1,524	3,803	6,700	8,379	6,183	6,,57
% margin	24.7%	8.9%	11.1%	12.7%	10.5%	10.1%
Taxes	(270)	968	1,720	2,528	1,886	1,877
% tax rate	(17.7%)	25.5%	25.7%	30.2%	30.5%	30.0%
Net Income	895	2,700	4,928	5,681	4,287	4,370
% margin	2.8%	6.3%	8.2%	8.62%	7.3%	7.1%
EPS	1.43	4.15	7.4	8.48	6.68	6.91
% y/y growth	(74.7%)	190.2%	78.3%	14.6%	(21.2%)	49.2%
Weighted Diluted Shares Outstanding	626.0	650.4	666.1	669.5	641.8	632.6

Table A.5 *Caterpillar-Bouchard-Koch Model: Downside Case (continued)*

Income Statement						
FYE Dec ($ millions)	FY2015P	FY2016P	FY2017P	FY2018P	FY2019P	FY2020P
Revenues						
Machinery and Power Systems	61,244	63,081	64,973	66,923	68,930	70,998
Financial Products	3,364	3,542	3,717	3,899	4,089	4,287
less: Corporate	(323)	(333)	(343)	(354)	(365)	(376)
Total Revenue	64,285	66,290	68,347	70,468	72,654	74,909
% y/y growth	3.7%	3.1%	3.1%	3.1%	3.1%	3.1%
Gross Profit	16,071	16,572	17,087	17,617	18,164	18,727
% margin	25.0%	25.0%	25.0%	25.0%	25.0%	25.0%
EBITDA	9,534	9,380	9,268	9,188	9,128	9,078
% margin	14.8%	14.1%	13.6%	13.0%	12.6%	12.1%
less: D&A	3,337	3,161	3,044	2,972	2,937	2,930
EBIT	6,197	6,219	6,225	6,216	6,191	6,148
% margin	9.6%	9.4%	9.1%	8.8%	8.5%	8.2%
% incremental margin	5.1%	1.1%	0.3%	(0.4%)	(1.1%)	(1.9%)
EBT	6,379	6,406	6,417	6,418	6,424	6,443
% margin	9.9%	9.7%	9.4%	9.1%	8.8%	8.6%

Taxes	1,914	1,922	1,925	1,925	1,927	1,933
% tax rate	30.0%	30.0%	30.0%	30.0%	30.0%	30.0%
Net Income	4,273	4,287	4,290	4,280	4,254	4,205
% margin	6.6%	6.5%	6.3%	6.1%	5.9%	5.61%
EPS	6.81	6.86	6.88	6.86	6.82	6.74
% y/y growth	(1.4%)	0.8%	0.2%	(0.2%)	(0.6%)	(1.1%)
Weighted Diluted Shares Outstanding	627.6	624.6	623.9	623.9	623.9	623.9

Table A.5 Caterpillar-Bouchard-Koch Model: Downside Case*(continued)*

Working Capital (ex-finance operation)

FYE Dec ($ millions)	FY2009A	FY2010A	FY2011A	FY2012A	FY2013P	FY2014P
Net Working Capital	8,901	12,002	16,563	18,886	15,191	16,312
Investment in (Benefit from) Working Capital	(4,450)	3,101	4,561	2,323	(3,695)	1,122

Working Capital Analysis (ex-finance operation)

	FY2009A	FY2010A	FY2011A	FY2012A	FY2013P	FY2014P
Receivables Days	62 days	71 days	62 days	56 days	57 days	57 days
Inventory Days	93 days	112 days	120 days	119 days	100 days	101 days
Payables Days	44 days	68 days	67 days	52 days	50 days	49 days

Fixed Assets

FYE Dec ($ millions)	FY2009A	FY2010A	FY2011A	FY2012A	FY2013P	FY2014P
Net PP&E	9,285	9,628	11,516	16,461	15,622	14,508

Free Cash Flow

FYE Dec ($ millions)	FY2009A	FY2010A	FY2011A	FY2012A	FY2013P	FY2014P
Net Income	895	2,700	4,928	5,681	4,287	4,370
plus: D&A	2,275	2,220	2,294	2,813	3,786	3,593
less: Capex	(2,472)	(2,586)	(3,924)	(3,350)	(2,947)	(2,479)
less: Investment in (Benefit from) Working Capital	(4,450)	3,101	4,561	2,323	(3,695)	1,122
Free Cash Flow	5,148	(767)	(1,263)	2,821	8,821	4,362

Uses of Free Cash Flow

FYE Dec ($ millions)	FY2009A	FY2010A	FY2011A	FY2012A	FY2013P	FY2014P
Dividends					1,366	1,475
Pension Contribution					500	500
Acquisitions					1,000	1,000
Debt (Paydown)/Increase					(2,926)	0
Share Buyback					3,029	1,387

Cash and Debt

FYE Dec ($ millions)	FY2009A	FY2010A	FY2011A	FY2012A	FY2013P	FY2014P
Cash and Short-Term Investments	2,648	1,840	1,844	5,490	5,490	5,490
Total Debt (ex-Finance Operation)	6,395	5,210	9,066	10,415	7,489	7,489
Net Debt	3,747	3,370	7,222	4,925	1,999	1,999
Dividends per Share	$1.68	$1.74	$1.82	$1.99	$2.19	$2.40

Table A.5 *Caterpillar-Bouchard-Koch Model: Downside Case (continued)*

Working Capital (ex-finance operation)						
FYE Dec ($ millions)	FY2015P	FY2016P	FY2017P	FY2018P	FY2019P	FY2020P
Net Working Capital	17,273	18,125	19,113	20,092	21,114	22,119
Investment in (Benefit from) Working Capital	960	852	988	979	1,022	1,005

Working Capital Analysis (ex-finance operation)						
Receivables Days	58 days	58 days	59 days	59 days	60 days	60 days
Inventory Days	102 days	103 days	104 days	105 days	106 days	107 days
Payables Days	48 days	47 days	46 days	45 days	44 days	43 days

Fixed Assets						
FYE Dec ($ millions)	FY2015P	FY2016P	FY2017P	FY2018P	FY2019P	FY2020P
Net PP&E	13,743	13,233	12,924	12,770	12,7391	12,805

Free Cash Flow						
FYE Dec ($ millions)	FY2015P	FY2016P	FY2017P	FY2018P	FY2019P	FY2020P
Net Income	4,273	4,287	4,290	4,280	4,254	4,205
plus: D&A	3,337	3,161	3,044	2,972	2,937	2,930
less: Capex	(2,571)	(2,652)	(2,734)	(2,819)	(2,906)	(2,996)
less: Investment in (Benefit from) Working Capital	960	852	988	979	1,022	1,005
Free Cash Flow	4,078	3,944	3,611	3,455	3,263	3,134

Uses of Free Cash Flow

FYE Dec ($ millions)	FY2015P	FY2016P	FY2017P	FY2018P	FY2019P	FY2020P
Dividends	1,604	1,749	1,915	2,099	2,300	2,521
Pension Contribution	500	500	500	500	500	500
Acquisitions	1,000	1,000	1,000	1,000	1,000	1,000
Debt (Paydown)/Increase	0	0	0	0 144	537	887
Share Buyback	975	695	196	0	0	0

Cash and Debt

FYE Dec ($ millions)	FY2015P	FY2016P	FY2017P	FY2018P	FY2019P	FY2020P
Cash and Short-Term Investments	5,490	5,490	5,907	6,542	7,246	8,027
Total Debt (ex-Finance Operation)	7,489	7,489	7,489	7,633	8,170	9,057
Net Debt	1,999	1,999	1,999	2,143	2,680	3,567
Dividends per Share	$263	$2.88	$3.15	$3.46	$3.79	$4.15

Table A.5 *Caterpillar-Bouchard-Koch Model: Downside Case (continued)*

Segment Revenue							
FYE Dec ($ millions)	**FY2009A**	**FY2010A**	**FY2011A**	**FY2012A**	**FY2013P**	**FY2014P**
Machinery and Power Systems—External Sales							
Construction Industries	8,507	13,572	19,667	19,334	18,561	19,489
Resource Industries	5,857	8,667	15,629	21,158	15,869	16,979
Power Systems	13,389	15,537	20,114	21,122	20,700	21,735
All Other	1,791	2,156	2,021	1,501	901	928
Total—Machinery and Power Systems	29,544	39,932	57,431	63,115	56,029	59,130
Financial Products	3,139	2,946	3,003	3,090	3,208	3,157
Eliminations	(287)	(290)	(296)	(330)	(296)	(311)
Total Revenue	32,396	42,588	60,138	65,875	58,941	61,975

Operating Profit Before Tax							
FYE Dec ($ millions)	**FY2009A**	**FY2010A**	**FY2011A**	**FY2012A**	**FY2013P**	**FY2014P**
Machinery and Power Systems							
Construction Industries	(768)	783	2,056	1,789	1,615	1,698
Resource Industries	288	1,789	3,334	4,318	2,698	2,920
Power Systems	1,660	2,288	3,053	3,434	3,366	3,532
All Other	625	720	837	1,014	450	451
Total—Machinery and Power Systems	1,805	5,580	9,280	10,555	8,129	8,601

	FY2009A	FY2010A	FY2011A	FY2012A	FY2013P	FY2014P
Financial Products	399	429	583	741	734	654
Corporate & Consolidating Adjustments	(1,627)	(2,046)	(2,710)	(2,723)	(2,941)	(3,176)
Total Operating Profit Before Tax	577	3,963	7,153	8,573	5,922	6,080
% Margin						
Machinery and Power Systems						
Construction Industries	(9.0%)	5.8%	10.5%	9.3%	8.7%	8.7%
Resource Industries	4.9%	20.6%	21.3%	20.4%	17.0%	17.2%
Power Systems	12.4%	14.7%	15.2%	16.3%	16.3%	16.3%
All Other	34.9%	33.4%	41.4%	67.6%	50.0%	48.7%
Total—Machinery and Power Systems	6.1%	14.0%	16.2%	16.7%	14.5%	14.5%
Financial Products	12.7%	14.6%	19.4%	24.0%	22.9%	20.7%
Corporate & Consolidating Adjustments	566.9%	705.5%	915.5%	825.2%	992.9%	1019.8%
Total	1.8%	9.3%	11.9%	13.0%	10.0%	9.8%

Financial Products Segment

FYE Dec	FY2009A	FY2010A	FY2011A	FY2012A	FY2013P	FY2014P
Total Receivables		22,743	24,758	27,234	24,093	25,426
Total Revenue		2,986	3,057	3,160	3,208	3,157
Operating Income		386	583	741	734	654
% margin		13%	19%	23%	23%	21%
Profit to CAT		349	453	555	554	497

Table A.5 *Caterpillar-Bouchard-Koch Model: Downside Case (continued)*

Segment Revenue						
FYE Dec ($ millions)	FY2015P	FY2016P	FY2017P	FY2018P	FY2019P	FY2020P
Machinery and Power Systems—External Sales						
Construction Industries	20,073	20,676	21,296	21,935	22,593	23,270
Resource Industries	17,828	18,363	18,914	19,481	20,066	20,668
Power Systems	22,387	23,058	23,750	24,462	25,196	25,952
All Other	955	984	1,014	1,044	1,075	1,108
Total—Machinery and Power Systems	61,244	63,081	64,973	66,923	68,930	70,998
Financial Products	3,364	3,542	3,717	3,899	4,089	4,287
Eliminations	(323)	(333)	(343)	(354)	(365)	(376)
Total Revenue	64,285	66,290	68,347	70,468	72,654	74,909
Operating Profit Before Tax						
FYE Dec ($ millions)	FY2015P	FY2016P	FY2017P	FY2018P	FY2019P	FY2020P
Machinery and Power Systems						
Construction Industries	1,751	1,805	1,861	1,918	1,978	2,039
Resource Industries	3,090	3,197	3,307	3,420	3,537	3,658
Power Systems	3,636	3,744	3,854	3,968	4,086	4,207
All Other	452	454	455	456	457	459
Total—Machinery and Power Systems	8,929	9,199	9,477	9,763	10,058	10,362

	FY2015P	FY2016P	FY2017P	FY2018P	FY2019P	FY2020P
Financial Products	698	725	749	773	800	827
Corporate & Consolidating Adjustments	(3,430)	(3,705)	(4,001)	(4,321)	(4,667)	(5,040)
Total Operating Profit Before Tax	6,197	6,219	6,225	6,216	6,191	6,148
% Margin						
Machinery and Power Systems						
Construction Industries	8.7%	8.7%	8.7%	8.7%	8.8%	8.8%
Resource Industries	17.3%/o	17.4%	17.5%	17.6%	17.6%	17.7%
Power Systems	162%	162%	162%	162%	162%	162%
All Other	47.4%	46.1%	44.9%	43.7%	42.5%	41.4%
Total—Machinery and Power Systems	14.6%	14.6%	14.6%	14.6%	14.6%	14.6%
Financial Products	20.7%	20.5%	20.1%	19.8%	19.6%	19.3%
Corporate & Consolidating Adjustments	106.8%	1112.1%	1164.9%	1220.3%	1278.2%	1338.9%
Total	9.6%	9.4%	9.1%	8.8%	8.5%	8.2%

Financial Products Segment

FYE Dec	FY2015P	FY2016P	FY2017P	FY2018P	FY2019P	FY2020P
Total Receivables	26,335	27,125	27,939	28,777	29,640	30,529
Total Revenue	3,364	3,542	3,717	3,899	4,089	4,287
Operating Income	698	725	749	773	800	827
% margin	21%	20%	20%	20%	20%	19%
Profit to CAT	528	547	564	582	601	620

Notes

Chapter 1

Page 1. But things . . . Caterpillar lost $1.17 million
Caterpillar financial loss in 1984: Caterpillar Annual Report 1984.

Page 1. However, turn things . . . Caterpillar was ranked
Caterpillar's number 46 Fortune 500 ranking: http://money.cnn.com /magazines/fortune/fortune500/2012/full_list.

Page 1. However, turn things . . . Its composite revenues
Caterpillar sales and dividend increases: Caterpillar annual reports.

Page 2. However, turn things . . . In November 2012
Caterpillar size relative to John Deere and Komatsu: www.finance.yahoo.com (accessed November 10, 2012). Data are for the trailing 12 months.

Page 3. Between January 2, 2001
Caterpillar share prices and dividends per share: Caterpillar annual reports.

Page 3. Hanging like a cloud . . . unemployed or underemployed in June 2014.
14.3% unemployed or underemployed: This was the U6 unemployment rate of the Bureau of Labor Statistics in June 2013, Table A-15, "Alternative Measures of Labor Underutilization," www.bls.gov/news.release/enosut.t15.htm.

Page 3. Some have responded bravely . . . only 8 percent of new businesses
Only 8 percent of new firms reach 29 employees within 10 years: "Why Washington Has It Wrong," *Wall Street Journal*, 259 (November 12, 2012), R1.

Page 4. James Tobin and Harry Markowitz are academic titans
James Tobin and Harry Markowitz: See James Tobin, http://en.wikipedia .org/wiki/James_Tobin, and Harry Markowitz, http://en.wikipedia.org /wiki/Harry_Markowitz.

Page 7. Take a peak at your 401(k) . . . the S&P 500 stock index
S&P 500 values: www.finance.yahoo.com (accessed January 15, 2013).

Page 7. Take a peak at your 401(k) . . . the consumer price index
See www.bls.gov.

Page 7. [Sidebar] Bad Management Makes a Difference . . . a company involved in generating electronic power
On Montana Power: a good summary can be found at www.answers.com/ topic/the-montana-power-company.

Page 7. The moral of the story? . . . yielded only 3.683 percent.
On yields: http://online.wsj.com/mdc/public/page/mdc_bonds.html?refresh =on (accessed July 10, 2014).

Page 8. There have been changes . . . the 2008 demise of Washington Mutual
"Washington Mutual," *New York Times* (October 11, 2011), www.nytimes .com.

Page 8. There have been changes . . . the meltdown
On Montana Power: www.answers.com/topic/the-montana-power-company.

Page 8. There have been changes . . . the sudden disappearance of Wall Street's Lehman Brothers
Lehman Brothers: "Lehman Brothers Holdings, Inc.," *New York Times* (April 4, 2012), www.nytimes.com.

Page 8. There have been changes . . . the bursting of the real estate price bubble
Declining real estate values: *Wall Street Journal*, 259 (September 21, 2012), A2; re net worth: Pew Research Center, "Wealth Gaps Rise to Record Highs Between Whites, Blacks and Hispanics," (Washington, DC: Pew Foundation, 2012).

Page 8. Meanwhile, investments . . . The average equity that homeowners held
Household equity in homes: A. Gary Shilling, September 12, 2012, http:// www.bloomberg.com/view/bios/gary-shilling/2.

Page 8. Meanwhile, investments . . . to only $93,150 in 2010
Pew Foundation on household net worth: Richard Fry and Paul Taylor, "A Rise in Wealth for the Wealthy: Declines for the Lower 93%," *Pew Research Social & Demographic Trends* (April 23, 2013), www.pewsocialtrends.org /2013/04/23/a-rise-in-wealth-for-the-wealthydeclines-for-the-lower-93.

Page 8. Contrast these dismal results . . . the performance of Caterpillar
Caterpillar stock prices: www.finance.yahoo.com (accessed January 15, 2013).

Page 8. Compare these dismal results . . . about 2.3 percent annually
Caterpillar average dividend: Caterpillar's 10-K filings.

Page 9. There are many reasons . . . in European sovereign risk markets
JPMorgan loss: http://en.wikipedia.org/wiki/2012_JPMorgan_Chase _trading_loss.

Page 9. There are many reasons . . . "the best banker in the world."
Jamie Dimon as best banker in the world: Howard Davidowitz, interviewed by Lauren Lyster on Yahoo Finance's "Daily Ticker," May 20, 2013, http:// news.yahoo.com/video/jamie-dimon-best-banker-world-122228391.html.

Page 9. The Mexican management team . . . the Foreign Corrupt Services Act
Walmart in Mexico: David Barstow, "Vast Mexico Bribery Case Hushed Up by Wal-Mart After Top-Level Struggle," *New York Times* (April 21, 2021), www.nytimes.com, and David Barstow and Alejandra Xanic von Bertrab, "The Bribery Aisle: How Wal-Mart Got Its Way in Mexico," *New York Times* (December 17, 2012), www.nytimes.com.

Page 9. GE Capital and Bank of America
Re GE, http://money.cnn.com/2008/10/09/news/companies/colvin_ge
.fortune/index.htm; re Bank of America: Shira Ovide, "Bank of America-
Countrywide: Worst Deal in History?" *Wall Street Journal* (June 29, 2011),
www.wsj.com.

Pages 10–11. The authors of this book . . . Esmark, the firm he founded
Esmark Story: Craig T. Bouchard and James V. Koch, *America for Sale: How
the Foreign Pack Circled and Devoured Esmark* (Santa Barbara, CA: Praeger,
2009).

Pages 10–11. The authors of this book . . . Signature Financial Holdings
Signature Financial: http://labusinessjournal.com/news/2013/jun/05
/upheaval-signature.

Page 11. Great Timing . . . American "Men of Steel"
Bouchard Story: Emily Lambert, "Men of Steel," *Forbes* (January 8, 2007),
http://www.forbes.com/global/2007/0108/060.html.

Page 15. [Sidebar] Even Apple . . . "headed straight for the discount rack."
On Apple's future: Nick Wingfield, "Product Questions and Threats of
Higher Tax Hit Apples Shares," *New York Times* (November 7, 2012),
www.nytimes.com.

Page 17. We began an investigative process . . . like Yogi Berra
Yogi Berra: Yogi Berra's observation has been recorded several different
ways, but is frequently cited because it captures a very basic element of the
truth. See "Language Log," www.itre.cis.upenn.edu.

Chapter 2

Page 23. "Nothing concentrates . . . Samuel Johnson
See www.wikipedia.org/wiki/Samuel_Johnson. This source points out that
Johnson's aphorism has been recorded in many different versions.

Page 24. Following Samuel Johnson . . . and that could not continue
Caterpillar losses: Annual reports, 1982–1984.

Page 24. To CAT executives . . . Mushashi's *Book of Five Rings*
Miyamoto Musasi (circa 1584–1645) was a Japanese rōnin, legendary
swordsman, and author. His *The Book of Five Rings*, concerning strategy and
tactics, deals with strategy, tactics, and philosophy and is considered by some
to be the equal of Sun Tzu's *The Art of War* and von Clausewitz's *On War*.

Page 24. Would (could) Caterpillar Change? . . . "creative destruction"
"creative destruction": Although Harvard University economist Joseph
Schumpeter was not the first to use this term, he was the individual who
popularized its use in *Capitalism, Socialism and Democracy* (New York:
Harper and Brothers, 1942).

**Page 25. In these circumstances . . . Caterpillar's marginalization or
eventual demise**
Harvard Business School: Christopher Bartlett and Susan Ehrlich,
"CATERPILLAR, Inc.: George Schaefer Takes Charge," Harvard Business
School Case 9-930-036, 1989, revised in 1991.

Page 26. Caterpillar has made decisions . . . difficult, almost existential choices

The road "less traveled": Robert Frost, "The Road Not Taken," *Mountain Interval* (New York: Henry Holt, 1916).

Page 26. Sometimes it's better . . . the Plaza Accord

Plaza Accord: See http://en.wikipedia.org/wiki/Plaza_Accord.

Pages 26–27. Sometimes it's better . . . the dollar appreciated about 50 percent

Exchange rates: http://online.wsj.com/public/page/news-currency-currencies-trading.html.

Page 27. The justification in 1985 for the dollar's depreciation

Current account deficit in 1985: "Big Deficit in Current Account," *New York Times* (March 19, 1985), www.nytimes.com.

Page 27. The justification in 1985 for the dollar's depreciation . . . The high interest rates

Thirty-year bond rates above 15 percent in 1982: http://online.wsj.com/public/page/news-fixed-income-bonds.html.

Page 28. What happened next . . . the yen/dollar exchange rate plummeted

Exchange rates: http://online.wsj.com/public/page/news-currency-currencies-trading.html.

Page 28. What happened next . . . did not occur at a constant rate

Japanese monetary reserves: http://www.imf.org/external/country/JPN/index.htm.

Page 28. The Plaza Accord heralded . . . the rate had fallen to 80

Yen/dollar exchange rate on November 7, 2012: http://online.wsj.com/public/page/news-currency-currencies-trading.htm.

Page 28. In 1986, on the heels . . . the "Plant with a Future" (PWAF)

A good summary may be found in Gary L. Neilson and Bruce A. Pasternack, "The Cat That Came Back," *Strategy + Business*, No. 40 (Fall, 2005), www.strategy-business.com/article/05304?pg=all. Neilson and Pasternack were senior executives in Booz Allen Hamilton's Chicago office and helped Caterpillar come to grips with its organizational challenges. See also, Caterpillar annual reports, 1986–1995. Our interview with Donald Fites, February 17, 2012 was quite helpful in understanding PWAF. There were hiccups along the way, however. See Eric N. Berg, "Thinking Long Term Is Costly to Caterpillar," *New York Times* (November 24, 1989), www.nytimes.com.

Page 31. In the 1980s Caterpillar . . . described them as "silos"

Donald Fites on the organization: Interview, Donald Fites, February 17, 2012.

Page 31. In the 1980s Caterpillar . . . headquarters in Peoria

Caterpillar reorganizes: Gary L. Neilson and Bruce A. Pasternack, "The Cat That Came Back," *Strategy + Business* (Fall 2005). Neilson and Pasternack were senior executives in Booz Allen Hamilton's Chicago office and helped Caterpillar come to grips with its organizational challenges.

Page 31. Our interview with A. J. Rassi and Gerry Flaherty

A. J. Rassi and Gerry Flaherty on Caterpillar's culture: Interview, October 29, 2012.

Page 33. Caterpillar in the 1970s and 1980s . . . inside the company
Caterpillar strategic planning and implementation: Interview, Donald Fites, February 17, 2012.

Page 33. Don Fites commented . . . it was frustrating"
Donald Fites on hierarchy and reorganization: Interview, February 17, 2012.

Page 34. Schaefer had a good sense . . . means to stimulate change
Glen Barton observation on the origin of the Strategic Planning Group: Comment made by Glen Barton during the editing of this book.

Page 35. Glen Barton, who became . . . substitute CAT for Eastman Kodak
Glen Barton on the visit to Kodak and Gerstner: Interview, February 6, 2012.

Page 35. Glen Barton, who became . . . "Chinese water torture method"
Donald Fites on Gerstner and the tipping point: Interview, February 17, 2012.

Page 37. If there were entrepreneurial . . . weren't a whole lot of guidebooks"
No guidebooks: Gary L. Neilson and Bruce A. Pasternack, "The Cat That Came Back," *Strategy + Business* (Fall 2005).

Page 37. As time passed . . . "Everyone owned their own numbers"
Managers owning their own numbers: Interview with Doug Oberhelman, February 3, 2012.

Page 38. Several decades later . . . Frank Crespo
Frank Crespo quote: Interview with Frank Crespo, March 23, 2012.

Page 38. But nothing was quite that certain . . . A. J. Rassi
A. J. Rassi on his change in responsibilities: Interview, October 29, 2012.

Page 38. Donald Fites became . . . Fites remarked
Donald Fites on timetable: Gary L. Neilson and Bruce A. Pasternack, "The Cat That Came Back," *Strategy + Business* (Fall 2005).

Page 38. [Sidebar] Caterpillar's business unit approach
Each business unit manages its own operations: Richard Craver, "Caterpillar to Decrease Production," *Winston-Salem Journal* (October 26, 2012), www.journalnow.com.

Page 39. Further, a business unit . . . Donald Fites said, "This made us
Donald Fites on transfer pricing: Interview, February 17, 2012.

Page 39. As time passed, Caterpillar . . . would not be pursued
On rates of return: Interviews with Doug Oberhelman, February 3, 2012, and Donald Fites, February 17, 2012.

Page 40. Donald Fites was straightforward . . . change of the first magnitude
Donald Fites on culture change and survival: Gary L. Neilson and Bruce A. Pasternack, "The Cat That Came Back," *Strategy + Business* (Fall 2005).

Page 40. Glen Barton, the company's chairman . . . "draconian decisions"
Glen Barton on draconian changes: Interview, February 6, 2012.

Page 40. Glen Barton, the company's chairman . . . employee base fell
Fall in employee base: Caterpillar annual reports.

Page 40. The United Auto Workers . . . criticized Caterpillar's cost-cutting moves
On cuts and outsourcing: Steven Greenhouse, "Caterpillar's New Driver: George A. Schaefer; Heavy Cost-Cutter with a Light Touch," *New York Times* (May 12, 1985), www.nytimes.com.

Page 41. Prepared simultaneously with . . . sources of Caterpillar's competitive advantage
Importance of dealers: Caterpillar annual report, 1990.

Page 42. Beginning in 2001 . . . improve its market position
Six Sigma explanation: www.en.wikipedia.org/wiki/Six_sigma. Our interview with Glen Barton, February 6, 2012, was critical. See also, Austin Webber, "Jerry Palmer Outlines the Company's Six Sigma Strategy," *Assembly* magazine (January 1, 2004), www.assemblymag.com/articles /print/83686-caterpillar-on-track-for-big-growth.

Page 43. Six Sigma methods . . . plant in Sanford, North Carolina, was able
Austin Webber, "Jerry Palmer Outlines the Company's Six Sigma Strategy," *Assembly* magazine (January 1, 2004), www.assemblymag.com/articles /print/83686-caterpillar-on-track-for-big-growth.

Page 44. When the reorganization was announced . . . for their own purchasing
Glen Barton on manufacturing and purchasing: Comment of Glen Barton during the editorial process.

Page 44. Owens's assessment . . . Caterpillar's overall situation
Jim Owens on organization and operations: Interview, February 13, 2012.

Pages 44–45. Owens also concluded . . . thus avoid costly disruptions
Process standardization: Interview, Chuck Laurenti, October 22, 2012.

Page 45. Six Sigma and this burst . . . Glen Barton unambiguously declared
Glen Barton on Six Sigma and costs: Interview, February 6, 2012.

Page 46. Those who follow . . . TQM) have followed the trajectory
On TQM: The disappointing productivity of TQM in the context of higher education can be found in James V. Koch and James L. Fisher, "Higher Education and TQM," *Total Quality Management*, 9 (8), 1998, 659–668; "TQM and Other Management Fads: Why Has Their Impact on Higher Education Been So Small?" *David Dodds Henry Lecture*, University of Illinois, March 3, 2003 (University of Illinois Press, 2003; and "TQM: Why Is Its Impact in Higher Education So Small?" *TQM Magazine* 15 (September 2003), 325–233. TQM's deficiencies also apply to for-profit firms.

Page 46. It is here that Caterpillar's focus . . . An illustration is its 2011 announcement
Caterpillar investment of $200 million in East Peoria plant: Steve Tarter, "Cat to Invest $640 Million to Upgrade Facilities," *Peoria Journal-Star* (November 12, 2011), www.pjstar.com.

Chapter 3

Page 49. "It's in Caterpillar's DNA," . . . thrust into international markets
Thomas J. Bluth on CAT's DNA: Interview, February 17, 2012.

Page 49. "It's in Caterpillar's DNA," . . . In 2011, for the first time
On the location of Caterpillar's sales: Caterpillar annual reports, 1964, 1984, 2004, and 2011.

Page 49. Caterpillar is hardly a newbie . . . the Netherlands and Tunisia
Caterpillar history: "Caterpillar, Inc.," Funding Universe, www.
fundinguniverse.com/company-histories/caterpillar-inc-history, and
www.cat.com.

Page 49. Caterpillar's high-energy chairman/CEO . . . outside the United States
Doug Oberhelman on where customers are located: *Caterpillar 2011 Year in Review.*

Page 50. Although slightly more . . . in 1963, international customers accounted for
Caterpillar annual report, 1963.

Page 50. Although slightly more . . . By 2003, that number had climbed
Caterpillar annual report, 2003.

Page 52. The globalization of Caterpillar vibrates . . . "outside of North America,"
Employment numbers: Rachel Potts, Caterpillar Public Affairs.

Page 53. Only four years after . . . $13.3 million in 1932
Falling Caterpillar sales, 1930-1932: Caterpillar annual reports.

Page 53. Selling to the Soviet Union
On the Soviet example: Caterpillar annual report, 1960; Caterpillar history:
"Caterpillar, Inc.," Funding Universe, www.fundinguniverse.com/company
-histories/caterpillar-inc-history, and www.cat.com.

Pages 53–54. In the case at hand . . . 1,300 tractors and 750 harvesters
"Caterpillar, Inc.," Funding Universe, www.fundinguniverse.com/company
-histories/caterpillar-inc-history, and www.cat.com.

Page 54. [Sidebar] Fast forward to December 2012
Russian trade restrictions removed: Sudeep Reddy, "Congress Scraps Russia
Trade Curbs," *Wall Street Journal,* 259 (December 7, 2012), A11.

Page 54. Caterpillar's demonstrative lesson . . . adheres to the Office of Foreign Assets Control
Office of Foreign Assets Control: http://www.treasury.gov/about
/organizational-structure/offices/Pages/Office-of-Foreign-Assets-Control
.aspx.

Page 55. The major difference . . . reduce its impact on the environment
Caterpillar's sustainability statement: "Caterpillar 2011 Sustainability
Report," www.caterpillar.com/cda/files/3694814/7/CAT-015_2011_SR
_PDF_v2.5.pdf.

Page 56. To the disappointment of a few . . . selling bulldozers to the U.S. government
On bulldozers in Palestine: "Caterpillar Cut from Investments Lists: Israeli
Role Cited," *Los Angeles Times* (June 27, 2012), http://latimesblogs.latimes
.com/world_now/2012/06/caterpillar-israel-palestine-investment
-controversy.html. A pro-Palestinian, anti-Israel, anti-Caterpillar perspective
on these issues is provided by Wissam Nassar, "The Electronic Intifada"
(August 27, 2012), www.electronicintifada.net.

Page 56. Caterpillar's indirect provision . . . U.N. Commission on Human Rights

United Nations urges divestment of Caterpillar stock: "UN Rep: Boycott Hewlett Packard, Caterpillar, Motorola" (October 25, 2012), www.examiner.com.

Page 57. At the end of the day . . . the company's Worldwide Code of Conduct

On the Worldwide Code of Conduct: Caterpillar, *Our Values in Action: Caterpillar's Worldwide Code of Conduct.*

Page 57. It's worth noting . . . facilities had used forced labor

On Ford and Germany: Reinhold Billstein (ed.), *Working for the Enemy: Ford, General Motors, and Forced Labor in Germany During the Second World War* (New York: Berghahn Books, 2000).

Page 59. In 1967, Japan's Komatsu . . . head to head with Caterpillar

On Komatsu: "Caterpillar, Inc.," Funding Universe, www.fundinguniverse .com/company-histories/caterpillar-inc-history, and www.cat.com.

Page 60. The magnitude of Komatsu's challenge . . . Gerald Flaherty

Gerald Flaherty on Komatsu: Interview, October 29, 2012.

Page 60. Caterpillar's responses were several . . . Ed Rapp comments

Ed Rapp and Komatsu: Interview, January 23, 2012, and subsequent conversations.

Page 61. [Sidebar] Insider's Edge: "My opponents . . ."

Sadaharu Oh quote: Sadaharu Oh, *A Zen Way of Baseball* (New York: Times Books, 1984).

Page 61. While dancing with its main rival Komatsu . . .future of the company resided

On international expansion: Caterpillar annual reports, 1963, 1983, and 2011.

Pages 61–62. The dollar/yen relationship . . . home base of Komatsu

On dollar/yen values: http://search.stlouisfed.org/search?&client=Research &proxystylesheet=Research-new&site=Research&output=xml_no_dtd &num=30&q=foreign+exchange+rate.

Page 63. Exchange rate difficulties . . . $1.17 million *every day*

Caterpillar financial losses: Caterpillar annual reports, 1982, 1983, 1984, and 1985.

Page 63. Caterpillar's 1981 annual report . . . a Japanese counterpart

On international wage differences: Caterpillar annual report, 1981.

Pages 63–64. Caterpillar's reaction was . . . restrictions be eliminated, not increased

Caterpillar supporting free trade: Caterpillar annual report, 1981.

Page 64. Caterpillar's position on free trade . . . Doug Oberhelman noted

Doug Oberhelman on trade policies: *Caterpillar 2011 Year in Review.*

Page 64. Caterpillar often has walked . . . did not ask the U.S. government for tariff protection

On President Obama's visit to Caterpillar: Karen Travers, "CEO Contradicts Obama on Rehiring Employees," www.abcnews.go.com /Politics/story?id=6866995&page=1#.UIGNudd2jyF.

Page 64. [Sidebar] Caterpillar's leaders . . . importance of free-trade principles to the company's prosperity
On Caterpillar not asking for tariff protection: John Pulliam, "Caterpillar CEO Decries Lack of Leadership," *Peoria Journal-Star* (April 2, 2012), www.pjstar.com.

Page 65. Fortunately for Caterpillar . . . the yen appreciated slightly more than 50 percent
On dollar/yen exchange rate: www.research.stlouisfed.org/fred2.

Page 65. Fortunately for Caterpillar . . . sales and revenue coming from outside the United States
On international sales: Caterpillar annual reports, 1981, 1985, and 1991.

Page 66. During the first decade . . . By July 11, 2013, however, the yen had declined
On exchange rates: www.research.stlouisfed.org/fred2.

Page 66. During the first decade . . . the strength of the Japanese yen
On Caterpillar price increases: www.seekingalpha.com (September 28, 2012).

Page 67. In fact, in recent years, the dollar . . . between 2003 and 2012
On the U.S. dollar vs. European currencies: http://search.stlouisfed .org/search?&client=Research&proxystylesheet=Research-new&site =Research&output=xml_no_dtd&num=30&q=foreign+exchange+rate.

Chapter 4

Page 69. When the words *China* and *PRC* . . . sell in the BRIC countries
Discussion of Caterpillar's facilities outside the United States: Caterpillar annual report, 2011.

Page 70. By the end of 2012 . . . individuals in the PRC
Number of Caterpillar employees in China: "Departure of Caterpillar Executive Linked to China Writedown—Source," *Fox Business*, www .foxbusiness.com (accessed January 20, 2013).

Page 70. Many non-Caterpillar individuals . . . Frank Crespo
Quotation from Frank Crespo: Interview, March 23, 2012.

Page 70. [Sidebar] China consumes
China consumption statistics: Roger Nusbaum, "China's Share of World Commodity Consumption" (May 17, 2011), www.SeekingAlpha.com.

Pages 70–71. Caterpillar has a long history . . . Doug Oberhelman
Doug Oberhelman on China: Interview, February 3, 2012.

Pages 70–71. Caterpillar has a long history . . . Sany, Doosan, and Hitachi
On Komatsu's leadership position in China: "China's Sany Heavy Poised for Economic 'Golden Age,'" Reuters (October 28, 2012), www.reuters.com.

Pages 70–71. Caterpillar has a long history . . . CAT trails Shantui, HBXG, and Zoomlion
Caterpillar's market shares in China: authors' conversations with financial analysts and Caterpillar personnel and James R. Hagerty, "Caterpillar's Shaky Ground in China," *Wall Street Journal* (January 28, 2013), www .wsj.com.

Page 71. Oberhelman's attitude . . . "Caterpillar in China" identified
Caterpillar facilities in China: http://china.cat.com/cda/files/1570321
/7/2013%20Caterpillar%20in%20China%20Brochure_Final%20Version
_14May2013.pdf.

Page 71. Oberhelman's attitude . . . "many investors were edgy"
Stephen Volkmann on Caterpillar profitability: quoted by Bob Tita and
James R. Hagerty, "Caterpillar Pushes Up Forecast as Profit Rises," *Wall
Street Journal*, 259 (April 25, 2012), www.wsj.com.

Page 71. [Sidebar] Insider's Edge: Within the next five years
Cost of doing business in China versus southern United States: Harold L.
Sirkin, Michael Zinser, and Douglas Hohner, *Made in America, Again: Why
Manufacturing Will Return to the U.S.* (Boston: Boston Consulting Group,
2012). The authors argue that by 2015, the cost of doing business in China
will be roughly equivalent to that in the southern United States once one
has taken into account differences in productivity and quality. More recent
support for this view was detailed in "China Starts Losing Edge as World's
Factory Floor," *Wall Street Journal* (January 16, 2013), www.wsj.com.

Page 72. Many American manufacturing firms . . . An August 2012 report
Economic Policy Institute on Chinese currency manipulation: Robert E.
Scott, "The China Toll," Economic Policy Institute (August 23, 2012),
www.epi.org.

**Page 72. Many American manufacturing firms . . . the *New York Times*
asserted**
The *New York Times* on Chinese currency manipulation: "Times Topics:
Renminbi (Yuan)," *New York Times* (May 31, 2012), www.nytimes.com.

**Page 72. Many American manufacturing firms . . . Treasury Secretary
Timothy Geithner already**
Treasury Secretary Timothy Geithner on Chinese currency manipulation,
January 2012: www.google.com/hostednews/afp/article/ALeqM5ixfHMb
AbLcYP5YxbivekEzeqttBQ?docId=CNG.871f4204301feda9723alcb343f5
afe.3.541.

**Page 72. Many Amercian manufacturing firms . . . political economist Paul
Krugman averred**
Paul Krugman on Chinese currency manipulation: Paul Krugman, "Taking
on China," *The New York Times* (March 15, 2010), www.nytimes.com.

Page 74. [Sidebar] Coca-Cola . . . commented David Brooks
Coca-Cola's problems in India: Laurie Burkitt, "China Shuts Coke Plant
Over Chlorine," *Wall Street Journal* (April 30, 2012), www.wsj.com. The
Brooks quote comes from "Coca Cola Apologises to China Over Excessive
Chlorine Content," *Times of India* (May 5, 2012), http://timesofindia
.indiatimes.com/business/international-business/Coca-cola-apologises-to
-China-over-excessive-chlorine-content/articleshow/13013261.cms.

**Pages 74–75. The posturing of political candidates aside . . . In this vein,
C. Fred Bergsten**
C. Fred Bergsten on Chinese currency manipulation: Howard Schneider,
"Some Experts Say China's Currency Is Not a Danger to the U.S. Economy,"
Washington Post (September 28, 2012), www.washingtonpost.com.

Page 75. State capitalism . . . CAT had been in China more than 35 years
Rich Lavin on doing business in China: Interview, February 10, 2012.

Page 75. Caterpillar does lean . . . a hefty rate of increase
Financial Times estimates of the revenue of state-owned Chinese enterprises:
Simon Rabinovitch, "March of the State Presses Private Companies,"
Financial Times (November 12, 2012), p. 6, www.ft.com.

Page 76. Caterpillar knows well . . . Chinese firm ERA Mining Machinery
Caterpillar's Siwei deal: Debbie Cai and Bob Tita, "Caterpillar Finds
Accounting Misconduct at Chinese Unit," *Wall Street Journal* (January 18,
2013), www.wsj.com; Ernest Scheyder, "Caterpillar Writes Off Most of
China Deal After Fraud," Reuters (January 19, 2013), www.reuters.com, for
Caterpillar's view of the Growth Enterprise Market, the price paid for the
original acquisition, and the $580 million write-off.

**Page 76. Caterpillar knows well . . ."deliberate, multiyear, coordinated
accounting misconduct,"**
"Caterpillar Takes Action to Address Accounting Misconduct at Siwei,"
Caterpillar Corporate Press Release, January 18, 2013. See also James
T. Areddy, "Unusual Roots for Firm in Caterpillar Scandal," *Wall Street
Journal* (January 20, 2013), www.wsj.com.

Page 76. The ERA purchase . . . $64 billion in 2012
$64 billion size of Chinese machinery market: Neil Munshi, "Caterpillar
Sees Stronger China Growth," *Financial Times* (January 28, 2013),
www.ft.com.

**Page 76. The ERA purchase . . . (Caterpillar language according to
Reuters)**
Risk language of Reuters: Ernest Scheyder, "Caterpillar Writes Off Most
of China Deal After Fraud," Reuters (January 19, 2013), http://news.yahoo
.com.

**Page 76. Caterpillar paid $653.4 million for ERA . . . "corporate secretarial
services"**
Ernest Scheyder. "Caterpillar Writes Off Most of China Deal After Fraud,"
Reuters (January 19, 2013), http://news.yahoo.com.

Page 76. There is little dispute . . . reported profit in fourth quarter 2012
Details of Caterpillar's purchase of Siwei: Debbie Cai and Bob Tita,
"Caterpillar Finds Accounting Misconduct at Chinese Unit," *Wall Street
Journal* (January 18, 2013), www.wsj.com.

Page 76. There is little dispute . . . renegotiated some of the terms
Caterpillar recovers $135 million: Bob Tita, "Caterpillar Lowers Cost of
Chinese Acquisition," *Wall Street Journal* (May 16, 2013), www.wsj.com.

Pages 76–77. Multiple lessons were learned . . . use of its cash
"Red flags": Duncan Mavin, "Caterpillar Tracks a Wayward China Path,"
Wall Street Journal (January 28, 2013), www.wsj.com.

Page 77. Second, even though CAT has asserted
"Rigorous and robust": "Departure of Caterpillar Executive Linked to
China Writedown—Source," *Fox Business*, www.foxbusiness.com (accessed
January 20, 2013).

Page 77. Finally, although it always . . . *TIME* magazine noted in September 2012
TIME magazine on difficulties of doing business in China, Michael Schuman, "The New Great Wall of China," *TIME*, 180 (September 24, 2012), p. 2, Business Section.

Page 77. A China veteran writing in *Bloomberg Businessweek* . . . cautioned Western businesses
Bloomberg Businessweek quote: Shaun Rein, "Foreigners in China Must Learn the Rules of the Road," *Bloomberg Businessweek* (September 14, 2012), www.businessweek.com.

Page 78. [Sidebar] Investors have largely been comfortable
Caterpillar share prices: http://finance.yahoo.com/q/hp?s=CAT+Historical +Prices.

Pages 78–79. Caterpillar's approach to China . . .nicely," says Oberhelman
Doug Oberhelman on long-term outlook in China: Interview, February 3, 2012.

Page 79. Doug Oberhelman is an aggressive leader . . . When he notes
Doug Oberhelman on 95 percent of consumers living outside the United States: *Caterpillar Year in Review, 2011.*

Page 80. Much of Caterpillar's American focus . . . In 2011, the company exported $19.44 billion
On Caterpillar exporting $19.44 billion in 2011: Rachel Potts, Caterpillar Public Affairs.

Page 80. Much of Caterpillar's American focus . . . access to the Port of Savannah
On Caterpillar expanding in Georgia: James R. Hagerty, "Caterpillar Strikes a Deal to Build Georgia Plant," *Wall Street Journal*, 259 (February 18, 2012), www.wsj.com.

Page 80. When Caterpillar weighs . . . high value on global perspectives and experience
David Goode on the internationalization of Caterpillar: Interview, March 26, 2012.

Page 81. Understanding, cooperation, and mutual respect . . . "Caterpillar's core values" will be sustained as time passes
Eugene Fife on Caterpillar's Worldwide Code of Conduct: Interview, May 3, 2012.

Page 81. Caterpillar's culture . . . did not translate to the German retail space
Walmart's problems: David Barstow and Alejandra Xanic von Bertrab, "The Bribery Aisle: How Wal-Mart Got Its Way in Mexico," *New York Times* (December 17, 2012), www.nytimes.com.

Chapter 5

Page 85. During the fall 2012 U.S. election . . . By 2011, only 42.56 percent of CAT's employees
Caterpillar employee numbers: Rachel Potts, Caterpillar Public Affairs.

Page 85. Thus if offshoring . . . Caterpillar can be classified as one of the major American malefactors
See Jordan Weissmann, "What's Good for Caterpillar Isn't So Great for America," *The Atlantic* (October 25, 2011), www.theatlantic.com.

Page 86. It is important at the outset . . . 616,000 insourced jobs in 2011
On foreign-owned plants in the United States: "Top Ten States for Insourcing," *Global HR News*, www.globalhrnews.com/story.asp?sid=589.

Page 86. [Sidebar] One of the most intriguing
On Caterpillar reshoring: Bob Tita, "Caterpillar to Shift Some Production to U.S.," *Wall Street Journal*, 258 (November 11, 2011), www.wsj.com.

Page 86. In 2008, 4.7 percent of all U.S. jobs . . . Connecticut followed with 7.1 percent
On direct foreign investment: Bureau of Economic Analysis, U.S. Department of Commerce, www.bea.gov, for aggregate numbers by year and the U.S. Bureau of the Census, *The 2012 Statistical Abstract*, for state data.

Pages 86–87. In 2008, 4.7 percent of all U.S. jobs . . . similar work in the American private sector
Matthew J. Slaughter on insourced workers being paid more: "Insourcing Jobs: Making the Global Economy Work for America," Tuck School, Dartmouth College, 2004. See also www.census.gov/compendia/statab/cats/foreign_commerce_aid/foreign_investment.html.

Page 88. Caterpillar produces dozens . . . only in the United States
On the items Caterpillar produces inside the United States: Rachel Potts, Caterpillar Public Affairs.

Page 88. In some industries . . . 337,000 new jobs in the United States between 2006 and 2010
On Information Technology Association of America study: Caron Carlson, "ITAA Study Pushes for Outsourcing," *eWeek* (October 31, 2005), www.eweek.com.

Pages 88–89. In some industries . . . McKinsey found that the typical firm
McKinsey on value created by offshoring: *Offshoring: Is It a Win-Win Game?* (San Francisco: McKinsey, 2003), and Diana Farrell and Jaeson Rosenfeld, *U.S. Offshoring: Rethinking the Response.* (New York: McKinsey, 2005).

Page 89. Ultimately, the benefits . . . firms locating overseas
On job losses and the economics of offshoring: U.S. Department of Labor, Bureau of Labor Statistics, www.bls.gov/mls/#tables; "Extended Mass Layoffs in 2010," Report 1038, Bureau of Labor Statistics, U.S. Department of Labor, November 2011; Diana Farrell and Jaeson Rosenfeld, "U.S. Offshoring: Rethinking the Response," McKinsey Global Institute, December 2005; and Mary Amiti and Shang-Jim Wei, "Demystifying Outsourcing: The Numbers Do Not Support the Hype over Job Losses," *Finance and Development* (December 2004), 36–39. Syud Amer Ahmed examined the impact of outsourcing on 86 U.S. manufacturing industries between 1998 and 2004 and found that "outsourcing has not had a large labor market impact." "Outsourcing and U.S. Manufacturing Employment," World Bank, June 2007. An excellent summary of the

evidence as of 2006 can be found in Gregory N. Mankiw and Philip Swagel, "The Politics and Economics of Offshore Outsourcing," NBER Working Paper No. 12398 (July 2006).

Page 91. United Auto Workers leaders . . . and ordinary Americans
On views of union leaders: Interview, David Chapman, president of UAW-974, East Peoria, IL, March 23, 2012, and an interview with a retired labor leader in 2008.

Page 93. Nevertheless, high levels . . . As Matthew J. Slaughter
Matthew J. Slaughter on hollowing out by insourcing: Matthew J. Slaughter, "How U.S. Multinational Companies Strengthen the U.S. Economy," United States Business Council Round Table, 2009.

Pages 93–94. The Foreign Corrupt Practices Act . . . local custom and practice
On the Foreign Corrupt Practices Act: U.S. Department of Justice, www.justice.gov/criminal/fraud/fcpa.

Page 94. The lessons attached . . . experience of Walmart in Mexico
On Walmart in Mexico: David Barstow, "Wal-Mart Hushed Up a Vast Mexican Bribery Case," *New York Times*, www.nytimes.com/2012/04/22/business/at-wal-mart-in-mexico-a-bribe-inquiry-silenced.html?_r=1.

Page 94. The lessons attached . . . Walmart's practices "extended beyond Mexico to China, India, and Brazil
On Walmart in China, Brazil, and India: Stephanie Clifford and David Barstow, "Wal-Mart Inquiry Reflects Alarm on Corruption," *New York Times* (November 15, 2012), www.nytimes.com.

Page 94. Caterpillar Chairman/CEO Doug Oberhelman reacted . . . Worldwide Code of Conduct
On Caterpillar's Code of Conduct: *Our Values in Action: Caterpillar's Worldwide Code of Conduct* (Caterpillar, 2012).

Page 94.[Sidebar] IBM paid a $10 million penalty
IBM pays $10 million to settle charge: "IBM to Settle Bribery Charges for $10 Million," *New York Times* (March 18, 2011), www.nytimes.com.

Page 94. When Caterpillar confronted . . . restated the standards of the Code
Caterpillar's reaction to Siwei accounting fraud: Debbie Cai and Bob Tita, "Caterpillar Finds Accounting Misconduct at Chinese Unit," *Wall Street Journal* (January 18, 2013), www.wsj.com.

Page 95. In light of Caterpillar's far-flung operations . . . says Mexico City security consultant Max Morales
On *gestores*: David Barstow, "Walmart Hushed Up a Vast Mexican Bribery Case," *New York Times*, www.nytimes.com/2012/04/22/business/at-Walmart-in-mexico-a-bribe-inquiry-silenced.html?_r=1.

Page 95. [Sidebar] Back in the 1950s, Caterpillar Chairman Louis Neumiller
Louis Neumiller on one Caterpillar: Caterpillar 2002 annual report, p. 18.

Page 96. Caterpillar's competitors . . . Eugene V. Fife's observation
Eugene V. Fife on Caterpillar's ethics: Interview, May 3, 2012.

Chapter 6

Page 97. Notwithstanding Caterpillar's . . . surprisingly low-key
Low-key, agreeable labor relations observation: Interview, Dave Chapman, president of UAW-974, March 23, 2012.

Page 97. *Wall Street Journal* reporters James R. Hagerty and Bob Tita noted . . . hardball in labor relations
Caterpillar plays hardball in labor relations, James R. Hagerty and Bob Tita, "Unions Confront Rising Tide," *Wall Street Journal*, 259 (May 7, 2012), A3. See also Mina Kimes, "Caterpillar's Doug Oberhelman: Manufacturing's Mouthpiece," *Bloomberg Businessweek* (May 16, 2013), www.businessweek.com.

Page 97. Caterpillar's corporate stance . . . emphasizes two points
Caterpillar's labor stance: Interview, Chris Glynn, February 3, 2012.

Page 98. Second, Caterpillar asserts . . . shutter the plant on February 3, 2012
Wages would be cut in half and cost competitiveness issues, James R. Hagerty and Chip Cummins, "Caterpillar, Rio Lock Out Workers in Canada," *Wall Street Journal* (January 2, 2012), www.wsj.com.

Page 98. Caterpillar, however, maintained . . . cost structure that simply was "not sustainable"
Cost structure "not sustainable": Steve Tarter, "Two Sides to the CAT Coin," *Peoria Journal-Star* (February 12, 2012), www.jstar.com.

Pages 98–99. Subsequently, in August 2012 . . . reported to have driven a "hard bargain"
On the machinists' strike and a hard bargain: Steven Greenhouse, "Caterpillar Workers Ratify Deal They Dislike," *New York Times* (August 17, 2012), www.nytimes.com.

Pages 98–99. Subsequently, in August 2012 . . . "Caterpillar to Unions: Drop Dead"
Pearlstein quote: Steven Pearlstein, "Caterpillar to Unions: Drop Dead," *Washington Post* (August 4, 2012), www.washingtonpost.com.

Pages 98–99. Subsequently, in August 2012 . . . unlikely to have endeared him to Caterpillar's management
Governor Pat Quinn's support for the machinists: "Striking Caterpillar Workers Receive Backing from Gov. Pat Quinn," www.ksdk.com/news /aricle/332627/3/Gov-Quinn-supports-striking-Caterpillar-workers -?odyssey=tab|topnews|bc|large.

Page 99. The first Caperpillar union to be certified . . . (UAW) prevailed in 1948
History of bargaining and UAW membership numbers: Isaac Cohen, "The Caterpillar Labor Dispute and the UAW, 1991–1998," *Labor Studies Journal*, 27 (Winter, 2003), 77–99.

Pages 99–100. Between 1948 and 1980 . . . when the company once again began to lose money
Caterpillar losing money, Komatsu, and pattern bargains: Toby Eckert, "CAT vs. UAW: Pattern Bargaining at Issue," *Illinois Issues* (March 1992),

Illinois Periodicals Online, www.lib.niu.edu/1991/ii920315.html. Eckert was a Springfield correspondent for the *Peoria Journal-Star.*

Page 100. It would lose $404 million . . . labor costs that were 30 percent below those of CAT
Komatsu's labor costs 30 percent lower: Caterpillar annual report, 1984.

Page 100. In 1991, the pattern bargain . . . payment the next two years
UAW bargaining proposal: Toby Eckert, "CAT vs. UAW: Pattern Bargaining at Issue," *Illinois Issues* (March 1992), Illinois Periodicals Online, www.lib.niu.edu/1991/ii920315.html. Eckert was a Springfield correspondent for the *Peoria Journal-Star.*

Page 100. [Sidebar] How things have changed . . . showed up to bid for the jobs
Wages offered in Muncie, Indiana: AllGov, "Caterpillar Closes 62-Year-Old Plant in Canada to Take Advantage of Cheaper, Non-Union Labor in Indiana," February 14, 2012, www.allgov.com.

Pages 100–101. Caterpillar had been consistent . . . off base in Caterpillar's view
Caterpillar and pattern bargaining: Toby Eckert, "CAT vs. UAW: Pattern Bargaining at Issue," *Illinois Issues* (March 1992), Illinois Periodicals Online, www.lib.niu.edu/1991/ii920315.html, and Interview, Donald Fites, February 17, 2012.

Page 101. Interestingly, on the other side . . . same output in 1991 as in 1979
Decline in UAW membership: "UAW Calculated Wrong on Strike: Both Company, Public Surprised It," *Chicago Tribune* (September 8, 1992), www.chicagotribune.com.

Page 102. In any event, negotiations . . . their personal finances and families
1991 UAW strike fund and memories of 1982 strike: Peter T. Kilborn, "Caterpillar's Trump Card: Threat of Permanently Replacing Strikers Gave Company Advantage Against Union," *New York Times* (April 16, 1992), www.nytimes.com.

Page 102. However, Caterpillar surprised the union . . . limit the effects of the strike."
Lockout stunned workers, neutralized UAW: "UAW Calculated Wrong on Strike: Both Company, Public Surprised It," *Chicago Tribune* (September 8, 1992), www.chicagotribune.com.

Page 103. Early in the dispute . . . less than $40,000 being paid by its competitor Deere
Caterpillar's early settlement offer: Peter T. Kilborn, "Caterpillar's Trump Card: Threat of Permanently Replacing Strikers Gave Company Advantage Against Union," *New York Times* (April 16, 1992), www.nytimes.com.

Page 103. Early in the dispute . . . would "close down Caterpillar."
Statement attributed to Owen Bieber: Interview with A. J. Rassi and interview with Gerald Flaherty, both on October 29, 2012.

Page 103. The UAW's failure to respond . . . were at an "impasse."
Negotiations at impasse: Stephen Franklin, *Three Strikes: Labor's Heartland Losses and What They Mean for Working Americans* (New York: Guilford

Press, 2001). Franklin's book provides excellent background on the Caterpillar strike in Decatur, Illinois.

Page 103. Nonunion individuals at all levels . . . Secretaries ran machines
Ronald Bonati and A. J. Rassi working on the line: Interview with Rassi, October 29, 2012.

Page 104. When it became known . . . telephone calls from prospective employees
On telephone calls from interested job applicants and power shift: Jonathan P. Hicks, "Caterpillar and Union Agree to Meeting," *New York Times* (April 11, 1992), www.nytimes.com.

Page 104. When it became known . . . hiring a large group of welders
Hiring welders from the Gulf Coast: Interview with A. J. Rassi, October 29, 2012.

Page 104. When it became known . . . and away from unions
On the balance of power tipping toward companies: Peter T. Kilborn, "Caterpillar's Trump Card: Threat of Permanently Replacing Strikers Gave Company Advantage Against Union," *New York Times* (April 16, 1992), www.nytimes.com.

Page 104. [Sidebar] Thank God for the Plant with a Future
Gerald Flaherty on the PWAF: Interview, October 29, 2012.

Pages 104–105. UAW personnel . . . couldn't tell the difference and neither could his customers
Peter Holt's observation on quality: Interview, March 30, 2012. For a confirmation, see "An Interview with Tony Green," *Interbusiness Issues* (September 1994), www.peorianmagazines.com. Green was the president of UAW-974 between 1984 and 1990.

Page 105. Donald Fites at the time . . . Our problem isn't supply, it's demand
Donald Fites's statement on CAT not losing sales and Bill Casstevens's comments at board meeting: Jonathan P. Hicks, "Union Leader Takes Case to Stockholders," *New York Times* (April 9, 1992), www.nytimes.com.

Page 105. Donald Fites at the time . . . things that are false."
Bill Casstevens's assertion that Fites was not telling the truth: Jonathan P. Hicks, "Union Leader Takes Case to Stockholders," *New York Times* (April 9, 1992), www.nytimes.com.

Page 105. This may have been . . . acrimonious and often nasty
History of negotiations, 1991–1998: Michael H. Cimini, "Caterpillar's Prolonged Dispute Ends," *Compensation and Working Conditions*, 3 (Fall 1998), 4–11.

Page 105. On April 14, 1992, . . . said negotiations must continue
On strike details and charges of unfair labor practices: Michael H. Cimini, "Caterpillar's Prolonged Dispute Ends," *Compensation and Working Conditions*, 3 (Fall 1998), 4–11.

Page 105. On April 14, 2002, . . . fallen as much as 40 percent
Production may have fallen 40 percent: Stephen Franklin, *Three Strikes: Labor's Heartland Losses and What They Mean for Working Americans* (New York: Guilford Press, 2001).

Pages 105–106. Public opinion . . . union disputed but did not counter with its own numbers
On strike details and proposals: Michael H. Cimini, "Caterpillar's Prolonged Dispute Ends," *Compensation and Working Conditions*, 3 (Fall 1998), 4–11.

Page 106. In 1993, Caterpillar . . . We have to accept defeat."
UAW workers return to work and worker statement that the union had been defeated: "Union Leaders Give Up on Caterpillar Strike," *New York Times* (December 4, 1995), www.nytimes.com.

Page 106. During the 1994 strike, . . . unfair labor practices
Strike is about unfair labor practices: Michael H. Cimini, "Caterpillar's Prolonged Dispute Ends," *Compensation and Working Conditions*, 3 (Fall 1998), 4–11.

Page 107. Meanwhile, Caterpillar . . . reached a long-term, six-year agreement
Agreement reached in 1998: "U.A.W. Members Back Contract With Caterpillar, First Since '91," *New York Times* (March 23, 1998), www.nytimes.com.

Page 107. A *Los Angeles Times* reporter . . . "throwback to another era."
Strike is a throwback to a previous era: Donald W. Nauss, "UAW Dispute with Caterpillar Just Crawls Along," *Los Angeles Times* (July 5, 1994), www.latimes.com.

Pages 107–108. [Sidebar] Tony Green was . . . adversarial relationship with CAT management
Tony Green on negotiations and UAW-974: "Interview with Tony Green," *Interbusiness Issues* (September 1994), www.peorianmagazines.com.

Page 108. As the Associated Press put it . . . boast about except survival."
Associated Press assessment of 1998 contract: Christopher Wills, "UAW OKs 6-Year Caterpillar Contract," March 23, 1998, www.apnewsarchive .com/1998/UAW-OKs-6-Year-Caterpillar-Contract/id-58f06310f470922fd 441c58a29c03043. A few observers scored the contract as a victory for the union. See Isaac Cohen, "The Caterpillar Labor Dispute and the UAW, 1991–1998," *Labor Studies Journal*, 27 (Winter 2003), 77–99. This was not the consensus view, however. See Victor G. Devinatz, "A Heroic Defeat: The Caterpillar Labor Dispute: 1991–1998," *Labor Studies Journal*, 30 (Summer 2005), 1–18.

Page 108. Despite holding out . . . Donald Fites
Donald Fites's statement that Caterpillar was not out to break the union: Jonathan P. Hicks, "Union Leader Takes Case to Caterpillar Stockholders," *New York Times* (April 9, 1992), www.nytimes.com.

Page 108. Despite holding out . . . "Who was going to run the plant?"
Donald Fites on who was going to run Caterpillar: Interview, February 17, 2012.

Page 109. This turnabout would not have occurred . . . as Fites later put it to us
Donald Fites's observation on taking risks as CEO: Interview, February 17, 2012; "agreeable" labor relations observation: Interview, Dave Chapman, president of UAW-974, March 23, 2012.

Page 110. In any case . . . "agreeable and about as good as they have ever been."
Agreeable labor relations: Interviews with UAW leaders and members, 2012.

Page 111. First, Caterpillar energetically strives . . . Glynn says, "We try to manage
Chris Glynn on managing so that employees don't need third parties: Interview, February 3, 2012.

Page 111. CAT's strategy is to manage so well . . . obtain a productive response
Discussion of Caterpillar's approach to labor relations: based in part on Interview with Chris Glynn, February 3, 2012.

Page 112. Every year . . . "There's no magic here."
Chris Glynn's observation that it isn't magic: Interview, February 3, 2012.

Page 112. Second, Caterpillar . . . under the title "Healthy Balance"
Doug Oberhelman on health programs and health costs: Interview, February 3, 2012.

Page 112. Another concrete means . . . its 2008 decision to ban smoking
Smoking policy and unfair labor practice charge: Jeff Muniz, "Workers Protest Caterpillar Smoking Ban," WEEK-TV News 25 (July 15, 2010), www.cinewsnow.com/news/local/19458444.html.

Page 115. Sixth, Caterpillar knows . . . collective bargaining issues P1 throught P5
P1 through P5 negotiating issues: Interview, Chris Glynn, February 3, 2012.

Page 115. Boeing, Inc. . . . encountered significant problems with the National Labor Relations Board
Boeing and the NLRB: Steven Greenhouse, "Labor Board Drops Case Against Boeing After Union Reaches Accord," *New York Times* (December 9, 2011), www.nytimes.com.

Page 116. Caterpillar also has been careful . . . to obtain its inputs when and where it sees fit
Contract language that grants Caterpillar flexibility: Interview, Chris Glynn, February 3, 2012.

Page 117. There is no shortage . . . "Hobbesian scenario"
Hobbesian scenario: Martin Regg Cohn, "How Canada Let Caterpillar Strip a Plant Clean," *Toronto Star* (February 4, 2012), www.TheStar.com /printarticle/1126357.

Page 117. There is no shortage . . . "dangerous precedents"
Dangerous precedents: Mike Moffatt, a University of Western Ontario economist, quoted in Linda Nguyen, "Caterpillar Tactics 'Dangerous Precedent,'" *Montreal Gazette* (January 27, 2012), www.montrealgazette .com/story_print.html?id=6059146.

Page 117. There is no shortage . . . globalization run amok
On globalization run amok: Martin Regg Cohn, "The Caterpillar Crisis Now Is Canada's Crisis," *Toronto Star*, (January 25, 2012), www.thestar .com/printarticle/1121470.

Chapter 7

Page 119. There isn't much doubt . . . they are so *#$% committed
Cummins dealer quote: Interview with a Cummins dealer who did not wish to be identified, June 7, 2011.

Page 119. One of the spinoff benefits . . . the dealers (189 in number in 2012)
Caterpillar dealer data: *Caterpillar Year in Review, 2012.*

Pages 119–120. Because Caterpillar's dealers . . . become strategic and tactical partners
Caterpillar-dealer relationship more of a partnership: Interview with Jim Parker, March 14, 2012.

Pages 119–120. Because Caterpillar's dealers . . . sell directly to customers and bypass our dealers
Donald Fites on not bypassing dealers on sales: gmx.xmu.edu.cn/ews/business/pmarketing/chapter12.htm.

Page 120. Hence, in the 1980s . . . very difficult to regulate
Donald Fites on competitive advantage of the dealer network and the result of the 1980s visits: Interview, February 17, 2012.

Page 120. The benefits of the company-dealer . . . pay dividends over time
Donald Fites on an equipment sale being like an annuity: Interview, February 17, 2012.

Page 120. The benefits of the company-dealer . . . some machines plummeted as much as 62 percent
Fall in sales in the Great Recession: Rachel Potts, Caterpillar Public Affairs.

Pages 122–123. Only a handful . . . Finning International
Finning data: Salman Partners, "Finning International, Inc.," December 14, 2012, www.salmanpartners.com.

Page 123. Another publicly held Caterpillar dealership is Toromont
Toromont data: Canaccord Genuity, "Toromont Industries, Ltd.," October 14, 2021, www.canaccordgenuity.com.

Page 123. Table 7.2 provides . . . outposts in 182 countries
Dealer data: *Caterpillar Year in Review, 2012* and Rachel Potts, Caterpillar Public Affairs.

Page 125. Caterpillar's dealers are notable . . . Peter Holt notes, "My great-grandfather
Peter Holt quote: in *Working as One: The Enduring Partnership of CAT Dealers and Caterpillar,* 2006, p. 15.

Page 125. Caterpillar's dealers are notable . . . Blake Quinn of the Quinn Group
Blake Quinn quote: *Working as One: The Enduring Partnership of CAT Dealers and Caterpillar,* 2006, p. 8.

Page 126. If all this might be mistaken . . . Voltaire's *Candide* and its
Voltaire: *Candide,* in *The Complete Tales of Voltaire,* William Walton, trans. (New York: H. Fertig, 1990).

Page 126. In contrast to the many . . . Jim Parker of Carter Machinery
Jim Parker quote: Interview, March 14, 2012.

Page 126. In contrast to the many . . . Don Fites observed in 1996
Donald Fites on trust between Caterpillar and its dealers: in Caterpillar, *Working as One: The Enduring Partnership of CAT Dealers and Caterpillar,* 2006, p. 15.
Page 127. Edward Rust . . . "superb feedback loop"
Edward Rust quote: Interview with Edward B. Rust, Jr., January 23, 2012.
Page 127. Gerald Flaherty, a retired . . . needed to do to compete with Komatsu
Gerald Flaherty about Caterpillar customer: Interview, Flaherty, October 29, 2012.
Page 128. Regardless of where . . . Dealers all over the world embrace them
Quote from Tom Gales, in Caterpillar, *Working as One: The Enduring Partnership of CAT Dealers and Caterpillar* (2006), p. 21.
Page 128. Ultimately, Caterpillar's insistence . . . Brazilian dealer Pedro Esteva
Quote from Pedro Esteva, in Caterpillar, *Working as One: The Enduring Partnership of CAT Dealers and Caterpillar* (2006), p. 16.
Page 129. Dealers also expect . . . 500,000 distinctive parts in its system
Peter Holt on inventory: Interview, March 30, 2012.
Page 129. The notable success of Caterpillar's . . . a dealer network like Caterpillar's
Quote from Caterpillar competitor who did not wish to be named: Interview, September 19, 2012.
Page 130. Thus in simple economic terms . . . at early stages of development
Sany's thrust into the United States: "Sany Committed to U.S. Market," *Wall Street Journal,* 259 (October 30, 2012), A16.
Page 130. In 1926 a team . . . a relationship based on "mutual respect"
1926 observation on company-dealer relationships: *Across the Table: Caterpillar Tractor Co. and Its Dealers in the United States and Canada,* p. 12. Originally published by Caterpillar in 1926; reprinted in 2011, gmx.xmu.edu.cn/cws/business/pmarketing/chapter12.htm.

Chapter 8

Page 133. "Each brought something different to the table,"
David Goode on the qualities of Caterpillar CEOs: Interview, David Goode, March 26, 2012.
Page 134. Glen Barton, who led Caterpillar from 1999 to 2004
On Glen Barton: www.referenceforbusiness.com/biography/A-E/Barton-Glen-A-1939.html#ixzz2CDthI4bl.
Pages 134–135. Let's give luck its due . . . turn out to have feet of clay
On feet of clay: This is an Old Testament image (Daniel 2:31-33) and expresses disappointment that even kings and heroes have fatal weaknesses.
Page 135. No board can purchase . . . vice presidents make the most presentations
Who makes the most presentations at Caterpillar board meetings: Interview, Edward Rust, January 23, 2012.

Page 135. The most obvious damage . . . Motorola had to declare bankruptcy

Motorola example: Rajul Pandita, "Diseconomies of Scale," www.buzzle .com/articles/diseconomies-of-scale.html.

Page 136. There is some empirical . . . this advantage increased over time

Evidence about insider CEOs: James S. Ang and Gregory L. Nagel, "Outside and Inside Hired CEOs: A Performance Surprise," 2011, www.docstoc.com /docs/79071183/Outside-and-inside-hired-CEOs-A-performance-surprise.

Page 136. There is some empirical . . . point in the opposite direction

On college presidents: James L. Fisher and James V. Koch, *The Entrepreneurial College President* (Westport, CT: Praeger, 2004).

Page 136. Regardless, Caterpillar's . . . buddy of the management

Eugene Fife on the role of board members: Interview, Eugene Fife, May 3, 2012.

Page 136. Regardless, Caterpillar's . . . the green flag and said, "Go ahead."

Eugene Fife on the Bucyrus acquisition: Interview, Eugene Fife, May 3, 2012.

Page 139. [Sidebar] Contrast Caterpillar's product strategy

Apple's product dependency and share price: Michael Wolff, "Is the Age of Apple Ending?" *USA Today* (November 12, 2012), 1B; for the share prices, http://finance.yahoo.com/q/hp?s=AAPL&a=8&b=7&c=1984&d=6&e =12&f=2013&g=d&z=66&y=396.

Page 142. We have already . . . decision-making methodology

Glen Barton on Six Sigma: Caterpillar annual report 2000, p. 1.

Page 142. We have already . . . in the space of five years

Reducing operating costs by $1.0 billion: Caterpillar annual reports, 2000–2004.

Page 143. Caterpillar's hefty spending . . . according to Rob Wertheimer of Vertical Research Partners

Rob Wertheimer on quality: Interview, November 26, 2012.

Page 143. [Sidebar] Boeing, one of the "Big Ten" companies . . . grounded all Dreamliners worldwide

Boeing Grounds Dreamliner: Jon Ostrower, Andy Pasztor, and Yoree Koh, "All Boeing Dreamliners Are Grounded World-Wide," *Wall Street Journal* (January 17, 2013), www.wsj.com.

Page 144. For as long as . . . price that may have been unwise

On Caterpillar's pricing: Christopher Bartlett and Susan Ehrlich, "Caterpillar, Inc.: George Schaeffer Takes Charge," Harvard Business School Case 9-930-036, 1989, revised in 1991.

Page 144. For as long as . . . trade-in for a new CAT product

Eighty percent of sales come back to the firm: Interview, Ken Adams, vice president of CAT Financial, February 6, 2012.

Page 144. [Sidebar] In contrast to Caterpillar, IBM's

IBM's revenue from services: "IBM Reports 2013 First-Quarter Results," IBM News Room (April 18, 2013), www-03.ibm.com/press/us/en/press release/40878.wss.

Page 145. One measure of Caterpillar's resolve . . . that of most of its competitors
Caterpillar's R&D expenditures: Caterpillar annual reports, 2010–2012.

Page 145. One measure of Caterpillar's resolve . . . active patents in its portfolio to demonstrate this
Research and development statistics: Interview, Tana Utley, Caterpillar's former chief technology officer and vice president of the Product Development & Global Technology Division, February 10, 2012.

Page 145. Although Caterpillar has jealousy . . . sold at premium prices
Caterpillar and its primary Caterpillar brand: www.caterpillar.com/brands.

Page 145. Although Caterpillar has jealousy . . . equipment such as wheel loaders
Caterpillar and SEM: www.caterpillar.com/brands/sem

Page 146. [Sidebar] Caterpillar group president Ed Rapp
Ed Rapp on the importance of China: Colum Murphy, "Caterpillar Strategy in China: Go Low," *Wall Street Journal,* 259 (November 28, 2012), www.wsj.com.

Page 146. In the estimation of Colum Murphy
Importance of low-priced market segment: Colum Murphy, "Caterpillar Strategy in China: Go Low," *Wall Street Journal,* 259 (November 28, 2012), www.wsj.com.

Page 147. Caterpillar maintains approximately 30 different brands
On the number of brands: Caterpillar's website lists 21 distinct brands, but several individuals we interviewed indicated that there are about 30 distinct Caterpillar brands.

Page 147. Contrast the decision on branding . . . Bucyrus in 2011
Bucyrus acquisition and switch to Caterpillar name: Interview, Doug Oberhelman, February 2, 2012, and Interview, Luis de Leon, February 20, 2012.

Page 147. We visited the former headquarters . . . this will increase job security
Anonymous Bucyrus worker quote: Visit to the former Bucyrus plant in South Milwaukee, Wisconsin, February 20, 2012.

Page 147. The Caterpillar–Bucyrus operation . . . since has left the company
Luis De Leon resigns: James T. Areddy, "Caterpillar Unit in Scandal Has Unusual Roots," *Wall Street Journal* (January 20, 2013), www.wsj.com.

Page 148. The Caterpillar–Bucyrus operation . . . Chinese subsidiary, ERA Mining Machinery
Luis de Leon on merger: Interview, February 20, 2012.

Page 148. Caterpillar has reason to protect its brand
Value of the Caterpillar brand in 2011, www.interbrand.com/en/best-global -brands/2012/Best-Global-Brands-2012.aspx.

Page 148. *Fortune* magazine's 2012
Most admired companies in 2012: www.money.cnn.com/magazines /fortune/most-admired/2012/snapshots/81.html.

Chapter 9

Page 151. [Chapter title] The Burning Platform

Burning platform metaphor: Kevin Giovanetto, *Giant Steps* (Peoria, IL: Caterpillar, 2002), p. 19. Ed Rapp, today a group president at Caterpillar, also used this metaphor at the time.

Page 151. In 2000 Caterpillar . . . $1.05 billion in profit on $20.18 billion of sales

Caterpillar consolidated sales and revenues, profits in 1991 and 1998–2002: Caterpillar annual reports.

Page 151. In 2000 Caterpillar . . . was "stuck on a plateau"

Glen Barton's view on stagnation: Kevin Giovanetto, *Giant Steps* (Peoria, IL: Caterpillar, 2002). Giavanetto, a consultant hired by Caterpillar, wrote three unpublished reports/books about events at the company during this period. His remarks provide a treasure trove of information and salient observations about Caterpillar's activities. Glen Barton provided an introduction to the book and noted that it would allow readers to "relive our Six Sigma journey," p. 6.

Page 153. Kevin Giovanetto, a Caterpillar consultant . . . in an internal Caterpillar report titled *Giant Steps*

December 19, 2000, meeting concerning Six Sigma: Kevin Giovanetto, *Giant Steps* (Peoria, IL: Caterpillar, 2002).

Page 154. [Sidebar] "The devil is in the details.

Jerome Hamilton statement re the devil is in the details: Interview, February 21, 2013.

Page 157. How does Six Sigma relate to lean manufacturing programs

Lean manufacturing founders: Much has been written about lean manufacturing techniques. A good summary is provided in Stephen A. Ruffa, *Going Lean: How the Best Companies Apply Lean Manufacturing Principles to Shatter Uncertainty, Drive Innovation, and Maximize Profits* (New York: AMACOM, 2008).

Page 158. Lean is about eliminating waste . . . became famous as the Toyota Production System (TPS)

Toyota Production System: The TPS has been described and dissected thousands of times. An early and central contribution is Taiichi Ohno, *Toyota Production System: Beyond Large-Scale Production* (Cambridge, MA: Productivity Press, 1988). Ohno was an engineer at Toyota and is considered one of the key individuals in the development of TPS.

Page159. Frank Crespo is Caterpillar's chief procurement officer

Frank Crespo on Caterpillar purchasing: Interviews on March 23, 2012, and February 8, 2013.

Page 161. Caterpillar was hardly the first . . . interesting models for benchmarking

GE and 3M total revenues and TEVs: total revenue from www.yahoofinance.com; TEVs computed by the authors.

Page 161. Jeffrey Immelt took the reins of GE . . . toward a more profitable course

Among the individuals who helped us understand GE's Six Sigma success were Tom Quidlen, president and CEO of GE Capital Corporate Finance; Paul Feehan, senior managing director at GE Corporate Lending; and Dustin Weinberger, senior vice president, GE Capital.

Page 162. 3M is now under the stewardship

3M's Six Sigma savings: Dinner conversation with Inge Thulin, CEO and chairman of 3M, February 7, 2012, his first day in those posts.

Page 162. 3M is now under the stewardship . . . 3M can point to $1 billion of cost savings

3M's Six Sigma experience: Among the individuals who helped us understand 3M's Six Sigma success were Executive Vice President Mike Roman and Vice President Jim Fall.

Page 162. In December 2000, Glen Barton convinced . . . to do four things

Glen Barton's goals: Interview, February 6, 2012, and Kevin Giovanetto, *Giant Steps* (Peoria, IL: Caterpillar, 2002).

Page 162. [Sidebar] I think it was a bold move

Ed Rapp's observations: Interview, February 8, 2013.

Page 163. The reader already knows how this story ends . . . 24.6 percent in 2006

Caterpillar's sales, net income, and PBT margins: Rachel Potts, Caterpillar Public Affairs. The 2002 PBT percentage of sales is from the 2002 annual report. The 2005 value is from Caterpillar's 10-K submission in 2005.

Chapter 10

Page 166. There is an almost irresistible tendency . . . McRib sandwich

McDonald's examples: Peter Bloom, "Diversification Can Be Deadly," *Washington Business Journal* (June 21, 2011), www.bizjournals.com /washington/fedbiz_dialy/2011/06/diversification-can-be-deadly.html and www.foodnetworkhumor.com.

Page 166. The common denominator in McDonald's product expansions

One-year return on McDonald's stock: Spencer Jakab, "McDonald's 300-Billionth Burger Delayed," *Wall Street Journal* (January 23, 2013), www.wsj.com.

Page 166. [Sidebar] McDonald's sold more than 300 billion

Number of McDonald's franchises: www.entrepreneur.com/franchises /mcdonalds/282570-0.html.

Page 167. Alas, it doesn't always work . . . National Semiconductor

National Semiconductor diversification failure: Peter Bloom, "Diversification Can Be Deadly," *Washington Business Journal* (June 21, 2011), www.bizjournals.com/washington/fedbiz_dialy/2011/06 /diversification-can-be-deadly.html.

Page 167. Alas, it doesn't always work . . . Northrup Grumman

Northrup Grumman exited from ship building in 2011: http://defense
-update.com/20110401_northrop-grumman-shipbuilding.html.

**Page 167. Alas, it doesn't always work . . . Hewlett-Packard was taken
aback**

Hewlett-Packard and Autonomy Corporation: Ben Worthen, Paul Sonne,
and Justin Scheck, "Long Before H-P Deal, Autonomy's Red Flags," *Wall
Street Journal* (November 26, 2012), www.wsj.com.

**Page 168. What do these examples . . . CAT enjoys very positive profit
margins on those sales**

Caterpillar's margin on compressor sales: Interview, Rob Wertheimer,
November 26, 2012.

**Page 169. Many heavy industry firms . . . Delta Airlines purchased a
pretroleum refinery**

Delta's purchase of an oil refinery: Jad Mouawad, "Delta Buys Refinery
to Get Control of Fuel Costs," *New York Times* (April 30, 2012),
www.nytimes.com.

Page 169. Many heavy industry firms . . . Alcoa, for example, dominated

Alcoa's bauxite and aluminum market power: George David Smith, *From
Monopoly to Competition* (Cambridge, UK: Cambridge University Press,
1988).

**Page 170. Caterpillar has constructed a record . . . "We don't do
refrigerators"**

Kent Adams on refrigerators: Interview, February 6, 2012.

**Page 170. Although some observers initially blanched . . . it paid a
premium of $8.8 billion for Bucyrus**

On Bucyrus acquisition's current value and after-market margins: Interviews
with Joel Tiss of BMO Capital, November 26, 2012, and Rob Wertheimer,
November 26, 2012.

Page 171. [Sidebar] Before its acquisition by Caterpillar, Bucyrus

Bucyrus margins and 45 percent of CAT's mining revenues being after-
market: Rob Wertheimer, Vertical Research Partners, Interview, November
26, 2012.

Page 171. Wall Street investors and analysts . . . character Wile E. Coyote

Caterpillar as Wile E. Coyote: Interview, Joel Tiss of BMO Capital,
November 26, 2012.

**Page 171. Wall Street investors and analysts . . . other analysts, such as Rob
Wertheimer**

Inflated inventory levels: Interview, Rob Wertheimer, Vertical Research
Partners, November 26, 2012.

**Page 172. An unspoken goal of Caterpillar CEOs . . . to diversify the
company's revenue**

Caterpillar diversifies its profit stream: Interview, Joel Tiss of BMO Capital,
November 26, 2012, for the 60 percent estimate and Trefis for the 20.9
percent estimate, Trefis, analysis for Caterpillar, October 10, 2012,
www.trefis.com/company?hm=CAT.trefis#.

Page 172. An unspoken goal of Caterpillar CEOs . . . Trefis estimated that up to 60 percent

Caterpillar margins: Trefis, analysis for Caterpillar, October 10, 2012, www.trefis.com/company?hm=CAT.trefis#.

Page 173. Among Caterpillar's four major areas of thrust . . . a great effort on CAT's part to change this

On growth prospects and Chinese construction market shares: Interview, Joel Tiss, BMO Capital, November 26, 2012.

Page 173. By contrast, according to Rob Wertheimer

Caterpillar's market shares in oil and gas and mining: Interview, Rob Wertheimer, Vertical Research Partners, November 26, 2012.

Page 173. Caterpillar operates Caterpillar Financial

Caterpillar Financial's size, customer base, and relation to GE Capital: Interview, Kent Adams, February 6, 2012.

Page 174. The emphasis of Caterpillar Financial . . . In Adams's words

On Caterpillar Financial's role: Interview, Kent Adams, February 6, 2012.

Page 175. Caterpillar's public filings . . . classified as "nonperforming

Nonperforming financial receivables: Caterpillar's Form 10-Q filing with the Securities and Exchange Commission, September 30, 2012.

Page 175. Caterpillar denies it has a Southern Strategy . . . this term is not part of its lexicon

George Boze on a Southern Strategy: quoted in Steve Tarter, "Despite CAT Moves, Illinois Still Remains Company's Production Hub," *Peoria Journal-Star* (February 27, 2012), www.pjstar.com.

Pages 175–176. Caterpillar denies it has a Southern Strategy . . . The diverse set of observers that has applied this label

Media references to Southern Strategy: "Caterpillar Picks Athens, GA for Another Plant," (November 18, 2012), www.sb-d.com www.sb-d.com /Issues/Winter2012/SouthernAutoCorridorcomNews/tabid/472/Default .aspx; the "Caterpillar Picks Athens, GA," (February 27, 2012), www .southernautocorridor.com; Mathew Burns, "Caterpillar Rolls Into Lee County," (June 24, 1996), www.webcitation.org/mainframe.php; John Bussey, "An Engine Down South," (July 4, 2012), www.wsj.com; "CAT Continues Its 'Southern Strategy,'" www.bizjournals.com, (August 13, 2010); George Boze as quoted in Steve Tarter, "Despite CAT Moves, Illinois Still Remains Company's Production Hub," (February 27, 2012), www .pjstar.com; "Caterpillar, Inc.," www.wikipedia.com (accessed November 18, 2012).

Page 176. What are right-to-work laws?

Right to work law definitions: http://legal-dictionary.thefreedictionary.com /Right-to-Work+Laws.

Page 176. The reduction in union power . . . most organized unions and the U.S. Democratic Party

Organized labor's financial contributions: Tom McGinty and Brody Mullins, "Political Spending by Unions Far Exceeds Direct Donations," *Wall Street Journal* (July 10, 2012), www.wsj.com.

Page 177. [Sidebar] Use of union dues for political purposes
United States Supreme Court "Opt Out" decision: *Communications Workers of America v. Beck,* 487 U.S. 735 (1988).

Page 177. [Sidebar] After the state of Michigan
Neil Shah and Ben Casselman, "Laws' Scant Effect on Wages," *Wall Street Journal* (December 11, 2012), www.wsj.com.

Page 178. Workers' wages typically . . . somewhat lower in right-to-work states
Wages lower in right-to-work states: Neil Shah and Ben Casselman, "'Right to Work' Economics," *Wall Street Journal,* 259 (December 15, 2012), A3; Elise Gould and Heidi Shierholz, "The Compensation Penalty of 'Right to Work' Laws," Economic Policy Institute Briefing Paper #299, February 17, 2011. See also Lonnie K. Stevans, "The Effect of Endogenous Right-to-Work Laws on Business and Economic Conditions in the United States: A Multivariate Approach," *Review of Law and Economics,* 5(1), 2007, 595–614. Both of these studies reach stronger conclusions on this issue than do many other economists. Gould and Shierholz note that "it is notoriously difficult to separate out the effect of a single public policy on wages across a statewide economy" (p. 9). That is precisely why the verdict may not yet be clear.

Page 178. Workers' wages typically are . . . according to the *Peoria Journal-Star*
Lower wage rates in Texas: Steve Tarter, "Two Sides to the CAT Coin," *Peoria Journal-Star* (February 12, 2012), www.pjstar.com.

Page 179. However, whatever the impact . . . Indeed, in 1992, Washington State adopted
Decline of dues payers in Washington State: State Budget Solutions www.statebudgetsolutions.org/publications/detail/why-government-employee-collective-bargaining-laws-must-be-reformed-now (accessed December 15, 2012).

Page 179. However, whatever the impact . . . portion of their dues from 82 percent to 11 percent
Union attitudes toward free-riding: Gary N. Chaison and Dileep G. Dhavale, "The Choice Between Union Membership and Free-Rider Status," *Journal of Labor Research,* 13 (Fall 1992), 355–369.

Page 179. It's no surprise that union . . . to join collectively in any way whatsoever
Organized labor's dread of right-to-work laws: Steven Greenhouse, "Strained States Turning to Laws to Curb Labor Unions," *New York Times* (January 3, 2011), www.nytimes.com.

Page 179. It's no surprise that union . . . statement by Randi Weingarten
Randi Weingarten on attacks on organized labor: Steven Greenhouse, "Strained States Turning to Laws to Curb Labor Unions," *New York Times* (January 3, 2011), www.nytimes.com.

Page 179. This view certainly is not new . . . In 1996 George Boze
George Boze on Caterpillar moving into the South: quoted in Steve Tarter, "Despite CAT Moves, Illinois Still Remains Company's Production Hub," *Peoria Journal-Star* (February 27, 2012), www.pjstar.com.

Pages 179–180. This view certainly is not new . . . The *Wall Street Journal* **seemingly agreed**
On wrecking the economy: "The Truth About Cat and Jobs," *Wall Street Journal* (August 22, 2012), www.wsj.com.

Page 180. Southern Strategy or not . . .
Caterpillar growth in right-to-work states: Caterpillar annual reports.

Pages 180–181. There are economic reasons . . . employees in the United States in 2011
Work stoppage data: www.bls.gov/news.release/archives/wkstp_02082012 .htm.

Page 182. Second, costs of production (including labor)
Regional CPI-U differences: http://data.bls.gov/cgi-bin/surveymost.

Page 182. Third, as Table 10.2 reveals . . . lost 900,000 jobs
Migration of businesses and jobs into right-to-work states: Mark Perry, Carpe Diem blog, "America on the Move in 2011: Away from Forced-Unionism States to Right-to-Work States," December 13, 2012, www .aei-ideas.org/channel/carpe-diem; www.washingtonpost.com/blogs/fact -checker/post/romneys-claim-that-right-to-work-states-get-more-good -jobs/2011/09/29/gIQAGsP17K_blog.html.

Page 182–183. Fourth, right-to-work states . . . .manufacturing activities in Clayton
Economic development financial incentives: Louise Story, "As Companies Seek Tax Deals, Governments Pay High Price," *New York Times* (December 1, 2012), www.nytimes.com.

Page 183. Although Texas is the undisputed leader . . . $759 per capita
Incentives received by Caterpillar and its operation in Texas: Louise Story, "As Companies Seek Tax Deals, Governments Pay High Price," *New York Times* (December 1, 2012), www.nytimes.com.

Page 183. Caterpillar has been highly . . . of the quality of the economic environment
Caterpillar's criticism of the economic climate in Illinois: Mitch Dudek, "Caterpillar CEO Criticizes Illinois' Workers' Comp, Pensions," *Chicago Sun-Times* (October 18, 2012), www.suntimes.com.

Page 183. Caterpillar has been highly . . . The *New York Times* **reported that Illinois spends $1.51 billion**
State of Illinois expenditures on incentives: Louise Story, "As Companies Seek Tax Deals, Governments Pay High Price," *New York Times* (December 1, 2012), www.nytimes.com.

Page 183. Caterpillar has been highly . . . deciding to base new facilities in other states
Caterpillar's employment in Illinois: Mitch Dudek, "Caterpillar CEO Criticizes Illinois' Workers' Comp, Pensions," *Chicago Sun-Times* (October 18, 2012), www.suntimes.com.

Page 183. [Sidebar] The impact of right-to-work laws is disputed
Washington Post on Romney statement: www.washingtonpost.com/blogs /fact-checker/post/romneys-claim-that-right-to-work-states-get-more-good -jobs/2011/09/29/gIQAGsP17K_blog.html.

Pages 183–184. Some might question whether . . . "Doug, why are you in Illinois?"

Oberhelman quote on Caterpillar's location: Mitch Dudek, "Caterpillar CEO Criticizes Illinois' Workers' Comp, Pensions," *Chicago Sun-Times* (October 18, 2012), www.suntimes.com.

Pages 183–184. Some might question whether . . . has given Caterpillar the back of its hand

State of Illinois financial incentives: Louise Story, "As Companies Seek Tax Deals, Governments Pay High Price," *New York Times* (December 1, 2012), www.nytimes.com.

Page 184. There is no doubt . . . even less attractive to prospective employers

State of Illinois a basket case: Josh Barro, "Illinois Is Pension Basket Case You Forgot About," *Bloomberg News*, www.bloomberg.com/news/2012-04 -09/illinois-is-pension-basket-case-you-forgot-about.html.

Page 184. Caterpillar has responded . . . contributed an additional $15 million

Caterpillar Visitors Center: Steve Tarter, "Caterpillar's $37 Million Showcase Nearly Ready," *Peoria Journal-Star* (September 24, 2012), www.pjstar.com.

Pages 184–185. A fifth reason Caterpillar's move to right-to-work states

UAW membership: Harold Meyerson, "The Lansing-Beijing Connection," *Washington Post* (December 11, 2012), www.washingtonpost.com.

Page 186. Southern Strategy or not

Optimal plant size: While Caterpillar executives did not always agree on what constitutes the optimal plant size for the company, their estimates ranged from between 500 and 1,500 in our interviews.

Chapter 11

Page 190. *Fortune* magazine's Geoff Colvin puts it this way

Geoff Colvin, "Caterpillar Is Absolutely Crushing It," *Fortune* (May 12, 2011), http://management.fortune.cnn.com/2011/05/12/caterpillar-is -absolutely-crushing-it.

Page 192. Not surprisingly, the share price

Caterpillar's beta value: www.yahoo.finance.com (July 15, 2013).

Page 192. Thus very few . . . many other well-known firms

Highly variable performances of other large firms: The beta coefficients of these large firms reflect their highly variable performances: Citigroup (1.98), Bank of America (1.92), U.S. Steel (1.78), and Advanced Micro Devices (2.54). www.yahoofinance.com (July 15, 2013).

Page 193. More so than any other individual, CEO Jim Owens

Owens on planning for the trough and goals: Interview, February 12, 2012.

Page 193. Owens became Caterpillar chairman . . . Doug Oberhelman, who was to succeed

Oberhelman quote: Geoff Colvin, "Caterpillar Is Absolutely Crushing It," *Fortune* (May 12, 2011), http://management.fortune.cnn.com/2011/05/12 /caterpillar-is-absolutely-crushing-it.

Page 194. Proof of the concept came in fall 2008 . . . Group President Ed Rapp

Ed Rapp on sales falling off the table: Interview, February 8, 2013.

Page 194. However, despite the lag . . . real gross domestic product in the United States would decline

Declining real gross domestic product: Federal Reserve Bank of St. Louis, http://research.stlouisfed.org/fred2/series/GDP?rid=53&soid=18.

Pages 194–195. However, despite the lag . . . a grueling time period for virtually every industrial firm

Caterpillar's declining sales: Caterpillar annual report, 2009.

Pages 195–196. Although most companies were confused . . . As Ed Rapp put it

Ed Rapp re Caterpillar being prepared: Interview, February 8, 2013.

Page 196. Chairman/CEO Jim Owens said it all

Jim Owens on this being the worst recession he had seen: Interview, February 12, 2012.

Page 196. Overall company end-of-year employment

Reductions in employment: Geoff Colvin, "Caterpillar Is Absolutely Crushing It," (May 12, 2011), http://management.fortune.cnn.com/2011/05/12/caterpillar-is-absolutely-crushing-it, and Caterpillar's 10K filings in 2009.

Page 196. Overtime hours were reduced

Production slowdown at Decatur plant: Tony Reid, "CAT Denies Extended Shutdown Rumors," *Decatur Herald-Review* (March 24, 2009), www.herald-review.com.

Page 196. The total value of inventories declined

Reduction in inventory: Colonel David Hicks, Colonel Linda Hurry, and Colonel William A. Spangenthal (all U.S. Air Force and Secretary of Defense Corporate Fellows), "Observations and Recommendations from Apple, Caterpillar, and General Dynamics," report to the Air University (Montgomery, AL), June 2010.

Page 196. Executive compensation was reduced

Reduction in managerial salaries: Peggy Cope, "To Survive the Worst, Plan During the Best of Times," *HRO Global*, 7 (Spring/Summer 2009), www.hroglobal.com/content/3832/survive-worst-plan-during-best-times.

Page 198. A portion of Caterpillar's trough . . . to minimize the bullwhip effect

Bullwhip effect: this term was popularized by Hau L. Lee, V. Padmanabhan, and Seungjin Whang, "The Bullwhip Effect in Supply Chains," *Sloan Management Review*, 38(Spring 1997), 93–102.

Page 198. A portion of Caterpillar's trough . . . this refers to situations in which small increases

Bullwhip quote taken from Timothy Aeppel, "'Bullwhip' Hits Firms as Growth Snaps Back," *Wall Street Journal* (January 27, 2010), www.wsj.com.

Page 198. By some reports, Caterpillar visited

Caterpillar visits 500 suppliers: Colonel David Hicks, Colonel Linda Hurry, and Colonel William A. Spangenthal (all U.S. Air Force and Secretary of

Defense Corporate Fellows), "Observations and Recommendations from Apple, Caterpillar, and General Dynamics," report to the Air University (Montgomery, AL), June 2010.

Page 200. It would be a mistake . . . *monitor* is a more accurate term)
Caterpillar monitoring suppliers: This view was imparted to the authors in several of their interviews with Caterpillar suppliers.

Chapter 12

Page 203. We've said many good things . . . Caterpillar's stock price rose
Caterpillar's share prices, DJIA, S&P 500 Index, and real GDP growth: www.yahoofinance.com reports that the adjusted closing price of a Caterpillar share was $3.58 on January 2, 1981, and $89.61 on December 31, 2012; the Dow Jones Average was 376.58 on January 2, 1981, and 4,442.07 on December 31, 2012; the S&P 500 was 136.34 on January 2, 1981, and 1,426.19 on December 31, 2012. The Bureau of Economic Analysis (www.bea.gov) reports that real GDP in terms of chained 2005 prices was $6,000.6 billion in first quarter 1981 and $13,647.6 billion in fourth quarter 2012.

Page 204. The owners of Caterpillar stock . . . has averaged a 2.5 percent dividend
Caterpillar dividends: Caterpillar annual reports and www.bloomberg.com.

Page 204. The owners of Caterpillar stock . . . only 1.3 percent for Dow Jones Industrial Average firms
S&P dividends: www.bloomberg.com.

Page 204. The owners of Caterpillar stock . . . invested in CAT in 1996 and held their shares
Caterpillar stock returns: Caterpillar annual reports and www.bloomberg .com.

Pages 204–205. All investors face thousands . . . 15,000 publicly traded companies
Number of publicly traded companies in the United States: http://wiki .answers.com/Q/How_many_publicly-traded_companies_are/in_the-US /and/the/world.

Page 209. Caterpillar's three-decade surge forward . . . an 86.3 percent decline in its operating profit the next year
Caterpillar's precipitous fall in profits in 2009: Caterpillar annual report, 2009.

Page 212. Even the most knowledgeable . . . CAT revised those figures down
Caterpillar's revised investor guidance: "Caterpillar Crawls to a Standstill After Years of Explosive Growth," *Forbes* (February 6, 2013), www.forbes.com.

Page 214. Gerard Vittecoq, Caterpillar's influential . . . true for a long time
Gerard Vittecoq on Caterpillar being in the right spot: Interview, February 2, 2012.

Page 215. The dealer network . . . a single truck might carry
Truck carrying capacity: reports of Caterpillar dealers and personnel in the field.

Page 216. Caterpillar has established conditions . . . EBIT margins ranged
Dealer margins: EBIT margins: Salman Brothers, "Toromont Industries, Ltd.," November 6, 2012; Salman Brothers, "Finning International, Inc.," December 14, 2012; Scotia Bank, "Finning International, Inc.," December 14, 2012.

Pages 217–218. Consider the market for mining trucks . . . 60 percent in 2011
Caterpillar's market share in mining: Caterpillar does not disclose market shares. We have made estimates based upon conversations with analysts and reliance upon the Parker Bay Company Global Mining Database.

Page 218. A similar dynamic plays out . . . between 30 and 40 percent
Caterpillar's market share in construction: Caterpillar does not disclose market shares. We have made estimates based upon conversations with analysts and reliance upon the Parker Bay Company Global Mining Database.

Page 218. Success breeds success . . . in China, for example
Caterpillar's prices in China: Authors' conversations with customers and competitors.

Page 221. Here is a simple example. In 2006, according to Trefis
Source of Caterpillar profits: Trefis, "Caterpillar" (August 27, 2012), www.trefis.com/search?q=caterpillar.

Page 222. At the same time, Caterpillar moved aggressively
Source of Caterpillar's sales and revenues: Construction's share of sales and revenues at Caterpillar: *Caterpillar Year in Review, 2012.*

Page 223. Joel Tiss, an analyst with BMO Capital Markets
Joel Tiss on Caterpillar's supplying of information: Interview, November 26, 2012.

Page 225. Even so, what the Lord giveth
The Lord giveth and taketh away: a paraphrase of Job 1:21 in the Bible.

Page 226. [Sidebar] Caterpillar's head economist
Don Johnson on leading indicators: Interview, February 8, 2013.

Page 226. According to the *Financial Times* . . . sales appear to have fallen about 30 percent
Financial Times reporting of market share data (in this case for crawler excavator sales in China): Leslie Hook, Paul J. Davies, and Neil Munshi, "Caterpillar Digs Further into Trouble in China," *Financial Times* (February 12, 2013), 15.

Page 226. That's not easy to do at a company like Caterpillar . . . declined by 74 percent
Fall in Caterpillar earnings in 2009: Caterpillar 10-K Filing 2009.

Page 227. Although we admire Caterpillar . . . CAT purchased the Bucyrus mining business
Bucyrus's $8.6 billion purchase price: Shruti Date Singh, "Caterpillar to Buy Bucyrus to Expand Mining Range," www.bloomberg.com (November 15, 2010).

Page 227. Caterpillar's hard-charging approach
Warning signs in China: Forbes, Simon Montlake, "Cat Scammed," *Forbes*, 191 (March 14, 2013), 36–38 at 38.

Chapter 13

Page 229. In recent years, Caterpillar has derived
Seventy percent of Caterpillar's sales outside the United States: Caterpillar annual reports and 10-K filings.

Page 230. The year 2002 was a momentous one
China's GDP: http://data.worldbank.org/indicator/NY.GDP.MKTP.CD/countries/CN?display=graph.

Page 230. Growth of this magnitude . . . By 2011, China dominated the world
China's consumption of commodities: "Julian Simon: Still More Right Than Lucky in 2013," Mark J. Perry's Carpe Diem Blog, www.aei-ideas.org (January 12, 2013).

Page 230. Global miners could not keep up . . . the Brazilian miner Vale was able to grow
Growth in Vale's activities: Capital IQ.

Pages 231–232. Increased profits and production drive . . . 37 percent annual compound rate
Rise in shipments of mining equipment: Parker Bay Company Mining Database.

Page 234. 1. Overburden has been growing
Definition of overburden: Wikipedia, "Overburden," http://en.wikipedia.org/wiki/Overburden.

Pages 234–235. 2. Unconventional plays are becoming . . . Rob Wertheimer of Vertical Research Partners notes
Rob Wertheimer of Vertical Research Partners on horsepower: Interview, November 26, 2012.

Page 235. Even though recovery rates . . . The Bakken shale formation in North Dakota
Bakken shale recovery rate: Chip Brown, "The Luckiest Place on Earth," *New York Times Magazine* (February 3, 2013), www.nytimes.com.

Page 237. Road building continues to be a very important source
Chinese road building: Rob Wertheimer, April 20, 2012.

Page 237. This spurt in road building . . . 30 excavators were sold
Chinese excavator sales: Rob Wertheimer, April 20, 2012.

Page 238. The sometimes explosive nature of investments
Small increases in construction expenditures translate to greater Caterpillar sales: Interview, Mike DeWalt, February 8, 2013.

Page 238. DeWalt also noted . . . 3 percent increase in U.S. GDP
GPD growth means greater Caterpillar sales: Interview, Mike DeWalt, February 8, 2013.

Page 238. A salient question for Caterpillar . . . rather unusual in a global context
Fixed asset investments by country: Adapted from Ichiro Muto and Tomoyuki Fukumoto, "Rebalancing China's Economic Growth: Some Insights from Japan's Experience," Bank of Japan Working Paper Series, No. 11-E-5, July 2011, p. 4.

Page 239. A 2012 International Monetary Fund (IMF) report . . . needs to be changed

International Monetary Fund report: Victoria Ruan, "IMF Warns of Risks in Investment Binge," *South China Morning Post* (May 30, 2013), www.scmp.com.

Page 240. If history provides . . . China needs to double its current fleet

Rob Wertheimer on China's stock of excavators: Interview, November 26, 2012.

Page 240. Wertheimer also observes . . . the rest of the world

Rob Wertheimer on Chinese equipment use hours: Interview, November 26, 2012.

Page 240. From Doug Oberhelman on down . . . "bleeding market share" to China's Sany

Caterpillar losing market share and misjudgments in China: Leslie Hook, Paul J. Davies, and Neil Munshi, "Caterpillar Digs Further into Trouble in China," *Financial Times* (February 12, 2013), p. 26.

Pages 240–241. From Doug Oberhelman on down . . . "complete business model" in that country

Ed Rapp on rolling out the complete business model: Interview, February 8, 2013.

Page 241. From Doug Oberhelman on down . . . Rapp also speaks of methodically developing a "pipeline of local leaders"

Ed Rapp on building a cadre of local managers: Interview, February 8, 2013.

Page 241. In the judgment of the *Financial Times*

Caterpillar losing market share and making misjudgments in China: Leslie Hook, Paul J. Davies, and Neil Munshi, "Caterpillar Digs Further into Trouble in China," *Financial Times* (February 12, 2013), p. 26.

Chapter 14

Page 245. Caterpillar will continue to pursue acquisitions . . . such initiatives can't be ruled out

Caterpillar's recent major acquisitions: See Table 8.1.

Page 247. In our base case scenario, Caterpillar's sales . . . averaged since its founding

A 9.6 percent historical Caterpillar annual growth rate in sales: Interview, Ed Rapp, February 8, 2013.

Page 247. Caterpillar has developed what we call *expectation curves*

Cost cutting at Caterpillar: Interview, Ed Rapp, February 8, 2013.

Pages 247–248. It is instructive to contrast Caterpillar's cost containment . . . a sign of managerial stature and success

"Managerial slack" has a long history in non-profit-maximizing models of the firm but is most associated with Richard M. Cyert and James G. March, *A Behavioral Theory of the Firm* (Englewood Cliffs, NJ: Prentice-Hall, 1963).

Page 254. Valuation of companies and their stocks . . . between 1984 and 2006

Fama and French on the lack of success of active fund managers: For an easy to understand summary, see Vanessa Sumo, "Measuring Chance," *Chicago Booth Magazine* (Fall 2012), www.chicagobooth.edu. The study is reported in Eugene F. Fama and Kenneth R. French, "Luck Versus Skill in the Cross-Section of Mutual Fund Returns," *Journal of Finance*, 65 (October 2010), 1915–1947.

Page 254. Numerous studies reveal . . . individual stock selections

Investor mistakes: A nontechnical summary can be found at "7 Common Investor Mistakes," *Investopedia* (August 5, 2011), http://www.investopedia.com/articles/stocks/07/mistakes.asp#axzz2L67D70sN. For a more scholarly approach that extends beyond economics and finance, see Daniel Kahneman, *Thinking, Fast and Slow*. (New York: Farrar, Straus, and Giroux, 2011).

Page 255. Hence, although we have no objection . . . on February 15, 2013)

Caterpillar's trailing 12-month EBITDA on February 15, 2013: www.yahoofinance.com.

Page 258. So how have Caterpillar's valuations changed . . . in the S&P 500 Index

P/E ratios: All data taken from www.yahoofinance.com except the mean P/E for S&P 500 Index firms, which is from www.multpl.com.

Page 258. Table 14.4 presents our estimates of Caterpillar's Total Enterprise Value . . . CAT's net income

Total enterprise values for Caterpillar: Authors' calculations from Caterpillar's annual reports and 10-K filings.

Page 262. You might ask why . . . probably would have been even lower

Other analysts' views of Caterpillar's 2014 consolidated sales and revenues: www.finance.yahoo.com/q/ae?s=CAT+Analyst+Estimates (April 4, 2013).

Chapter 15

Page 270. A well-known Buddhist proverb . . . the same key opens the gates of hell

Buddhist proverb: www.phys.washington.edu/users/vladi/phys216/Feynman.html.

Page 270. A well-known Buddhist proverb . . . in the *Summa Theologica* of St. Thomas Aquinas

Christian roots of the Buddhist proverb in *Summa Theologica*: www.newadvent.org/summa. See also Book of Revelations (1:18).

Pages 270–271. We've also noted . . . indexed their investments to the entire market

On investment results: According to Amanda B. Kish of the Motley Fool, over the most recent five-year period, 57.6 percent of domestic equity funds underperformed the S&P Composite 1500 Index. Broken down by market cap, 61.8 percent of large-cap funds underperformed the S&P 500 Index,

78.2 percent of mid-cap funds missed the mark compared with the S&P Mid Cap 400 Index, and 63 percent of all small-cap funds trailed the S&P Small Cap 600 Index. www.fool.com/investing/mutual-funds/2011/03/14 /more-proof-of-a-losing-investment-strategy.aspx (March 11, 2011).

Pages 270–271. We've also noted . . . John Bogle and other advocates of investment indexing

Indexing and John Bogle: See John Bogle, *Don't Count on It!: Reflections on Investment Illusions, Capitalism, "Mutual" Funds, Indexing, Entrepreneurship, Idealism, and Heroes* (Somerset, NJ: Wiley, 2010), for an excellent explanation of his views.

Page 271. Because Caterpillar as a company has performed . . . undervalued Caterpillar

Someone who has not undervalued Caterpillar: Undervaluing Caterpillar's share price: Ray Merola, "The Market Has Chronically Undervalued Caterpillar Stock," *Seeking Alpha* (February 26, 2013), http://seekingalpha .com/article/1224261-the-market-has-chronically-undervalued-caterpillar -stock?source=email_rt_article_title.

Acknowledgments

This book represents several years of intensive effort by Craig Bouchard and Jim Koch, but it would never have come to fruition without the superb efforts of many other individuals. We start by recognizing the huge contributions of our wives, Melissa Bouchard and Donna Koch, who stimulated us, encouraged us, and tolerated us in just the right ways at just the right times.

At Caterpillar, Rachel Potts and Jim Dugan of Caterpillar Public Affairs were especially critical to our work and in arranging numerous opportunities for us to learn and interpret what we later concluded was the Caterpillar Way. However, we also are indebted to a host of other individuals connected in various ways to Caterpillar, including Chairman/CEO Doug Oberhelman, numerous CAT senior executives, several board members, and a fascinating variety of CAT competitors, suppliers, customers, current and former employees, CAT dealers, journalists, investment analysts, union leaders, trade association personnel, elected officials, and ordinary citizens who provided us with information, advice, and counsel— sometimes unsolicited—about the company. It was surprisingly easy to convince people to talk about CAT because most observers recognize that CAT has broken the traditional industrial mold.

Our agent, Carole Greene, was very helpful with editing and provided astute suggestions about content and approach. At McGraw-Hill, Donya Dickerson deserves special praise for pushing us to bring the project to completion. She is both talented and patient, and we benefitted from both.

All errors of commission or omission, however, remain the responsibility of the authors.

Index

About the Authors

Craig T. Bouchard is the chairman of the board and chief executive officer of Signature Group Holdings (OTCQX:SGGH), the chairman of the board and chief executive officer of Cambelle-Inland, and the founder of Shale-Inland. Craig holds a bachelor's degree in social sciences, and a master's degree in economics from Illinois State University, an MBA from the University of Chicago, sits on the board of the Department of Athletics at Duke University, and has been a trustee of Boston University and the Foundation of the University of Montana. Craig was a finalist for the 2005 Ernst and Young Entrepreneur of the Year Award (Illinois), is an alumnus of Leadership Greater Chicago, and holds U.S. Patent 4,212,168 Power Producing Dry-Type Cooling Systems. www.craigbouchard.com.

James V. Koch is board of visitors professor of economics and president emeritus at Old Dominion University. He was named one of the 100 most effective college presidents in the United States in an Exxon Foundation study. His wide-ranging writing and research have focused on topics ranging from the economics of drug enforcement to the sources of entrepreneurial activity. He has served as a consultant to more than 100 universities, law firms, and businesses and has been a sought after board trustee. Dr. Koch earned a B.A. from Illinois State University and a Ph.D. in economics from Northwestern University. www.jamesvkoch.com.